Modern Language Association o

# Approaches to Teaching
# World Literature

## *Joseph Gibaldi*, Series Editor

# Approaches to Teaching

# Medieval

# English Drama

Edited by

## Richard K. Emmerson

The Modern Language Association of America
New York     1990

© 1990 by The Modern Language Association of America
All rights reserved. Printed in the United States of America

Library of Congress Cataloging-in-Publication Data

Approaches to teaching medieval English drama / edited by Richard K.
   Emmerson.
      p.     cm. — (Approaches to teaching world literature ; 29)
   Includes bibliographical references.
   ISBN 0-87352-531-0        ISBN 0-87352-532-9 (pbk.) :
   1. English drama—To 1500—Study and teaching.     2. English
drama—To 1500—History and criticism—Theory, etc.     3. Mysteries
and miracle-plays, English—Study and teaching.     4. Mysteries and
miracle-plays, English—History and criticism—Theory, etc.
5. Theater—England—History—Medieval, 500-1500—Study and
teaching.     I. Emmerson, Richard Kenneth.     II. Series.
PR641.A8      1990
822'.1'07—dc20       89-78012

Cover illustration of the paperback edition: Two episodes in the life of
Abraham: Abraham as host to angels who announce the birth of his son and
the sacrifice of Isaac. Mural mosaic, basilica of San Vitale, Ravenna, 6th
century. Photograph: Alinari/Art Resource.

Third printing 1993

Published by The Modern Language Association of America
10 Astor Place, New York, New York, 10003-6981

# CONTENTS

# PREFACE TO THE SERIES

In *The Art of Teaching* Gilbert Highet wrote, "Bad teaching wastes a great deal of effort, and spoils many lives which might have been full of energy and happiness." All too many teachers have failed in their work, Highet argued, simply "because they have not thought about it." We hope that the Approaches to Teaching World Literature series, sponsored by the Modern Language Association's Publications Committee, will not only improve the craft—as well as the art—of teaching but also encourage serious and continuing discussion of the aims and methods of teaching literature.

The principal objective of the series is to collect within each volume different points of view on teaching a specific literary work, a literary tradition, or a writer widely taught at the undergraduate level. The preparation of each volume begins with a wide-ranging survey of instructors, thus enabling us to include in the volume the philosophies and approaches, thoughts and methods of scores of experienced teachers. The result is a sourcebook of material, information, and ideas on teaching the subject of the volume to undergraduates.

The series is intended to serve nonspecialists as well as specialists, inexperienced as well as experienced teachers, graduate students who wish to learn effective ways of teaching as well as senior professors who wish to compare their own approaches with the approaches of colleagues in other schools. Of course, no volume in the series can ever substitute for erudition, intelligence, creativity, and sensitivity in teaching. We hope merely that each book will point readers in useful directions; at most each will offer only a first step in the long journey to successful teaching.

Joseph Gibaldi
Series Editor

# PREFACE TO THE VOLUME

Anyone who has attended the many sessions devoted to medieval drama at the annual meetings of the Modern Language Association and other organizations or who has witnessed a recent revival of these plays knows that medieval drama is alive and flourishing. This liveliness was particularly evident during two different yet related events that transpired in May 1985. The first event took place during the annual International Congress on Medieval Studies at Western Michigan University, when—at meetings on three sultry days in crowded unair-conditioned rooms and in competition with hundreds of other scheduled sessions—the several papers on the topic The Cycle Plays and the Critic: Reassessments and Recommendations drew large and intellectually engaged audiences. The use of historical, cultural, anthropological, and musicological research was extensively debated, and Theresa Coletti's call for a new generation of theoretical studies of the drama was rousingly supported. A few weeks later many appreciative spectators from all over North America gathered in Toronto to watch twenty-five companies perform the Towneley cycle.

This unique combination of scholarly energy and popular festivity is the driving force behind the phenomenal increase in the study of medieval drama. What has not always received so much attention, however, are the difficulties inherent in teaching these plays to even the advanced undergraduate. This is unfortunate, for, as John C. Coldewey rightly states in his contribution to this volume, students face "some daunting problems" when confronting medieval plays, and these problems are "not good news for the teacher who relishes a simple body of material or straightforward subject guidelines." This volume does not provide those guidelines, straightforward or otherwise. It does, however, offer help for the new teacher who must sort out this sometimes foreboding material, encourage the experienced teacher to rethink the classroom presentation of familiar plays, and suggest for us all new ways to integrate more medieval drama into undergraduate courses. As Kathleen M. Ashley notes, because medieval drama scholarship and criticism is still in its beginning stage, it is possible for teachers and students to be "in the exciting position of being toe-to-toe with the scholars." What follows is intended both to extend and to improve the teaching of medieval drama to undergraduates by helping make this possibility a reality.

The topic of this volume is probably the most challenging to date in the Approaches to Teaching World Literature series. Although the volume concentrates on the extensive cycle plays of the late Middle

Ages and pays scant attention to what Glynne Wickham in *The Medieval Theatre* calls "Theatres of Recreation"—folk festivals, mummers' plays, tournaments, and so forth—it nevertheless covers a wide spectrum of drama. The plays discussed here are drawn from England and the Continent. They were written over six centuries in Latin, Anglo-Norman, and Middle English; they represent a variety of dramatic genres staging an impressive range of religious topics; and they were produced by monastic and civic communities in numerous ways.

Following the series' model, this volume is divided into two major sections. Part 1, "Materials," draws on the wealth of information supplied by teachers of medieval drama who participated in the survey that preceded the preparation of this volume. Throughout, this section relies on the experienced advice of these teachers concerning the selection of textbooks, the assignment of student readings, and the recommendation of significant works of scholarly research and critical commentary.

The section "Editions and Translations" concentrates on the most important and widely used anthology, giving both an overview and a critique of its selections and their classroom use. Other anthologies and editions are also discussed in relation to the courses in which medieval drama is taught. Because I believe that a teacher should be a coach whose foremost responsibility is to help students wrestle with primary texts, "Required and Recommended Readings for Students" briefly discusses helpful primary materials, as well as some secondary works that have been successfully assigned as background reading and for class reports. The much longer section, "The Instructor's Library," discusses in depth important scholarly works and specialized secondary studies helpful in preparing to teach medieval drama. "Aids to Teaching," which concludes the first part of this volume, is limited to audiovisual aids easily available to teachers.

Part 2, "Approaches," surveys the various genres of medieval drama and the rich array of approaches and teaching strategies that have been pursued successfully in the classroom. Although reflecting the individual perspectives of their authors, the essays share a common faith in the value of interdisciplinary study and an insistence on both the literary and the theatrical elements of medieval drama. These essays are intended less to describe paradigmatic courses than to offer critical perspectives, structures, and methods that may be borrowed and modified by those wishing to teach everything from a single medieval play in a survey course to an entire genre in a graduate course.

The volume's introduction and afterword, by two distinguished scholars who have contributed greatly to the study and the teaching of medieval drama, are personal meditations on the rewards enjoyed by an increasing number of teachers who are devoting their energies to guiding students through these demanding texts. The volume concludes with a list of participants in the survey of medieval drama instructors, a bibliography of works cited in "Materials" and "Approaches," an index of dramatic texts, and an index of names.

In conclusion, I am delighted to acknowledge my gratitude to numerous scholars for what they have taught me concerning medieval drama and for their assistance with this volume. I particularly value the continuing support of my colleagues in the National Endowment for the Humanities Seminar on Medieval and Renaissance Drama (University of Chicago, 1978-79), especially David Bevington—the seminar director—and Michael Hall and Pamela Sheingorn, whose encouragement of and help with this project have been especially valuable. For specific assistance at key moments, I am also pleased to thank Jane Chance, Barbara Palmer, Milla Riggio, and Jerry Ward, as well as the staff of Georgetown University Library and of the Folger Shakespeare Library. For their good-natured patience when they were first subjected to my experimenting with many of the volume's approaches and strategies, I am grateful to the students of my medieval drama courses at Georgetown University. I also appreciate the help of Joseph Gibaldi, who, as a fellow medievalist, provided expert advice, and the good judgment of the manuscript's readers and the members of the MLA Committee on Teaching and Related Professional Activities, whose suggestions at various points improved this volume. Most important, for their unflagging understanding and loving sustenance, I thank my wife, Sandi, and my daughter, Ariel.

The volume is dedicated to the memory of Grosvenor Fattic, who introduced me to medieval drama and whose untimely death is mourned by his many friends.

RKE

# INTRODUCTION
## V. A. KOLVE

Thirty years ago, a series devoted to teaching the major monuments of our literary tradition would not have assigned a volume to the drama of medieval England. In comparison with *The Canterbury Tales*, the *Divine Comedy*, and *Sir Gawain and the Green Knight*, to name only works that have already found places in the MLA Approaches series, the drama seemed remote and difficult in its Latin liturgical traditions, rough and primitive in its vernacular manifestations. Its history was thought interesting, to be sure, for scholars saw in these texts a steady, almost inevitable movement from ritual to drama, from Latin to the vernacular languages, and from simple to complex dramatic forms. Describing the drama's migration from monastery and cathedral to the streets and open places of towns, scholars charted a parallel movement from religious themes austerely expressed toward increasingly secular invention and interpolation. And they saw all this as culminating (with an assist from the Protestant Reformation) in the great drama of Tudor and Elizabethan England. The end redeemed the beginnings.

That history, it seems fair to say, had greater appeal for many than did the dramatic texts themselves. The essays in this volume offer vivid testimony to how much all that has changed. The evolutionary account of the drama's development, so deeply influenced by nineteenth-century Darwinist theory, has been discredited on many grounds, but most especially for its cavalier attention to actual chronology. The Latin drama of the church was in fact performed and valued throughout the medieval period; different in kind from the vernacular cycles, it neither evolved into them nor was superseded by them. Latin plays from the twelfth and thirteenth centuries moreover are often longer and artistically more ambitious than those from the fourteenth and fifteenth centuries, reversing another evolutionary tenet, the expectation that development is always from simple to complex. Other aspects of this history have come to seem problematic or deficient as well. Because we no longer distinguish so confidently between ritual and drama as modes or between sacred and secular as categories, simple narratives of change (to say nothing of "progress") from one to the other have lost their authority. Above all, we have learned to pay closer attention to the texts themselves, drawing on other disciplines (theology, music, art history, cultural anthropology) and other medieval genres (sermons, lyrics, Gospel harmonies, universal histories) to recover a sense of the power and the place these plays once held within clerical and popular devotion.

We have, in sum, come a long way toward learning to prize the achievement of the early drama for its own sake, quite apart from what it led to in Elizabethan times; and we have done so most specifically by recovering the interest of its religious action—respecting, but not privileging, the secular within it. A lot of work is being done. The texts are being scrupulously reedited in the light of recent codicological theory; the drama records are being searched anew and published in uniform, accessible editions; the iconographic context of the drama is being reconstructed, civic center by civic center, in subject lists of both extant and lost art; the music that carried or enhanced this drama is being published and quite extensively recorded; and the texts are once again being staged—in churches and theaters and dining halls, on village greens and city streets. I know of no other field in medieval literary culture that has been so extensively recolonized, so extensively remapped.

In learning to read this drama better, we have discovered one further use for it that has brought it into the mainstream of our teaching. To modern students, often so ignorant of the Bible that even the story of Abraham and Isaac is new, it offers fundamental access to large areas of medieval culture, both lettered and visual. Anyone who has ever studied this drama and its contexts will visit parish churches and medieval cathedrals no stranger to the art they display or the functions they serve. Such students will listen to medieval plainchant and polyphony sensitive to the expressive potential of medieval music. They will bring to medieval religious lyric that knowledge of sacred story on which its emotional power depends, just as they will read Langland, Chaucer, Gower, Julian of Norwich, even medieval fabliau, alert to much that might otherwise remain hidden or inaccessible. Medieval drama offers useful background to all these other texts and genres—the list could be readily extended—precisely because it occupies culturally central ground.

That is of course no accident. Although the major dramatic forms—

cycle play, moral play, miracle play—shared with many medieval genres a wish to celebrate the mystery of God's love for humankind, they added an intention specifically pedagogical. They sought to instruct their audiences in the stories central to the Christian faith, in the sacraments necessary for their salvation, in the schemata (such as the seven deadly sins and the ten commandments) that are at the heart of Christian moral teaching. One of the reasons these plays were staged for more than two hundred years is that they taught so well. And we have found that they teach our graduates and undergraduates no less usefully still, for an imaginative experience of what it was like to be a medieval Christian is approachable through these works. The teaching of medieval drama, like the staging of it in its own time, is community building; but whereas the drama once linked church to town and guild to guild and God to humankind, in this secular age it serves chiefly to restore communion with something essential in the human past. Ruth Wallerstein, the great teacher who first quickened my love for literature, rebuked the skepticism some of us brought to her classes in seventeenth-century religious poetry with an aphorism: "The truth of the Bible," she used to say, "doesn't *depend* on the credibility of Judges or the edibility of Jonah." And she was surely right. Whether we choose to receive the Judeo-Christian story as historical myth or sacred history, there is significant human witness at its center. Because medieval drama drew on the resources of an entire culture to mirror the human condition and to imagine its transcendence, the texts lay continuing claim to our attention and respect.

And so I have taken a teacher's pleasure in reading an early version of this book, exhilarated by the view it offers of what is happening in other people's classrooms. David Bevington's splendid anthology, *Medieval Drama*, published in 1975, has transformed what we can do in those rooms, most of all because it makes accessible to students (through its facing-page translations) a rich selection of the Latin and vernacular drama of the twelfth and thirteenth centuries. I agree with C. Clifford Flanigan's claim in these pages that the high Gothic drama—imbedded in the ritual of monasteries and cathedrals, learned in its theology, subtle in its artistic means—poses a great challenge to our present scholarship and critical understanding. But if we conceive of the cycle drama, the drama of the towns, as richly as Kathleen M. Ashley urges in her contribution to this collection, that drama too remains only partially understood. We must do more, she tells us, than correctly read a text. We must make some effort to stage it in our minds; we must reconstruct its festival occasion, its place in the communal year, its relation to cycles of work and play and worship; we must investigate its political subtexts, its implicit assertions of class and civic and national identity, its role in popular devotion; and we must understand better the anarchy that is occasionally set loose within its orthodoxy. Though there is much to be done before this synthesis can be achieved, it is a project abundantly detailed in the essays that follow.

That does not mean our enterprise is all new. The books we have been drawing on, supplementing, and arguing with over the past thirty years—E. K. Chambers's *Mediaeval Stage* (1903) and Karl Young's *Drama of the Medieval Church* (1933)—are great books still, richer and more sophisticated by far than the simplified version of drama history that later books drew from them. Young's texts remain trustworthy, furnishing an archival resource of extraordinary scope; and Chambers's extensive exploration of folk drama and custom, his publication (in an appendix) of all the records of performance he had been able to discover, his profoundly learned account of the Feast of Fools, and his frequent recourse to the most interesting anthropological theory of his own time (that of the Cambridge "school")—all anticipate the questions, emphases, and publishing projects that have distinguished the scholarship of the past three decades. And there is much in *The Mediaeval Stage* and *The Drama of the Medieval Church* that awaits modern reformulation still; the value of those books has not been exhausted.

We have, to be sure, begun some inquiries Chambers never imagined. The feminist reading of these texts, here outlined by Theresa Coletti, is genuinely new and full of promise. A semiotic reading of the kind provided by Peter W. Travis can reveal powerful unities at the center of these cycles. The iconographic inquiry described by Pamela Sheingorn is still largely before us. Marxist theory (though it finds no singular advocacy in these pages) likewise throws a powerful light on the history of drama and its relation to political and economic power. But we would do well to recognize that much in our program for the future (especially that part so persuasively outlined by Kathleen M. Ashley) in fact continues Chambers's own.

That we shall do it better seems a reasonable hope, for there are many of us, building on past scholarship with new kinds of theoretical and methodological refinement. We have certain practical advantages, not to be underestimated: copying machines and word processors, sometimes even research assistants and research grants. We have seen these plays in performance—a crucial experience unavailable to our learned predecessors—in York and Chester and Wakefield and London, in Toronto and Irvine and places between. And we have our many classrooms, where students share with us in the work of recovery. We ought indeed to do better than Chambers and Young, though none of us is likely ever to do so much alone.

This book, then, celebrates a communal enterprise; and I value it especially because it presents teachers talking to teachers about medieval drama at its vital center, in ways not deformed by the need to publish something (marginally) new or perish. The authors of these essays have felt free to address the things that matter most in this drama, the things that speak to us in the name of all we share with the past. These days, it is clear, we seldom think of our subject as theater history merely.

*Part One*

# MATERIALS

*Richard K. Emmerson*

# Editions and Translations

## *Teaching an Anthology of Medieval Drama*

The textbook most widely used by those who participated in the survey of medieval drama teachers is David Bevington's *Medieval Drama*, which is recommended as the basic anthology by virtually all teachers whose courses focus specifically on medieval drama. Described by one participant as "the best overall survey of all major forms," it receives praise for its excellent essays introducing the various types of medieval drama, its helpful headnotes, and its presentation of the plays in their original languages. Latin and Anglo-Norman texts are accompanied by translations in parallel columns, whereas the Middle English texts are printed in standardized spelling and are generously glossed in the margins or, for those passages where students may need greater assistance, translated in the footnotes. The footnotes also include thoughtful explanatory notes. Most important, its presentation of the plays shuns the old evolutionary model that characterized drama scholarship through midcentury and that influenced Joseph Quincy Adams's *Chief Pre-Shakespearian Dramas*, the anthology that *Medieval Drama* replaced. Among the criticisms directed against Bevington's anthology as a textbook are that its bibliography is meager, that its introductions tend to place literary over theatrical concerns, and that it is expensive. Some survey participants also questioned whether assigning any single-volume textbook was the best way to teach medieval drama, but even they praised the scope and the value of Bevington's textbook.

The anthology's sixty-four selections are organized into six sections. The first two sections are particularly helpful because they provide English translations of texts not otherwise easily available for classroom use. As C. Clifford Flanigan points out later in this volume, the first part of *Medieval Drama*, "Liturgical Beginnings," hints at something like the traditional evolutionary view of drama, but the selections Bevington edits are key documents and plays that serve as background for students, rather than as the early links in a Darwinian chain. Classroom discussion can compare selected texts—for example, the *Quem quaeritis* from the *Regularis concordia* with the *Visitatio sepulchri* from the Fleury manuscript—not to trace how the drama "developed" but to consider the nature of the dramatic in the liturgy and the liturgical in the drama. The selections in this first part are limited by the liturgical focus, which necessarily, though unfortunately, excludes the works of Hrotsvitha, a' tenth-century nun whose six plays are increasingly gaining attention in the undergraduate classroom, especially in women's studies courses. Hrotsvitha's *Dulcitius* and

*Abraham* are now translated, though, in the anthologies of medieval women's literature edited by Elizabeth Alvida Petroff and by Katharina M. Wilson.

The excellent selection of twelfth-century Anglo-Norman and Latin church drama in part 2 is varied in topics, provenance, and types. It includes two of the most interesting Old Testament church plays, the Anglo-Norman *Jeu d'Adam* and the Beauvais *Play of Daniel*, as well as plays from the life of Christ, such as Hilarius's *Raising of Lazarus*, and two early versions of the saint's play, the Fleury *Conversion of Paul* and *Saint Nicholas and the Son of Getron*. (Altogether, Bevington prints five of the ten texts in the Fleury playbook.) Two of the finest medieval church plays, the Benediktbeuern Christmas and Passion plays, are edited from the *Carmina Burana* manuscript. The only disappointment is the omission of the *Ludus de Antichristo* from Tegernsee, a play that would round out the topics and the types presented in this section by exemplifying the dramatic treatment of Christian eschatology and some early features that came to be associated with the morality play, such as the staging of characters who are personified concepts. Happily, this play is available in John Wright's translation, *The Play of Antichrist*.

Part 3 prints twenty-eight selections from Corpus Christi drama; they comprise more than 430 pages and about forty percent of the anthology. This prominence is appropriate because the cycle drama is the form most often taught in medieval drama courses. More than half of the selections are from the Towneley (also known as the Wakefield) cycle, which means that fifteen of the cycle's thirty-two plays are anthologized. The advantage of this selection is that it is possible, by judicious assignment, to give students the flavor of one cycle. It also means that five of the six plays associated with the Wakefield Master—*The Killing of Abel, Noah, The Second Shepherds' Pageant, Herod the Great,* and *The Buffeting*—are included. One resulting disadvantage is that other cycles are underrepresented. For example, only two plays from Chester—*Balaam and Balak* and the saddlers' play of Christ's appearances to the disciples—are included. The N-Town collection (sometimes labeled the Hegge plays or, misleadingly, *Ludus Coventriae*) is better represented by significant portions of its important Passion play, two other plays, and its Banns. York similarly receives greater attention with six plays, including two associated with the York Realist, the pinners' *Crucifixion* and the butchers' *Death of Christ*. The anthology also includes the well-known Brome *Sacrifice of Isaac*, although no selection from the Coventry plays, which are still available in the second edition of Hardin Craig's *Two Coventry Corpus Christi Plays*.

In general, the plays included in part 3 are well chosen and representative. By printing both the York *Shepherds' Play* and the

Towneley *Second Shepherds' Play*, the N-Town *Death of Herod* and the Towneley *Herod the Great*, and the York and Towneley plays dealing with Christ's trial and Crucifixion, as well as the N-Town Passion sequence, *Medieval Drama* encourages comparisons between the cycles based on their differing treatments of similar events, themes, and characters. The selections, however, tend to overrepresent the Old Testament plays in comparison with their actual number in the cycle manuscripts. Bevington thus reflects much scholarship on the mystery plays, which, following the lead of V. A. Kolve's *Play Called Corpus Christi*, has concentrated on the Old Testament plays to investigate such issues as the principles supporting a hypothetical protocycle or a cycle's typological structure. As a consequence, plays that deal with events after the Resurrection are underrepresented, a problem evident in many anthologies and modernized cycles. For example, there are no plays on the Ascension, the Pentecost, the Assumption of the Virgin, or Antichrist.

The final three parts of *Medieval Drama* include nine plays, three each from the categories of saint's or conversion plays, morality plays, and humanist drama. The choices are logical and expected. Part 4 includes the only two Middle English saint's plays, *The Conversion of St. Paul* and *Mary Magdalene* from the Digby manuscript, as well as the Croxton *Play of the Sacrament*. Part 5 collects three of the most important morality plays, *The Castle of Perseverance* and *Mankind* from the Macro manuscript and *Everyman*. The last section of the anthology includes three plays—*Johan Johan*, *The Play of the Weather*, and *Wit and Science*—that, if the responses to the questionnaire are an accurate indication, are taught primarily in courses surveying medieval and Renaissance drama. The brief folk plays and the pre-Shakespearean Elizabethan plays anthologized by Adams are not included.

One respondent summarized the general opinion of Bevington's *Medieval Drama*: "I cannot overemphasize the excellence of this anthology as a one-volume teaching text and as a general reference." Nevertheless, some teachers of medieval drama, even while praising Bevington's selections from other types of drama, question the wisdom of assigning several plays drawn from various cycles, rather than assigning one complete cycle. It is the composite cycle in part 3, therefore, that receives the greatest criticism: "The worst feature is that it anthologizes a collection from different cycles." Critics fear that, unless teachers emphasize to students that they are reading a selection of plays that were never produced together in the Middle Ages and that are, in fact, brought together for editorial and pedagogical convenience, they may mistakenly believe that they are reading an authentic medieval cycle. In this, *Medieval Drama* follows Adams's *Chief Pre-Shakespearian Dramas*, as well as John Matthews Manly's *Specimens of the Pre-Shakespearean Drama* and Alfred W.

Pollard's *English Miracle Plays, Moralities and Interludes*, which include composite cycles. Critics maintain that it would be better to assign one cycle in a form found in an actual manuscript, even at the expense of depriving students of access to the other cycles, than to teach a cycle that is artificial and modern. There is much to be said for this point of view, which develops one of the principles Bevington follows in the anthology's other sections, where he prints complete plays. It can be argued, though, that it is also misleading to have students base their judgment of the mystery plays on only one cycle and not be aware of the unique features of others.

Although *Medieval Drama* in part 3 follows the tradition of earlier anthologies, it does not suffer from their many weaknesses. For example, their introductions and commentaries are hopelessly dated, and they all assume an evolutionary view of the drama's development. Whereas for Adams "the earlier drama was of interest primarily because of what grew out of it," Bevington, as he explains in his preface, "offers medieval drama as an artistic achievement in its own right rather than as a historical antecedent to Elizabethan greatness" (xiii). The earlier collections, furthermore, often censor the texts or provide snippets of plays. They remain available as reprints, but they are expensive, often misleading, and therefore not recommended for classroom use. *Medieval Drama* remains, as one teacher wrote, "not only the best but perhaps the only choice" for a medieval drama course that seeks to survey genres while providing some depth and variety.

## Teaching a Single Mystery Cycle

Teachers who believe that it is misleading to teach a composite cycle or who prefer not to assign an anthology often teach a single mystery cycle, either complete or through extensive selections. Survey respondents who described such courses noted that they were almost always intended for upper-level undergraduate or graduate students. John C. Coldewey's essay in this volume describes such a course focusing on the Chester cycle and considers the advantages and disadvantages of concentrating on one cycle. Other teachers prefer to have students read a selection of plays from the various cycles, as well as a complete cycle; several assign a cycle in addition to an anthology. These assignments may take the form of supplementary reading of the standard critical editions that are placed on reserve. Sometimes students are asked to become experts on one cycle and to present class reports of plays not read by others or to become the explicators of a cycle when particular selections are assigned. A cycle may also be assigned to the entire class from a required textbook. In such cases teachers must first select the common cycle and then order a text appropriate for classroom use, a process that requires some careful thought.

*The Towneley Cycle.*   The cycle that has received the most scholarly attention and that is most often taught is Towneley. Traditionally associated with Wakefield, its provenance remains a subject of scholarly debate. Assigning Towneley is complicated by the present state of available texts. A new edition of the manuscript (ed. Cawley and Stevens) is scheduled to be published in 1991 by the Early English Text Society (EETS). But until its appearance, teachers who wish to teach the plays in Middle English must choose between an edition of the complete cycle that is expensive and more than ninety years old—*The Towneley Plays* (ed. England and Pollard)—or an edition of only six plays, A. C. Cawley's *Wakefield Pageants in the Towneley Cycle.* Those who wish to teach the plays from a modernized text must choose between the fine modernization by John Russell Brown, *The Complete Plays of the Wakefield Master,* which includes only the six plays of the Wakefield Master, or the full modernization by Martial Rose, *The Wakefield Mystery Plays,* which is problematic. As the only complete translation of a cycle, it is useful for those wishing to teach a complete cycle while not having to deal with problems of language. Rose's introduction is sometimes eccentric, however, and his translation—occasionally fabricating whole stanzas for "dramatic" purposes—is often unreliable. It is perhaps for these reasons that as many respondents explicitly warned against as recommended assigning Rose's translation.

*The Chester Cycle.*   Available in a modern critical edition and commentary by Robert Lumiansky and David Mills, Chester is an excellent choice for a graduate course concentrating on one cycle, because it is the subject of a full range of scholarly, documentary, and critical materials. The critical edition is too expensive for most undergraduate courses, however, even for one concentrating on Chester, such as Peter H. Greenfield describes. Teachers who wish to assign Chester along with other medieval drama need to look elsewhere for texts. An early adaptation of the cycle in modern English, Maurice Hussey's *Chester Mystery Plays,* is still in print, but it includes only sixteen plays, cuts even these, and is not particularly faithful to the manuscripts. Another option is the recent modernization by Edward Burns, *The Chester Mystery Cycle: A New Staging Text.* Although a successfully performed acting text, it should be assigned with caution. Burns has conflated a few plays, shortened several others, and omitted some that make the Chester cycle unique, such as *Balaam and Balak* and *The Coming of Antichrist.*

*The York Cycle.*   One of the best choices to teach in depth, the York cycle is available in Richard Beadle's recent critical edition, *The York Plays,* which corrects and supercedes Lucy Toulmin-Smith's 1885 edition. Its price, however, makes it more likely to be put on library reserve than to be ordered for classroom use, even for specialized graduate courses. A selection is available in *York Mystery Plays: A Selection in Modern Spelling* (ed. Beadle and King), which edits twenty-two of York's forty-seven plays, thus providing a healthy sense of the cycle. The single-cycle text most often recommended by survey respondents, it makes available six of the eight plays associated with the York Realist, a playwright who has, like the Wakefield Master, taken on a life of his own. Although omitting *Cain and Abel* and *Abraham and Isaac*, two plays important for teachers who wish to highlight typological links, the anthology does include the skinners' *Entry to Jerusalem*, which, as Martin Stevens has recently argued (*Four Middle English Mystery Cycles* 50–52), is central to the cycle. Its general introduction, headnotes, and attention to staging are also praiseworthy. The J. S. Purvis modernization, *The York Cycle of Mystery Plays*, is out of print.

*The N-Town Plays.* The fourth of the extant collections of mystery plays, N-Town is being edited for the Early English Text Society by Steven Spector. Until it is available, the standard edition remains K. S. Block's *Ludus Coventriae: Or, The Plaie Called Corpus Christi*, which is, unfortunately, expensive and unsuitable for undergraduate courses. Furthermore, both *Representative Medieval and Tudor Plays* (ed. Loomis and Wells) and *The Corpus Christi Play of the English Middle Ages* (ed. Davies), which include large portions of N-Town and plays from other manuscripts, are out of print. Those who wish to teach the N-Town plays should consider, therefore, Peter Meredith's *The Mary Play from the N. Town Manuscript*, a handsome edition that includes a complete apparatus and an intelligent introduction. It provides a reasonable way to deal with a significant yet not overwhelmingly long sequence in depth and should be valuable for teachers who wish to pursue a feminist approach to the plays along the lines discussed by Theresa Coletti. Furthermore, it can be paired with the N-Town Passion sequence in Bevington's *Medieval Drama* or with Meredith's forthcoming edition of the Passion Play to provide students with a good sense of this difficult but fascinating manuscript.

Teachers need to take particular care in selecting texts of medieval cycles for classroom use. They should check the quality of the modernizations against a critical edition to determine faithfulness to the language and the spirit of the original and should analyze editions to ensure that they print complete plays and do not distort the texts. Teachers who believe that students should read a single "real, medieval cycle," rather than an composite "artificial, modern cycle," would not wish to assign simply a different modern version that distorts meaning, chops or omits plays, or creates new synoptic plays. Choosing a Middle English text involves other problems. The edition's format should be examined, as well as the extent to which the language, which can be difficult for beginning students, is standardized and glossed. Unfortunately, at present there is no totally satisfactory way to assign a complete cycle in an undergraduate course. The standard editions are expensive, and the many paperback editions and modernizations do not include complete cycles, are inaccurate, or in other ways distort the cycles. A carefully edited, intelligently introduced, and generously glossed teaching edition of a complete cycle remains a desideratum.

## Teaching Medieval Drama in a Survey Course

One of the challenges of teaching the typical medieval literature survey course through which most students are introduced to the rich variety of literature from the Middle Ages is to prevent the course from becoming "just one damn thing after another." Courses may be arranged by genre to study the drama as the major form of the fifteenth century or may interweave the drama with other literary types to highlight certain topics or themes (see, for example, Mark Allen's essay). Because these courses usually study works spanning several centuries and genres, Bevington's *Medieval Drama* is both too extensive and too expensive to be assigned. In fact, drama is usually a relatively small part of such courses, although it should be a much greater part than is suggested by the available general anthologies of medieval literature. For example, Thomas J. Garbáty's *Medieval English Literature* includes only the *Flood* and *Crucifixion* from York, the *Second Shepherds' Play*, and *Everyman*, whereas D. W. Robertson, Jr.'s *Literature of Medieval England* includes only the Towneley *Killing of Abel, Second Shepherds' Play*, and *Everyman*. Ann S. Haskell's *Middle English Anthology* and J. B. Trapp's *Medieval English Litera-ture*—volume 1 of the *Oxford Anthology of English Literature*—similarly give short shrift to the drama, and *Middle English Literature* (ed. Charles W. Dunn and Edward T. Byrnes) includes no drama. Although the editors of these and future anthologies obviously must make difficult choices, one can't help but feel that the relative neglect of medieval drama reflects a bias that until recently has excluded the drama from the canon of medieval literature or that has concentrated on a few "representative" plays that are, in fact, highly unrepresenta-tive.

Teachers who wish to remedy this problem supplement these meager selections by providing handouts or assigning several more plays from a modest and inexpensive collection, such as A. C. Cawley's *Everyman and Medieval Miracle Plays*. The most widely assigned paperback anthology in survey courses, it represents a compromise: "Bevington is rich but expensive, Cawley is thin but cheap." Several other teachers complained that Cawley has been difficult to assign because it has been in and out of print, but it is now again available.

Well edited, it includes fourteen cycle plays and *Everyman*. Unfortunately, its selections duplicate the plays available in the standard medieval literature anthologies, and its introduction is inadequate, somewhat diminishing its usefulness. It does include the Coventry Shearmen and Taylors' play, though, as well as the Cornish *Death of Pilate*, which is useful, since Bevington's *Medieval Drama* does not include selections from the Cornish *Ordinalia* and Markham Harris's translation is now out of print.

Instead of using a one-volume anthology of medieval literature, such as Garbáty's or Robertson's, some teachers prefer to assign students a range of literature available in a variety of paperback texts. Students consequently read fewer types of literature but in greater depth. An ideal text for such courses is Peter Happé's *English Mystery Plays*, which prints the plays in Middle English with glosses. The third most often recommended anthology (after Bevington and Cawley), it is praised as inexpensive, portable, and useful, and it is lauded for presenting a well-rounded selection from each of the four cycles. It includes thirty-eight plays—ten from York, nine from Towneley, eight from Chester plus its Banns, and five plays plus the Passion sequence from N-Town. It also includes the Brome *Sacrifice of Isaac* and the Coventry Shearmen and Tailors. Later in this volume Robert W. Hanning describes how he uses Happé's anthology to focus student attention on the nature of the cycle plays. Quite a different option is Tony Harrison's *Mysteries*, the text of Bill Bryden's highly successful National Theatre production. It makes no pretense of being other than a personal composite and modern cycle that is unified by Harrison's sense of the dramatic. Less successful is the new acting version by Kenneth Pickering and others, *The Mysteries at Canterbury Cathedral*, which concludes with the Resurrection and Ascension. Keith Miles has adapted the Coventry plays and added extracts from other cycles in his book *The Coventry Mystery Plays*, but the result is disappointing. R. G. Thomas's *Ten Miracle Plays*, ideal for upper-level students studying the drama in Middle English, is unfortunately out of print.

All these anthologies focus on the cycle plays. Teachers who wish to teach a range of medieval drama discover that, other than assigning several paperback collections or providing numerous and lengthy duplicated handouts, they have few alternatives to Bevington's *Medieval Drama*. Teaching editions of the Continental liturgical and church music drama are unavailable, for example. Both *Medieval Church Music-Dramas: A Repertory of Complete Plays* (ed. Collins), with musical scores and accompanying English translations, and *Medieval French Plays* (trans. Axton and Stevens) are out of print, although Oscar Mandel's *Five Comedies of Medieval France*, now reprinted, does include Jean Bodel's *Jeu de Saint Nicolas* and later comedies.

Morality and saint's plays are available in standard editions from the

Early English Text Society: *The Late Medieval Religious Plays of Bodleian MSS Digby 133 and e Museo 160* (ed. Baker, Murphy, and Hall), which includes *The Conversion of St. Paul* and *Mary Magdalene*; *Non-Cycle Plays and Fragments* (ed. Davis), which includes the Croxton *Play of the Sacrament*; and *The Macro Plays* (ed. Eccles), which includes *The Castle of Perseverance* and *Mankind*. Like almost all the society's editions, however, these are too expensive for courses other than a graduate seminar focusing on a particular manuscript or play. The one relatively inexpensive paperback standard edition of a morality play is Cawley's *Everyman*. This play is also available in a Poculi Ludique Societas performance text (ed. Astington) and in a scholarly edition with an extensive introduction and notes (ed. Cooper and Wortham). Unfortunately, no single paperback anthology includes the three most important morality plays. For example, G. A. Lester's *Three Late Medieval Morality Plays*: Mankind, Everyman, Mundus et Infans lacks the important *Castle of Perseverance*. This play is included in Peter Happé's *Four Morality Plays*, but its other selections—Skelton's *Magnyfycence*, Bale's *King Johan*, and Lindsay's *Ane Satire of the Thrie Estatis*—are more suitable for a course surveying medieval and Renaissance drama. *English Moral Interludes* (ed. Wickham), *Tudor Plays: An Anthology of Early English Drama* (ed. Creeth), and *English Morality Plays and Moral Interludes* (ed. Schell and Shuchter) are not in print.

One of the surprising discoveries that emerged from the survey of medieval-drama teachers was the sizable number of courses not focusing primarily on medieval literature in which medieval drama is taught to non-English majors. For such courses, teachers particularly recommend Cawley's *Everyman and Medieval Miracle Plays* as "the most suitable text." Another option is John Gassner's *Medieval and Tudor Drama*, which provides a much fuller range than Cawley's book, including plays by Hrotsvitha, a mummers' play, some liturgical selections, eleven Corpus Christi plays, a selection from the Cornish Passion play, *Everyman*, and three Tudor plays. Its introduction is disappointing, however, and Gassner wins few friends by arguing that the plays he modernizes are "not great dramatic literature" (xi). Also still available is *Medieval Mysteries, Moralities, and Interludes* (ed. Hopper and Lahey).

For many teachers "the single most important criterion for the selection of medieval plays" is what is available in the *Norton Anthology of English Literature*, volume 1 (gen. ed. Abrams). This anthology is the most widely assigned textbook for the standard survey of English literature, which in some institutions is called the "Norton course." Its major advantages are its widespread availability and its Middle English texts, which are well glossed. However, its introductory comments on the drama are criticized for being both outdated and wrong. It includes the York *Crucifixion,* as well as the *Second Shepherds' Play* and *Everyman,* which, not surprisingly, are the two most anthologized medieval plays. These two plays are usually included as well in textbooks surveying drama from antiquity to the modern theatre, such as *Plays for the Theatre* (ed. Brockett) and *Western Theatre: Revolution and Revival* (ed. Gillespie and Cameron). *Everyman,* particularly popular in introductory genre courses, is included in such standard texts as Alvin Kernan's *Character and Conflict* and Laurence Perrine's *Dimensions of Drama,* as well as in world literature anthologies such as *Literature of the Western World* (ed. Wilkie and Hurt) and *The Norton Anthology of World Masterpieces* (gen. ed. Mack). Not only is *Everyman* the best-known medieval play, but it may well be one of the most often taught works of medieval literature.

# Required and Recommended
# Readings for Students

Many teachers of medieval drama require their students to read beyond the drama itself from regularly assigned textbooks or from critical and background studies placed on library reserve in preparation for class reports and critical papers. Most survey courses limit this reading to the major source of medieval drama, the Bible. Teachers stress that it is a mistake to assume that students know the biblical stories; students should be required to read the key scriptural passages—particularly from Genesis and the Gospels—in conjunction with the drama. Often fruitful class discussions develop from an initial comparison between the remarkably brief biblical account and the richly developed dramatic version, and these discussions can help students better understand not only the medieval characteristics of the plays but the process involved in the dramatic transformation of narrative and traditional myth. In some upper-level courses, students are also directed to the Apocryphal sources of the drama. Such works as the *Protevangelium of James* and the *Gospel of Nicodemus*— available in *The Apocryphal New Testament* (trans. James) and in *New Testament Apocrypha* (ed. Hennecke and Schneemelcher)—help flesh out the medieval understanding of the lives of Mary and Christ.

A few courses require students to read as background or to present class reports on medieval texts and art relevant to the drama. Selections from Middle English works available in Early English Text Society editions—such as *A Stanzaic Life of Christ* (ed. Foster), *The Northern Passion* (ed. Foster), and *Mirk's Festial* (ed. Erbe)—are occasionally assigned. Several teachers stressed the importance of introducing advanced students to the contemporary Lollard polemic against plays, which is available in a complete edition in Clifford Davidson's *Middle English Treatise on the Playing of Miracles*. A snippet from the treatise, along with a few other brief documents, forms the first part of Peter Happé's *Medieval English Drama: A Casebook*. The work of medieval art most often cited in the classroom is the *The Holkham Bible Picture Book* (ed. Hassall), a fourteenth-century manuscript that helps visualize in medieval terms such dramatic events as the Crucifixion and the Last Judgment. Teachers also place facsimiles of books of hours on library reserve as visual representations of late medieval spirituality, particularly its emphasis on the Virgin Mary and Christ's suffering. *The Hours of Catherine of Cleves* (ed. Plummer) and *The Rohan Master: A Book of Hours* (ed. Meiss and Thomas) are popular choices.

Other primary sources occasionally placed on reserve allow students to get as close as possible to the manuscripts and the documents related to the drama. Students find examining facsimiles of the play manuscripts to be both fascinating and exasperating. As one teacher wrote, since modern editions are "just too tidy," it is important that students get a sense of the originals. A carefully planned class exercise that compares a printed text with a manuscript source can introduce a discussion of how a manuscript culture differs from our own and make clear the kinds of problems faced by modern editors. Facsimiles are now available for all the cycles; the one for the Macro plays (ed. Bevington) provides facing-page transcriptions. Other recent scholarship that can support various teaching strategies includes the handsome volumes published by the Records of Early English Drama. Simply directing students to the volumes and expecting them to get a sense of the records does not work, however, for the editors provide no interpretive framework for the documents, and the comprehensiveness of the volumes can overwhelm students with a mass of detail. Specific assignments that focus on selected records keyed to plays being read in class should be developed along the lines suggested by Peter H. Greenfield in his essay in this volume. The two collections most often recommended for student assignments are *Records of Early English Drama: Chester* (ed. Clopper) and the two-volume *Records of Early English Drama: York* (ed. Johnston and Rogerson).

*Medieval Drama*, edited by A. C. Cawley and others as the first volume of *The Revels History of Drama in English*, is often recommended as the basic history for students in upper-level courses. Several teachers also recommended, as background for students who have little previous exposure to medieval literature, a quick overview, such as David M. Zesmer's *Guide to English Literature from* Beowulf *through Chaucer and Medieval Drama*, or a general introduction to the thought and outlook of the Middle Ages, such as Robert Ackerman's *Backgrounds to Medieval English Literature* or C. S. Lewis's *Discarded Image*. A cogent and insightful introduction to medieval culture that is firmly grounded in the original texts is William R. Cook and Ronald B. Herzman's *Medieval World View*. A classic study is Johan Huizinga's *Waning of the Middle Ages*, but, as Martin Stevens argues in his essay, assigning Huizinga may do as much harm as good. It is probably better to assign historical studies that concentrate on England, such as Stephen Medcalf's *Later Middle Ages*. Two essays giving advanced students a sense of the communal aspects of the cycle plays are Charles Phythian-Adams's "Ceremony and the Citizen: The Communal Year at Coventry," and Mervyn James's, "Ritual, Drama and the Social Body in the Late Medieval English Town."

The critical work most often assigned for supplementary reading is V. A. Kolve's *Play Called Corpus Christi*, a readable book that is filled with insights and that provides an ideal way of dealing with many aspects of medieval drama students consider alien. Another influential scholarly study is O. B. Hardison's *Christian Rite and Christian Drama in the Middle Ages*, which, although perhaps too difficult for the average student, may be assigned to a bright student for a class report. Other important works of scholarship recommended for upper-level students are Robert Potter's *English Morality Play*, Rosemary Woolf's *English Mystery Plays*, and Martin Stevens's *Four Middle English Mystery Cycles*. Teachers often place two handy collections of essays on reserve: *The Drama of the Middle Ages* (ed. Davidson, Gianakaris, and Stroupe) and *Medieval English Drama* (ed. Taylor and Nelson).

Increasingly, teachers are focusing on the theatrical elements of medieval plays such as costuming, production, staging, and performance. In this volume the essays by Peter H. Greenfield, Milla C. Riggio, Míceál F. Vaughan, and Martin W. Walsh suggest ways to highlight the theatrical in the classroom. Students may be assigned one of the standard histories of the theater available in paperback, such as Glynne Wickham's *Medieval Theatre* and William Tydeman's *Theatre in the Middle Ages*. Both publish plates and other useful illustrations and consider both Continental and English drama. Richard Axton's *European Drama of the Early Middle Ages*, which includes short chapters on the earlier drama, and Glynne Wickham's *History of the Theatre*, with numerous black-and-white illustrations and excellent color plates, are also made available to students. Recently praised as "a treasure for anyone studying, reading, or producing medieval drama" (Urkowitz), *The Staging of Religious Drama in Europe in the Late Middle Ages* (ed. Meredith and Tailby) is packed with illuminating documents in translation. Available in paperback, it is sometimes required for courses that highlight the theatrical aspects of medieval drama.

# The Instructor's Library

Scholarly and critical study of medieval drama has exploded in the past twenty years and has revolutionized our understanding of these plays. Scholars have systematically collaborated to edit critical editions and facsimiles of the dramatic texts; collect and publish civic, ecclesiastical, and other documents related to the production of the plays; and develop comprehensive lists of artwork and other manifestations of medieval culture related to the drama. At the same time, critics have focused on the literary and aesthetic qualities of the plays, and theatre historians have stressed their essential theatricality. Several amateur and semiprofessional companies in Canada, England, and the United States have produced numerous plays, confronting the texts and testing the collective results of research and literary interpretation with the practical experience of staging. What follows is an overview of major reference tools, important works dealing with the religious, social, and cultural background of the drama; historical and critical studies of the drama; and studies of the medieval theatre. The goal is to provide teachers with a good sense of the shape and the present state of scholarly and critical discussion of the drama.

Recent scholarship and productions have swept away many misconceptions concerning the nature and the character of medieval drama. The beginning teacher should approach the older standard histories of English literature, such as *Literary History of England* by Albert Baugh and others, with caution. Unfortunately, even some recent histories continue to perpetuate these misconceptions and cast doubt on the integral importance of the plays. For example, in *The History of English Literature*, Peter Conrad states, "Dramatic representation begins in England as a humble and naive reincarnation of the initial Christian incarnation, a miming of mystery. The miracle of these fourteenth-century plays is the advent, but also the enactment of it" (126). Although less blatant, J. A. Burrow's overview of Old and Middle English literature minimizes the importance of the plays by devoting only one paragraph to all medieval drama. Tellingly, Burrow's essay appears in *The Oxford Illustrated History of English Literature* (ed. Pat Rogers), which includes a forty-eight-page chapter devoted to Shakespeare.

Beginning teachers are advised to eschew general histories of English literature in favor of *Medieval Drama*, (ed. Cawley et al.), the more specialized volume 1 of *The Revels History of Drama in English*. Praised as a "very sensible book" and an "ideal overview," it is up-to-date and comprehensive. A. C. Cawley studies "The Staging of Medieval Drama," David Mills and Peter F. McDonald discuss "The Drama of Religious Ceremonial," and Marion Jones considers "Early Moral Plays and the Earliest Secular Drama." Other useful histories are

Richard Axton's *European Drama of the Early Middle Ages*, Stanley J. Kahrl's *Traditions of Medieval English Drama*, and Arnold Williams's *Drama of Medieval England*. Although they are packed with interesting details and are still occasionally cited in scholarship, Hardin Craig's *English Religious Drama of the Middle Ages* and A. P. Rossiter's *English Drama from the Early Times to the Elizabethans* are outdated and not recommended.

One respondent wrote that "medieval drama as a field has produced more distinguished articles than books." Several of the best articles are available in collections, but others must be searched out. Because scholarship in the field is developing rapidly, teachers are encouraged to keep track of the most up-to-date work published in recent journal articles. Most major scholarly journals occasionally publish articles on medieval drama, but, because some of the best work frequently appears in their pages, the following are particularly recommended: *Comparative Drama, Leeds Studies in English, Medieval and Renaissance Drama in England*, and *Research Opportunities in Renaissance Drama*. The last of these offers a medieval supplement that includes an overview of recent scholarship and reviews of productions. An annual, it is mailed to members of the Medieval and Renaissance Drama Society. Particularly helpful for their articles concerning theatrical aspects are *Theatre Notebook* and *Medieval English Theatre*. Also recommended are the newsletters of the two collaborative research projects that have greatly influenced the study of medieval drama: Early Drama, Art, and Music (EDAM), centered at the Medieval Institute, Western Michigan University; and Records of Early English Drama (REED), coordinated from the University of Toronto.

## Reference Works

Carl J. Stratman's standard, two-volume *Bibliography of Medieval Drama* lists scholarly studies of medieval drama, although even the second edition (1972) is increasingly dated. Sidney Berger has published a continuation that updates this important reference tool. Also helpful are the entries by Anna J. Mill, Sheila Lindenbaum, Francis Lee Utley, and Barry Ward in "Dramatic Pieces," published in volume 5 of *A Manual of Writings in Middle English, 1050–1500* (ed. Hartung). Those wishing to pursue more specific topics should consult C. Clifford Flanigan, "The Liturgical Drama and Its Tradition: A Review of Scholarship, 1965–1975"; Peter J. Houle, *The English Morality and Related Drama: A Bibliographical Survey*; D. Jerry White, *Early English Drama: Everyman to 1580*; Graham A. Runnalls, "Medieval French Drama: A Review of Recent Scholarship"; and Kathleen C. Falvey, "Italian Vernacular Religious Drama of the Fourteenth through the Sixteenth Centuries: A Selected Bibliography on the *Lauda dramatica* and the *Sacra rappresentazione.*" *Annals of English Drama 975–1700* (ed. Harbage and Schoenbaum) is a chronological listing of plays, both extant and lost, although it implies a certainty about dating that cannot be supported by the evidence.

With the increased availability of standard editions, scholars have begun to publish related research tools. These include concordances and facsimiles of the major dramatic texts. For example, Jean D. Pfleiderer and Michael J. Preston have compiled *A Complete Concordance to the Chester Mystery Plays*, based on the Lumiansky and Mills edition, and *A KWIC Concordance to the Plays of the Wakefield Master*, based on the Cawley edition. Under the auspices of the School of English at the University of Leeds, Leeds Texts and Monographs has been publishing the Medieval Drama Facsimiles. Already available in this series are three of the Chester manuscripts (ed. Lumiansky and Mills), the York manuscript (ed. Beadle), the Towneley manuscript (ed. Cawley and Stevens), the N-Town manuscript (ed. Meredith and Kahrl), and the Digby plays (ed. Baker and Murphy). David Bevington has also published the Macro plays in the Folger Facsimile series.

Other important reference tools include the volumes published by the Records of Early English Drama (REED) project, which collects the civic, ecclesiastical, and other records of dramatic activity in England before 1642. Eight volumes have been published, and another twenty-eight are projected. The Malone Society has also been publishing relevant records. A helpful tool for organizing and understanding these and other records is Ian Lancashire's *Dramatic Texts and Records of Britain*, comprising a chronological list of 190 dramatic texts, topographical lists of dramatic records from about four hundred sites in Britain and other countries, several detailed indexes, an introductory overview of the records, a handy bibliography, and maps and other illustrations. It is a highly recommended reference work, more valuable for the teacher than any single REED volume.

Volumes in the Early Drama, Art, and Music Reference series are indispensable for teachers interested in the relationship between the visual arts and drama. These include subject lists of art from the locales of two of the major cycles: *York Art* (ed. Davidson and O'Connor) and *Chester Art* (ed. MacLean). Also recommended is Pamela Sheingorn's *Easter Sepulchre in England*. Handy for their iconographic details and extensive illustrations are Louis Réau's three-volume *Iconographie de l'art chrétien* and Gertrud Schiller's two-volume *Iconography of Christian Art*.

## Background Studies

One of the most difficult challenges facing teachers of medieval drama is its alterity. Because the plays are not simply literary texts but cultural performances, teachers should draw on the insights of a wide range of disciplines to introduce students to a world and a culture that are very different from our own. The essays in this volume by Kathleen M. Ashley and Peter W. Travis illustrate a few of the insights to be gained from the social sciences. Clearly, the teaching of medieval drama is enriched by an understanding of its historical, social, economic, religious, and cultural backgrounds. The following discussion only hints at the wealth of scholarship on backgrounds relevant to medieval drama. A good starting place for those who wish to pursue specific areas in detail is *Medieval Studies: A Bibliographic Guide* (ed. Crosby, Bishko, and Kellogg). Its section on drama (840–46) is disappointing, but it provides a handy overview of scholarship in other areas of medieval studies. Also recommended are the concise and usually excellent entries on all facets of the Middle Ages in the *Dictionary of the Middle Ages* (ed. Strayer). Because they focus on how a range of social, cultural, and religious backgrounds relate to the drama, the essays in *Contexts for Early English Drama* (ed. Briscoe and Coldewey) should also be consulted.

Readable histories include R. W. Southern's *Making of the Middle Ages*; G. R. Coulton's more dated but informative work, *Medieval Panorama: The English Scene from Conquest to Reformation*; and David Knowles's *Evolution of Medieval Thought*, the best one-volume intellectual history of the Middle Ages. Excellent overviews of various facets of medieval culture include William R. Cook and Ronald B. Herzman's *Medieval World View*, Ernst Robert Curtius's *European Literature and the Latin Middle Ages*, and Henry O. Taylor's wide-ranging two-volume *The Mediaeval Mind*. A classic study is Johan Huizinga's *Waning of the Middle Ages*, highly readable but not always reliable. A more up-to-date work is Steven Ozment's *Age of Reform, 1250–1550*. Stressing the impressive achievements of this period, Ozment suggests the essential continuity of late medieval and early modern thought and culture, a continuity evident in the drama. Given the importance of the communal aspects of late medieval drama, teachers should also be aware of the social and economic conditions of the late Middle Ages as studied in M. M. Postan's *Medieval Economy and Society*, Mervyn James's "Ritual, Drama and the Social Body in the Late Medieval English Town," and the essays in *Crisis and Order in English Towns, 1500–1700* (ed. Clark and Slack). A fascinating work that begins with a study of Shakespeare's *Richard II* but that develops insights concerning the body politic that can be applied to a range of medieval drama is Ernst H. Kantorowicz's *King's Two Bodies*.

Students and teachers should have a good sense of the biblical sources for the plays and the various ways in which the Bible was studied and communicated to the laity in the Middle Ages. Although first published in 1941, Beryl Smalley's *Study of the Bible in the Middle*

*Ages* remains the place for teachers to begin investigating this complex topic. Also helpful are several essays in volume 2 of *The Cambridge History of the Bible: The West from the Fathers to the Reformation* (ed. Lampe), especially R. L. P. Milburn's " 'People's Bible': Artists and Commentators" and Francis Wormald's "Bible Illustration in Medieval Manuscripts." The definitive work is Henri de Lubac's *Exégèse médiévale: Les quatre sens de l'Ecriture*, but, rather than working through the subtleties of medieval exegetical theories, those unfamiliar with the medieval Christian understanding of the world as a text that God spoke into creation will probably more profitably read Augustine's influential *On Christian Doctrine*. As Pamela Sheingorn argues later in this volume, medieval exegetical practice influenced the structure, the language, and even the staging of medieval drama through its understanding of biblical typology. A lucid study of typology is Erich Auerbach's "Figura." More specialized is Jean Daniélou's *From Shadows to Reality*. Some of the ways in which medieval audiences learned biblical stories, their interpretation, and their applicability to everyday life are examined by G. R. Owst's *Literature and Pulpit in Medieval England*, David Jeffrey's "Franciscan Spirituality and the Rise of Early English Drama," and Stanley J. Kahrl's "Secular Life and Popular Piety in Medieval English Drama." David C. Fowler's *Bible in Middle English Literature* surveys biblical influence on medieval drama, ranging from the liturgical to the morality plays and including the Cornish *Ordinalia* (3–52).

Teachers should have a solid understanding of the religious foundations of medieval culture, especially the liturgy, which was complex, developing throughout this period and reflecting particular regional concerns. Those unfamiliar with the liturgy should acquaint themselves with the introductory section, "The Liturgy of the Church of Rome," and the chapter "The Dramatic Element in Liturgy" in volume 1 of Karl Young's *Drama of the Medieval Church* (15–111) and the early essays in O. B. Hardison's *Christian Rite and Christian Drama in the Middle Ages*. A now classic study of the liturgy and its history is Joseph A. Jungmann's *Mass of the Roman Rite*. Helpful in studying particular aspects of the forms, the origins, and the texts of the liturgy are the essays and the annotated bibliographies in *The Study of Liturgy* (ed. Jones, Wainwright, and Yarnold). Excellent on the earliest texts and the music of the liturgical drama are C. Clifford Flanigan, "The Roman Rite and the Origins of the Liturgical Drama"; Timothy J. McGee, "The Liturgical Placements of the 'Quem quaeritis' Dialogue"; and William L. Smoldon, "The Melodies of the Medieval Church Dramas and Their Significance."

The last essays remind us of the close relationship between drama and music in the Middle Ages, even for the late medieval vernacular plays that are neither liturgical nor musical dramas. A helpful, although technical, history is Richard H. Hoppin's *Medieval Music*, which deals with all aspects of medieval music, from the earliest chants to the elaborate polyphonies of the fifteenth century. Similarly informed musicologically, yet more concerned with literary and dramatic texts, is John Stevens's *Words and Music in the Middle Ages*, which devotes two chapters to the liturgical drama. Richard Rastall's brief but insightful essay "Alle hefne makyth melody" focuses on music in the nonliturgical drama of the late Middle Ages. Rastall extends this study in his essay in *Contexts for Early English Drama*. More specialized and detailed is Rastall's study of music in the Chester cycle (in Lumiansky and Mills's *Essays and Documents*) and Nan Cooke Carpenter's "Music in the *Secunda pastorum*." JoAnna Dutka's *Music in the English Mystery Plays* provides indexes to songs and instruments, a glossary, and intelligent commentaries for the nonspecialist who wishes to focus class attention on music.

Drama, by its very nature as performance, draws on the visual arts, as well as the musical and verbal arts. An influential and still useful study of the relationship between art and drama is M. D. Anderson's *Drama and Imagery in English Medieval Churches*, which assumes that "medieval drama and imagery reflect the same traditions of theology, mysticism and popular instruction" but which also occasionally sets forth a "far-fetched" conjecture (3). Teachers interested in approaching plays through iconographical analysis should consider the solid methodological advice in Pamela Sheingorn's "On Using Medieval Art in the Study of Medieval Drama." Also recommended are Sheingorn's "Visual Language of Drama" and Clifford Davidson's *Drama and Art*. The insights derived from studying the relation between the visual arts and medieval drama are exemplified in the essays by David Bevington, Richard Emmerson, Ronald B. Herzman, and Pamela Sheingorn in *"Homo, Memento Finis": The Iconography of Just Judgment in Medieval Art and Drama* (ed. Bevington et al.); the chapter "Hierarchy in the Mystery Plays" in Murray Roston's *Renaissance Perspectives in Literature and the Visual Arts* (63–97); and Theresa Coletti's "Devotional Iconography in the N-Town Marian Plays."

Three art historical studies, classics in their own right, provide cultural background: Emile Mâle's *Gothic Image*, Millard Meiss's *Painting in Florence and Siena after the Black Death*, and Erwin Panofsky's two-volume *Early Netherlandish Painting*. Art historians have questioned the conclusions of these studies. Furthermore, they deal with Continental art; because of its popular nature, medieval drama is usually studied more profitably in relation to native English traditions. A dependable history of English medieval art is Margaret Rickert's *Painting in Britain: The Middle Ages*. More specialized sources include A. Caiger-Smith's *English Medieval Mural Paintings*, W. O. Hassall's *Holkham Bible Picture Book*, and Earnest William

Tristram's *English Wall Painting of the Fourteenth Century*. Although concentrating on the Continent, Adolf Katzenellenbogen's *Allegories of the Virtues and Vices in Mediaeval Art* studies the visual treatment of allegories that play key roles in the morality plays.

## Critical and Literary Studies of the Drama

In addition to recent scholarship devoted to basic research tools necessary for the study of medieval drama in its historical context, critical studies of the plays have flourished as scholars have increasingly gained an appreciation of their literary qualities, their integral place in late medieval culture, and their status as an urban and popular art form. Rather than attempting to be comprehensive, the following discussion concentrates on those books and articles that have been most influential and that were most often cited by the respondents in the survey of medieval drama teachers. Several of the most important essays have been collected in two handy anthologies: *The Drama of the Middle Ages* (ed. Davidson, Gianakaris, and Stroupe) and *Medieval English Drama* (ed. Taylor and Nelson), which includes Jerome Taylor's "Critics, Mutations, and Historians of Medieval English Drama," a survey of the approaches and critical disputes that dominated the study of medieval drama in the decades after the Second World War. Other useful collections of critical essays are Sandro Sticca's *Medieval Drama*, which gathers papers on French, German, Latin, and English plays; and Neville Denny's *Medieval Drama*, which includes original essays on a range of literary and theatrical topics, medieval and Tudor.

One of the most influential studies of medieval drama is O. B. Hardison's *Christian Rite and Christian Drama in the Middle Ages*, which reexamines the original texts and challenges the dogma that controlled the historical study of medieval drama before the Second World War. The book undermined the evolutionary assumptions of scholarship enshrined in E. K. Chambers's *Mediaeval Stage* and helped reestablish the legitimate relation between literary art and religious experience. Subsequent scholars followed Hardison, seeking insights from the study of ritual, devotional texts, theological treatises, popular spirituality, and Christian iconography. Ultimately, this emancipation of medieval drama from the confines of a narrow literary history devoted to the detection of the pre-Shakespearean has led to a scholarship that eagerly draws from a full range of interdisciplinary approaches and insights to better understand the plays as unique dramatic texts valuable in their own right. If Hardison revolutionized the scholarly understanding of the origins of medieval drama by emphasizing the continuing lively relationship between drama and religion, Harold C. Gardiner's *Mysteries' End* destroyed the common-place notion that the plays died of exhaustion.

Recommended studies of liturgical and church drama include Mary Marshall's "Aesthetic Values of the Liturgical Drama," a spirited essay that protested against the common prejudice that the liturgical drama was "lifeless, a dreary little undifferentiated amoeba of modern drama, without plot, without character, almost without conflict, whose only value is historical" (28). More recent studies have moved beyond the apologetic and have concentrated on particular features of the church drama. The Fleury manuscript particularly has been the focus of much study, including several essays studying the music, the iconography, the dramaturgy, and the theology of its plays collected in *The Fleury Playbook* (ed. Campbell and Davidson). C. Clifford Flanigan's "Fleury *Playbook*, the Traditions of Medieval Latin Drama, and Modern Scholarship" is particularly recommended. The most popular Anglo-Norman play, the *Mystère d'Adam*, is the subject of Erich Auerbach's classic essay, "Adam and Eve."

V. A. Kolve's *Play Called Corpus Christi* is the most often cited critical study of the cycle plays. Although scholars disagree about some of its conclusions, the study is praised for radically altering the scholarly interpretation of the cycle plays and is recommended to teachers as "absolutely the first place to start." Many of Kolve's arguments concerning the central importance of the feast of Corpus Christi, the structural principles underlying the cycles, their sense of play and "religious laughter," and their use of anachronism and comedy have become commonplace in recent interpretations of the plays. Reading *The Play Called Corpus Christi* is the critical equivalent of studying a composite cycle: it provides important insights into the cycle drama as play, rather than specific readings of individual plays. Another cogent study of the nature of medieval drama is Martin Stevens's "Illusion and Reality in the Medieval Drama."

An excellent study that examines particular plays in greater detail is Rosemary Woolf's *English Mystery Plays*, a New Critical reading that analyzes the treatment of similar episodes by the various cycles. Comparing one theme, character, or topic developed in more than one cycle is an approach that has yielded impressive dividends in the hands of several scholars. Particularly recommended are Thomas P. Campbell's "Eschatology and the Nativity in English Mystery Plays," Robert W. Hanning's "'You Have Begun a Parlous Pleye': The Nature and Limits of Dramatic Mimesis as a Theme in Four Middle English 'Fall of Lucifer' Cycle Plays," and David J. Leigh's "The Doomsday Mystery Play: An Eschatological Morality." Recent scholarship has also concentrated on the unifying thematic and structural features of the individual cycles, an approach pursued in Martin Stevens's *Four Middle English*

*Mystery Cycles: Textual, Contextual, and Critical Interpretations*, which analyzes the extant cycle manuscripts and the documentary evidence.

Individual cycles have also been the subject of scholarly study, although, perhaps because so much groundwork remains to be done, essays tackling specific problems have been more successful than books studying whole cycles. The best book devoted to a single cycle is Peter W. Travis's *Dramatic Design in the Chester Cycle*. Other recommended works on the Chester cycle include the Early English Text Society commentary by Lumiansky and Mills, their *Chester Mystery Cycle: Essays and Documents*, Lawrence M. Clopper's "History and Development of the Chester Cycle," and Kathleen M. Ashley's "Divine Power in the Chester Cycle and Late Medieval Thought." The Towneley plays have also received much scholarly attention, including one of the finest early critical studies, Arnold Williams's *Characterization of Pilate in the Towneley Plays*. More recent are Jeffrey Helterman's *Symbolic Action in the Plays of the Wakefield Master*, Lawrence J. Ross's "Symbol and Structure in the *Secunda pastorum*," and Míčeál Vaughan's "Three Advents in the *Secunda pastorum*." Barbara D. Palmer's " 'Towneley Plays' or 'Wakefield Cycle' Revisited" summarizes the continuing debate concerning the provenance of these plays.

The staging and the records relating to the York cycle have been extensively studied, as have the plays of the York Realist. See, for example, J. W. Robinson's "Art of the York Realist" and Clifford Davidson's "Realism of the York Realist and the York Passion," which is revised and included in Davidson's *From Creation to Doom: The York Cycle of Mystery Plays*. An important essay on the variety of drama performed in York is Alexandra F. Johnston's "Plays of the Religious Guilds of York: The Creed Play and the Pater Noster Play." Gail McMurray Gibson's "Bury St. Edmunds, John Lydgate, and the N-Town Cycle" is a detailed, though speculative, essay on the provenance of the N-Town cycle. Other recommended studies of N-Town include Kathleen M. Ashley's " 'Wyt' and 'Wysdam' in the N-Town Cycle" and Theresa Coletti's "Sacrament and Sacrifice in the N-Town Passion."

The most comprehensive and influential overview of the morality plays is Robert Potter's *English Morality Play*. Generic and formal studies of the moralities have been less successful, perhaps because their authors have concentrated on one dominant motif or pattern; in fact, the morality plays are too rich for this kind of categorizing. Examples of such studies include Merle Fifield's *Rhetoric of Free Will: The Five-Act Structure of the English Moral Play*, Michael R. Kelley's *Flamboyant Drama: A Study of* The Castle of Perseverance, Mankind, *and* Wisdom, and Edgar Schell's *Strangers and Pilgrims: From* The Castle of Perseverance *to* King Lear. In contrast, W. A. Davenport's *Fifteenth-Century English Drama: The Early Moral Plays and Their*

*Literary Relations* stresses the variety of late medieval drama, including *Everyman, Mankind, Wisdom,* and *The Castle of Perseverance.* A famous study that includes an analysis of the vices so dominant in the morality plays is Bernard Spivack's *Shakespeare and the Allegory of Evil.*

The saint's plays until recently have received less scholarly attention. David Jeffrey's "English Saints Plays" is a serviceable overview, and the essays in *The Saint Play in Medieval Europe* (ed. Davidson) help establish the foundation for future studies of "what may well have been the most popular type of drama in the medieval period" (ix). Studies of other forms and traditions include Alan Brody's *English Mummers and Their Plays,* E. K. Chambers's *English Folk-Play,* and Robert Longsworth's *Cornish Ordinalia: Religion and Dramaturgy.* General histories often have some helpful information concerning Continental processions and plays, but the medieval dramas of France, German, Italy, and Spain are not well known by students of English drama. Good introductions include the essays by Robert Potter and Lynette Muir in *Contexts for Early English Drama.* The standard survey of French drama is Grace Frank's *Medieval French Drama.* A more recent study is Alan E. Knight's *Aspects of Genre in Late Medieval French Drama*; Knight's discussions of theoretical issues are useful for teachers of English drama.

## Studies of the Medieval Theater

The distinction between literary and theatrical studies of medieval drama is, at best, practical and, at worst, misleading. The drama can be understood fully only when both literary and theatrical approaches are used, as is evident in several of the essays in this volume. The distinction is kept in this introductory section primarily to emphasize the importance of the theatrical, which—as Robert Potter laments—is sometimes overlooked by those who most often teach medieval drama, members of English departments. Although Chambers's two-volume *Mediaeval Stage* paid ample attention to dramaturgy, later scholarly emphasis on the literary, the religious, and the artistic qualities of the plays means that theatrical aspects have sometimes been ignored. The success of modern revivals and the steady work of several historians, however, have once again established the importance of studying the theatricality of these plays.

The work of Glynne Wickham represents the foremost scholarship on the medieval stage. His most important contribution is the three-volume *Early English Stages, 1300–1600;* also useful for teachers is *The Medieval Theatre,* which includes a surprisingly lengthy "Calendar of Twentieth-Century Revivals of English Mystery Cycle and Other Major Religious Plays of the Middle Ages in England" (234–38).

Recommended for the broad overview is William Tydeman's *Theatre in the Middle Ages*, which is also valuable for Continental drama. Other general studies include Alois M. Nagler's *Medieval Religious Stage* and Allardyce Nicoll's *Masks, Mimes, and Miracles*.

The best recent study of the staging of specific medieval plays is William Tydeman's *English Medieval Theatre, 1400–1500*, which illustrates several staging types in essays devoted to particular plays: *Mankind*, the Croxton *Play of the Sacrament*, *The Castle of Perseverance*, the York Passion sequence, and *Fulgens and Lucres*. More controversial but still recommended as a study of a particular staging form is Richard Southern's *Medieval Theatre in the Round*, which should be read in conjunction with Natalie Crohn Schmitt's "Was There a Medieval Theater in the Round?" Also controversial is Alan H. Nelson's *Medieval English Stage*, which examines "how, when, where, and for whom the Corpus Christi plays were performed" (11).

Studies of particular dramatic genres and types include some helpful analyses of the early church drama, such as David Bevington's "Staging of Twelfth-Century Liturgical Drama in the Fleury *Playbook*," Dunbar H. Ogden's "Use of Architectural Space in Medieval Music Drama," and Fletcher Collins's *Production of Medieval Church Music-Drama*. Among recent studies concentrating on the staging of the cycle plays are several essays collected in *The Staging of the Chester Cycle* (ed. Mills); "The Doomsday Pageant of the York Mercers, 1433," by Alexandra F. Johnston and Margaret Dorrell; and "Staging the N-Town Cycle," by Stanley Kahrl and Kenneth Cameron. Recommended studies of the morality plays are David Bevington's *From* Mankind *to Marlowe: The Growth of Structure in the Popular Drama of Tudor England*, one of the most influential books written on late medieval and Tudor drama, and the essays in *The* Wisdom *Symposium* (ed. Riggio). On the staging of other forms, see Neville Denny's "Arena Staging and Dramatic Quality in the Cornish Passion Play" and Glynne Wickham's "Staging of Saint Plays in England."

Finally, several essays consider various theatrical questions surrounding the recent revivals of medieval plays and the increasing documentary evidence related to late medieval drama. Reviews of the Toronto productions are particularly recommended, including Sheila Lindenbaum's "York Cycle at Toronto: Staging and Performance Style" and Martin Stevens's "*Processus Torontoniensis*: A Performance of the Wakefield Cycle." The essays in *Records of Early English Drama: Proceedings of the First Colloquium* (ed. Dutka) consider the relation between documentary detail and staging. John R. Elliott's essay in *Contexts for Early English Drama* surveys evidence for medieval acting practices. Two essays in *Aspects of Early English Drama* (ed. Neuss) concentrate on the practical application of historical research to staging: Peter Meredith's "Scribes, Texts and Performance," which tackles the problems of determining performance practice based on the meager manuscript evidence; and Meg Twycross's " 'Apparell comlye,' " which provides an insightful discussion of possible stage costuming.

# Aids to Teaching

Perhaps because drama depends heavily on many visual and aural elements beyond its texts, almost all the survey respondents noted that they incorporate some form of audiovisual material in their courses to encourage interpretation of the dramatic texts and to answer theatrical questions that arise from the staging of the plays. Many teachers, for example, use slides of medieval abbeys, cathedrals, castles, town walls, and other extant architecture and photographs of manuscript illuminations, stained glass, wall paintings, altarpieces, and other medieval art to enrich the background lectures and to support the discussions of relevant iconography. One respondent, noting that "there is no easy way to build up visual resources," explained that she has collected photographs from museums, trips abroad, books, and performances of the plays. Several teachers mentioned similar collections that they have personally developed over the years. One effective use of artistic materials is described in Pamela Sheingorn's contribution to this volume. More general but also helpful, especially for the inexperienced teacher, is Norine Cashman's *Teacher's Guide to Classroom Use of Slides for Medieval Studies*, an inexpensive pamphlet available from TEAMS (Consortium for the Teaching of the Middle Ages).

Some teachers debate the value of using films in a medieval drama course. On the one hand, several teachers use films, especially of dramatic performances, noting variously that films "are worth the investment" because "they bring the plays to life." On the other hand, some labeled the available films as "not authentic" or as simply "too expensive to buy or even rent," and one teacher noted that "students do not find them very interesting." Significantly, a few argued that a film simply takes time away from more worthwhile classroom discussion. Nevertheless, as Michael L. Hall argues in his discussion of how he has successfully used *Jesus Christ, Superstar* in teaching medieval drama, a film—when shown outside the classroom and then discussed with specific objectives in mind—can be an effective pedagogical tool. Teachers who wish to show films in their courses find two pamphlets prepared under the auspices of the Consortium for the Teaching of the Middle Ages helpful: Sue Ellen Holbrook's pamphlet, *Teacher's Guide to Finding Films and Videocassettes for Medieval Studies*, and Jonathan C. Enos's pamphlet, *Teacher's Guide to Classroom Use of 16mm Films and Videocassettes*.

Some of the highly successful University of Toronto productions of medieval drama have been filmed and are available on videotape for rent or purchase from the University of Toronto Media Centre (121 St., George St., Toronto, ON M5S 1A1). *The Castle of Perseverance* is available in two forms, a full-length recording lasting almost four and a half hours and a one-hour recording of its key scenes. Videotapes of thirty plays from the York cycle, ranging in length from seven to twenty-nine minutes, are also available, as are a forty-minute Middle English version of the Wakefield *Killing of Abel*, a modernized full version of the *Second Shepherds' Play*, and a two-hour Passion play based on the N-Town manuscript. In addition to these videotapes of actual performances, the center has available *The Origins of Liturgical Drama*, a thirty-five minute videotape written by Marcie Epstein; *The York Cycle in the Fifteenth Century*, a short discussion of the cycle's organization written by Alexandra Johnston; and *The Staging of Medieval English Drama*, David Parry's exploration of the various theatrical forms of medieval drama; and many other videotapes on a range of medieval topics that provide background for the drama. Because new tapes are regularly added to this excellent collection, teachers are urged to have their names placed on the Media Centre's mailing list.

The *Visit to the Sepulcher*, a performance of the Fleury *Quem quaeritis* directed by Fletcher Collins and filmed at the abbey of St.-Benoit de Fleury, is highly recommended. It is available as a 16mm film or on videocassette from Theatre Wagon (437 E. Beverley St., Staunton, VA 24401). Films of the *Second Shepherds' Play*, available from Films for the Humanities (PO Box 2053, Princeton, NJ 08540), and of the University of California production of Neville Denny's revival of the Cornish *Ordinalia* are also useful. The Early English Drama series produced by Ohio State University under the direction of Stanley J. Kahrl includes two videotapes of the early liturgical and church music drama, three dealing with the mystery plays, and one each devoted to *Mankind* and *The Nature of the Four Elements*. Designed for classroom use, the episodes begin with presentations of relevant background intended to place the plays in their cultural context and conclude with panel discussions. A videocassette of the recent performance of *The Play of Antichrist* is available from American Medieval Players (1146 W. Farwell, Chicago, IL 60626). Some of the short films listed in *Index to 16mm Educational Films*, such as *The Medieval Guilds* and *Medieval Times: The Role of the Church*, also provide useful background for students unfamiliar with medieval life and culture.

Perhaps not surprisingly, the most widely used teaching aids are phonographic and cassette recordings of the plays, which teachers praise as effective tools for helping students with sometimes difficult language and for providing a sense of the richness of the drama. One respondent noted, furthermore, that audio recordings are preferable to films and videotapes because they are not as prone "to silly 'interpretations.'" Several teachers also play for their classes examples of liturgical and other medieval music not explicitly related to the drama.

Such music is available in fine recordings by the New York Pro Musica, the Ensemble for Early Music, the Folger Consort, the Waverly Consort, and other groups dedicated to early music noted in Derrick Henry's book, *Listener's Guide to Medieval and Renaissance Music*. Martial Rose briefly discusses some ways in which musical recordings can be used in conjunction with drama in his introduction to *The Wakefield Mystery Plays* (48–54). A general examination of pedagogical strategies using recordings to introduce students to medieval literature is Frederick E. Danker's "Teaching Medieval Literature: Texts, Recordings, and Techniques." A basic reference work is Herbert H. Hoffman's *Recorded Plays: Indexes to Dramatists, Plays, and Actors*.

Several medieval plays are available in two recorded anthologies. The Caedmon record *Wellsprings of Drama* (disc, TC 1030; cassette, CDL 51030) includes recordings from a *Quem quaeritis* trope, the N-Town Banns, the Brome *Sacrifice of Isaac*, the Chester *Noah*, and *Robin Hood and the Friar*. A much more extensive boxed collection of records is the Dover anthology, *First Stage* (99705-99722). It includes the Towneley *Creation and Fall of Man, Noah, Abraham and Isaac, Jacob and Esau, Nativity, Betrayal, Trial and Crucifixion*, and *Resurrection*, as well as *The Castle of Perseverance, Everyman, Mary Magdalene, Play of the Sacrament, Pride of Life*, and *Robin Hood and the Friar*. Caedmon has also recorded the *Second Shepherds' Play* (disc, TC 1032; cassette, CDL 51032) and *Everyman* (disc, TC 1031; cassette, CDL 51031), which is also available from London Records (Argo ZSW 552). A Middle English recording of the Towneley *Noah* is available from Golden Clarion Literary Services (RR 1, Box 669, Hudson, PQ JOP 1HO, Can.). Some teachers also recommend the four-and-a-half-hour tape of the 1980 BBC radio production of *The Mysteries* and the shorter cassette of music from the production available from the National Theatre. Probably the most elaborate recording of a medieval play, the one most often recommended by the respondents, is the New York Pro Musica's version of *The Play of Daniel* (Decca Records DL 79402), which is beautifully performed and makes use of several authentic late medieval instruments, although its inventive treatment of the play extends beyond the available medieval evidence.

*Part Two*

# APPROACHES

# INTRODUCTION

The essays that follow are written by experienced teachers of medieval drama; many of them have also contributed to the scholarship on the dramatic genres, theatrical elements, and rich background of these plays. As a group, the essays seek a balance between those that provide extensive scholarly introductions to ways of presenting these plays from certain theoretical perspectives and those that are more focused and describe specific strategies that their authors have successfully used in the classroom. Although arising from teaching experiences, the essays do not provide syllabi or other materials to be simply appropriated by others; they do provide a range of models that other teachers may shape for their own needs to structure courses, highlight key dramatic features, assign materials for encouraging class discussion, and focus on staging and production issues. In "Medieval Drama: Genres, Misconceptions, and Approaches," Martin Stevens provides an introductory synthesis for many of the major concerns of part 2 by surveying the dramatic genres, citing significant scholarly trends that have altered our understanding of these plays, and recommending some generally applicable approaches for teachers, whatever their interests.

The essays in the "Critical and Theoretical Approaches" section are distinguished by their greater length and emphasis on theoretical issues. These contributions to medieval drama scholarship and pedagogy are as helpful for the experienced teacher who has been unable to keep up with the sometimes bewildering array of recent theoretical approaches as they are for the younger teacher whose area of specialization is not medieval drama. The essays begin with C. Clifford Flanigan's inquiry into the reasons for teaching Latin liturgical texts in courses primarily concerned with English drama. Then follow two wide-ranging essays, the first concentrating on an approach, the second on a topic. Kathleen M. Ashley demonstrates how an understanding of the dramatic forms as cultural performances helps students recognize the centrality of the theatrical in medieval public life, and Peter W. Travis investigates the rich potential of using the body of Christ as an interpretive paradigm for the cycle plays. The remaining two essays follow different approaches to achieve similar results—to engage student interest in the drama through the examination of significant issues and images important to both medieval and modern audiences. While recognizing the obstacles to be overcome in applying feminist theory to medieval drama, Theresa Coletti shows how this relatively new approach can illuminate a variety of Corpus Christi plays. Although the typological approach to the drama is more traditional in scholarship, its potential in the classroom has not always been fully realized. Drawing on modern critical theory as well as medieval exegetical and visual sources, Pamela Sheingorn demonstrates specific ways in which this approach can be applied to the Brome *Sacrifice of Isaac*, one of the most widely taught medieval plays.

The essays in the remaining two sections are shorter and less theoretical, describing in practical terms some ways that teachers have successfully solved the difficult problems of teaching medieval drama. "Courses and Strategies" begins with Peter H. Greenfield's description of a course designed for general students that fulfills a core requirement and ends with John C. Coldewey's reflections on teaching medieval drama to advanced undergraduate and graduate students. Because both essays concentrate on the Chester cycle and are concerned with the in-depth study of the texts in the light of recent scholarship dealing with social and economic evidence, they should be read together as examples of how similar pedagogical goals may be pursued at two levels of the curriculum. The three middle essays deal specifically with imaginative teaching strategies that may be pursued in undergraduate courses. The essays by Mark Allen and Michael L. Hall, which concentrate on plays widely available in literature and drama survey textbooks, are comparative in approach. Allen explains how students can be introduced to the art and the themes of the *Second Shepherds' Play* and *Everyman* through contemporary Middle English lyrical treatments of the Nativity and death; Hall explains how focusing on the use of anachronism and humor in a modern theatrical version of the Passion play can help students understand comparable features in medieval drama. Robert W. Hanning's essay describes his method of introducing English majors to the mystery plays in a medieval literature survey course, a familiar course in many English departments. In contrast to Coldewey's emphasis on a single cycle, Hanning's approach selects plays from various cycles to pursue three critical issues central to the nature of the mystery plays.

As Robert Potter argues in the first essay of "Staging and Performance," to be fully understood, medieval plays must be experienced in performance. His essay is a good-humored yet serious plea for teaching the theatrical elements of medieval drama. Several teachers have found that one successful way to deal with the theatrical is to ask students to attend productions or to participate in a dramatic performance staged for the class or for a larger audience. Martin W. Walsh relates how such class projects have occasionally led to the big time when his students joined their peers and professional actors from Canada, England, and the United States in the impressive University of Toronto productions that have been staged regularly over the past decade. Milla C. Riggio further explains how valuable such firsthand involvement can be for students, who become immersed in the culture and the outlook of the Middle Ages. In the last contribution to this section, Míceál F. Vaughan shows how literary interpretation of one of the most popular medieval works, *The Second Shepherds' Play*, depends on a practical theatrical question. His essay underscores one of the guiding themes of this book: literary and theatrical questions are intertwined.

# PROLOGUE

## Medieval Drama:
## Genres, Misconceptions, and Approaches

### *Martin Stevens*

---

Medieval drama is too vast in time, place, generic manifestations, and theatrical performance modes to admit of easy generalizations and comprehensive treatment. Even the monumental two-volume history by E. K. Chambers published at the turn of the century, *The Mediaeval Stage*, the study that more than any other opened the subject for scholarly and pedagogical consideration, limited its coverage essentially to the English stage. Although Chambers recognized the widespread occurrence of the Latin extraliturgical music drama of the medieval church, he never treated, except for passing references, the wide variety of vernacular drama as it was performed throughout Europe or, unknown at the time, as it was transplanted to sixteenth-century Mexico. The world still awaits a comprehensive history of the European drama of the Middle Ages, although Chambers's book remains a milestone of scholarly study that no teacher of the drama can afford to dismiss; the book's delineation of medieval drama still governs the teaching of the subject.

The absence of a comprehensive history of the drama is complemented by an absence of a volume of representative vernacular texts covering the European medieval drama. The masterworks of this drama or even parts thereof—plays like Arnoul Greban's *Mystère de la Passion* (the most popular Passion play of its time in France or anywhere else), the Lucerne *Osterspiel*, the *Laudario* of the Confraternity of Saint Andrew of Perugia, and the intriguingly informative collection of Spanish plays in the *Códice de autos viejos*—have thus far not been published in school editions or in accessible translations into

English. There is even a paucity of easily available and reasonably priced editions and collections of the English medieval drama. These limitations have dictated the approach and the scope of this essay. Apart from David Bevington's collection of the Latin church drama in his *Medieval Drama*, the primary focus of the available anthologies, histories, and university courses is still on the English vernacular drama, especially on the great mystery cycles and the moralities; therefore, this essay adopts a similar concentration. Nevertheless, we must pause to consider the scope of the medieval drama and must not forget that generalizations about the nature of the English drama and its performance usually have implications for the European drama as a whole.

## A Generic Survey of the Medieval Religious Drama

The scope of the drama is notable by its expanse of time. Most histories of the medieval drama begin with the decline of the Roman *spectacula*, a term that covers everything from chariot racing to gladiatorial combat to vulgar farce. The *spectacula* are important only because they stand as background for the attitude of influential Christian commentators toward what can broadly be called theatrical representations. From Tertullian's *De spectaculis* through the church Fathers and, in later times, Gratian, Pope Gregory IX, Bishop Robert Grosseteste—the list is almost inexhaustible—influential church leaders opposed the practice of theatrical performance as it was represented by the often obscene and entirely unspiritual heritage of the *spectacula*. The antitheatrical attitude of the church is, however, not as inclusive as is often assumed, for it is usually expressed only by those who are, in effect, puritans, whether Catholic or Protestant, and it is not so all-inclusive as to forbid any kind of performance. Indeed, the paradox of the church's role in the demise of the Roman drama and in its medieval resurgence has often been noted. The religious drama arose directly out of the liturgy, and for much of the medieval period the church not only condoned the drama but promoted it. The objections raised in later times by reformers, such as Gerhoh von Reichersberg in his *De investigatione Antichristi* (c. 1161), are usually directed against the interference of plays with devotional obligations and to the age-old view that the representation of God in any form is sacrilege. There is, in fact, some reason to assume that the antitheatrical bias is encapsulated by the figure of Antichrist, who is almost always invoked in the tracts as the ultimate example of the evil impersonator of God. That is clearly still the attitude of the fourteenth-century Wycliffite *Tretise of Miraclis Pleying*, and it just as clearly subsumes the eventual, though temporary, closing of the theaters by the Puritans during the Reformation.

The iconoclasm of the Protestant reformers is most widely blamed for the demise of the medieval stage. Yet even that view must be accepted with caution for two reasons. First, in England under Queen Elizabeth I, the traditional performances of Corpus Christi cycles stopped, but the spirit and the structure of the medieval drama became absorbed in the drama of the high Renaissance, and its form influenced such popular entertainments as Midsummer shows, royal entries, and processional disguisings like the York "shewe of Armour," in which citizens paraded through the city "in their owne persone with their best Armor and furniture" (Johnston and Rogerson 441). The medieval elements in Shakespearean drama have only begun to be noted, though in 1965 O. B. Hardison discussed the formal influences in *Christian Rite and Christian Drama in the Middle Ages*. Second, on the Continent the medieval drama had a resurgence during the time of the Counter-Reformation. The two most popular European performances that emerged during that time and that hold to this day are the controversial Oberammergau Passion play and the Salzburg Festival performance of *Everyman* (*Jedermann*). Robert Potter traces the connection between the medieval drama and modern literature in general to the first modern performance of *Everyman* by William Poel in the Master's Courtyard of the Charterhouse in London in 1901 (1–5), a performance that strongly influenced the drama of William Butler Yeats, George Bernard Shaw, T. S. Eliot, and Hugo von Hofmannsthal and that was attended by Max Reinhardt, who may have used it to help inspire Hofmannsthal's version of *Jedermann* at Salzburg (M. Stevens, "Reshaping" 118). Poel's *Everyman* has been noted for its open and outdoor staging, its illusionistic design, and its audacity in presenting God on stage, which, as Potter notes, was a violation of the law at the time (3). The medieval stage thus becomes a formative influence in the development of the modern theater, one that extends even to the design of Bertolt Brecht's epic theater and his theory of *Verfremdung* (Martin Stevens, "Illusion" 450).

Medieval drama is also notable for its variety of genre and staging. Some commentators go so far as to consider the tournament a dramatic performance (Wickham, *Early English Stages*, vol. 1). The Old English *scop*, minstrels, acrobats, and a variety of traveling mimes were also theatrical performers. To limit our discussion to the conventional kinds of theatrical forms, we can discriminate between two types of drama, the Latin church drama and vernacular plays. The first, sometimes imprecisely called the liturgical drama, is in essence formal and cultic in quality: it is sung in plainchant and is often closely related to worship. Its audience can be confined to monastic communities, and, when it is, the drama speaks directly to the initiated. Single-episode church dramas are, moreover, usually commemorative; that is, they are played on feast days as a mimetic event reliving the historical moment being celebrated. For example, the Beauvais play of Christ's appearance to the pilgrims and to Thomas was performed at Easter Monday vespers, the time in the liturgical calendar when the appearances of Christ are commemorated. The more elaborate church plays are composite dramas that are not tied to specific liturgical holidays, plays like the Anglo-Norman *Ordo repraesentationis Adae* of the twelfth century and the Christmas and Passion plays of the Benedictine monastery of Benediktbeuern in Bavaria. These latter works were designed to edify and inspire; they were highly wrought literary experiences that were clearly conscious of theatrical art. One may think of them as comparable to such present-day high-art forms as opera and oratorio.

By contrast, the tradition of the popular stage manifested itself in the vernacular drama of the late Middle Ages in all its generic variety. Included in this drama were, first and foremost, the biblical plays performed outdoors, usually as folk celebrations on holidays. The English mystery cycles, of which four complete works survive (known as York, Wakefield or Towneley, N-Town, and Chester), are the most notable illustrations of the type. They range over salvation history from creation to doomsday, and they may be construed in the broadest sense as lives of Christ. In this sense the Old Testament plays must be regarded as prefigurations—that is, they present dramatic foreshadowings of the Incarnation, with the suggestion that the Old Testament types—such as Adam, Abel, Noah, Isaac, Moses, and David—were all played to resemble Jesus. The time format for the English cycles was the seven ages of the world, with the climax coming at the Crucifixion (the sacred event usually excluded from the drama of the church except in symbolic form, such as the *Depositio* sequence), and the end being doomsday, which, in theatrical terms, was the grand closing scene at which all the characters made a curtain call. Continental versions of the cycles were the Passion plays, of which the play at Lucerne, performed for two full days in the Weinmarkt (the main marketplace of the old city, which still stands), is a good example. The Continental Passion plays differed in only one respect from the cycle plays: they did not enter eschatological time but stopped with the Resurrection, appearances, or Assumption. Their scope and manner of performance tended to be similar to the English form, with tradespeople or religious guilds taking charge of productions and lay audiences as spectators, usually in the heart of a city. While stages varied, two modes of production dominated: one was stationary; the other was on wagons drawn through the streets of the city, making stops at designated stations.

A second genre was the moral play, which was especially popular in England and which in its form as outdoor drama complemented the mystery cycle in size and manner of performance. One of the famous examples is *The Castle of Perseverance*, for which, as for virtually all examples of the genre, the central character was *"Humanum Genus"* or "Mankind" or "Everyman." The moral play of this variety simply exchanged the life-of-Christ format of the cycle plays for the life of human beings: where in the cycle the scope is the seven ages of the world, in the moral plays it is the seven ages of humankind. The typical course may not have been the ages as defined by Jaques in *As You Like It* (2.7.139–66), but one could expect the span of life to embrace mewling infancy, youth, the various occupations of youth, middle age (with its "fair round belly"), old age (of the "slippered pantaloon"), and the onset of death ("Sans teeth, sans eyes, sans taste, sans everything"). The central action of the moral play is the battle of vices and virtues for the human soul, a battle that leads to the ultimate repentance of the main character. While the scenario may sound cut-and-dried, the stage pictures of the aging man drawn for us by Jaques give the play its animation and its abiding interest. Its humor and its pathos reside to a large extent in the central figure of Mankind as he meets the typical crisis stages of life, in the spectacle of the battle between vices and virtues, and in the elaborate costuming of the characters.

The most famous example of the morality—*Everyman*, which de-rives from a Dutch original (*Elkerlijk*)—is unrepresentative of the genre: its dramatic moment is the death, not the life, of the *Humanum Genus* figure. But even in this more restricted play, one awaits in suspense the defection of all of Everyman's companions—first those who constitute the gifts of fortune (Fellowship, Cousin, Kin, Goods), then those who constitute the gifts of nature (Discretion, Strength, Beauty, Five Wits), and finally those representing the gifts of grace (Good Deeds, Knowledge) (Cawley, *Everyman* xx–xxii). *Everyman* captures the existential moment of departure, and thus the play is an action of worldly divestiture. The spectacular element is the enactment of the dramatized personifications against whom Everyman reacts. At Salzburg, for example, a moment of high theatrical interest occurs when a huge chest opens of its own accord and the character Goods (named Mammon by Hofmannsthal) springs up decked out in gold and fingering coins that sift through his hands. The moral play is a collage of dramatized iconographic scenes. The appearance on stage of allegorical figures is perhaps the most important earmark of the moral play, but no sweeping generalization can be made about its topic, performance, or scope. *Everyman*, in fact, has been linked with a genre of interludes (Wickham, *English Moral Interludes* viii–ix), which technically are simply performances between courses at a feast. Such moral plays as *Nature* and *Nice Wanton* fit this category. These plays were typically performed in banquet halls and thus require a different kind of staging plan from the great outdoor extravaganzas.

A third type of popular play is the saint play, for which we find the richest examples in France, Spain, and Italy. A good many plays of this genre also existed in England, but only three texts survive: the two plays in the Digby manuscript named *Mary Magdalene* and *The Conversion of St. Paul* and the lively *Play of the Sacrament*. No doubt the many English saints plays noted copiously in records (Davidson, *Saint Play* 31–122) came to their demise during the Reformation, when many of the play texts must have been destroyed. By contrast, more than a hundred saint-play texts survive from the Middle Ages in Europe, many as yet unedited (Muir 123–80). Saint plays typically involve the performance of miracles, and, in fact, they are often called miracle plays, though that term has been used inaccurately to describe mystery plays and craft cycles, *mystery* being derived from medieval Latin *misterium*, meaning "occupation" or "handicraft" (s.v. *OED*, "Mystery"). The performance of a miracle—for example, a bleeding host or the severing of Jonathas's hand in the *Play of the Sacrament*—is often the central spectacle in a saint play. Its dramatic highlight is typically the conversion of the main character. The French Miracles of the Virgin usually show the Virgin intervening to prevent a catastrophe in daily bourgeois life, but saint plays can also portray the life of a saint, sometimes emphasizing martyrdom. Saint plays can be enormously long; for example, the fifteenth-century French play *Sainte Barbe* runs to twenty thousand lines and was performed over a period of five days. The English play *Mary Magdalene* not only is long and complex but also combines elements of the mystery cycles (historical scenes from the life of Christ) and morality characters (World, Flesh, and the Devil). Consequently generalizing about the form and the nature of saint plays is difficult, but the genre must be recognized as one of the most important in the medieval drama.

For more elaborate treatments of the subject, one should turn to the discussions in David Bevington's *Medieval Drama* and to the survey by Arnold Williams, *The Drama of Medieval England*, or, for a more sweeping coverage and emphasis on theater history, William Tydeman's *Theatre in the Middle Ages*. Here it may be best, first, to focus on some generalizations that have come into dispute in the study of the medieval drama and, second, to examine some viable approaches to the teaching of the drama.

## Misconceptions

1. *The drama after its liturgical beginnings moved to the church porch and eventually to the marketplace.* This view of the growth of the drama assumes that a literary form, like a biological species, grows organically over the years. As O. B. Hardison argues in chapter 1 of *Christian Rite and Christian Drama in the Middle Ages*, the study of the medieval

drama was fundamentally influenced by the social Darwinism of the turn of the century, when scholars like John Matthews Manly and E. K. Chambers, who were spiritually removed from their subject, saw the medieval drama as a primitive organism that, as it moved away from its connection with worship, grew into ever more complex and, therefore, more interesting new forms. This view is both patronizing and inaccurate. Hardison demonstrated that Karl Young's monumental two-volume history and anthology, *The Drama of the Medieval Church*, was compiled according to the simple-to-complex formula, rather than according to date. As a result, early scholars of the drama were misled into perceiving the development of the drama as an organic growth.

The facts show otherwise. The Latin church drama did not, through some sort of mutation, develop into the vernacular drama of the cathedral porch (such as we see in the Anglo-Norman *Ordo repraesentationis Adae*), nor did it develop into the vernacular cycles of the late Middle Ages. Instead, the drama of the church existed side by side with the Corpus Christi cycles performed in the heart of the city. The two were different genres—indeed, different art forms, since the first was sung drama and the second colloquial. Single-scene church plays persisted throughout the Middle Ages. Nor is it true, as we can attest in other realms of literature, that the primitive is necessarily simple and that the course of history is ineluctably toward the perfection of the species. This is not to deny that early forms have the capacity for influencing late forms, but usually that influence is a matter of adaptation to new demands and contexts. Thus, for example, the essential medieval stage—the *sedes* or fixed place and the *platea* or open stage—was, no doubt, the shaping force of the Elizabethan playhouse. The medieval drama, which depended in large part on journey or procession from one *sedes* to another, emphasized constant movement. Because its theatrical space and time and its action were all-inclusive, it produced a dramaturgy that stood in direct opposition to the measured world of the ancient Greek stage with its unified conceptions, as seen by later critics, of time, space, and action. Shakespeare and his fellow dramatists inherited the medieval dramatic plan. If the subject was honed down to the rise and the fall of kingdoms, the dimensions were, nevertheless, on a scale that the Middle Ages passed on. The drama did not grow; it adapted to new needs. Nor did it necessarily improve; it changed. Few playwrights of the Renaissance and perhaps none of the eighteenth century or of contemporary America can approach the great theatrical art that the Wakefield Master left us. The medieval drama requires, as a first step toward its assessment, the respect of its students. The Darwinian thesis did not provide that.

2. *The Corpus Christi play can be traced in a direct development from procession to finished text: the growth of the Chester cycle provides the*

*example*. It is a commonplace that the establishment of the feast of Corpus Christi, proclaimed by Pope Urban ɪᴠ in 1264 and instituted by Pope Clement ᴠ at the Council of Vienne in 1311, is the nominal beginning of the popular drama in the Middle Ages. The old histories attempted to provide a direct succession from feast to procession to fully formed play. As I have shown in *Four Middle English Mystery Cycles* (258–72), Chambers relies on the myth and the folklore of Chester historians, rather than on ascertainable dates, to arrive at a tightly constructed historical outline of what he regarded as the first of the popular cycles in England and, by implication, anywhere. The Corpus Christi holiday, which is the feast of the Holy Sacrament, provided for a major procession through the city. After the establishment of the holiday, Corpus Christi guilds were quickly formed, and civic ceremonial required the leading citizens, usually in livery, to proceed through the city in association with the ambulatory display of the Sacrament. Not long thereafter, other guilds, especially craft and trade guilds, joined the procession to portray a biblical scene based on the patron saint of the guild or an association expressed in trade symbolism (for example, the fishers and the shipbuilders would parade with a replica or a picture of Noah's ark). In time, the static scenes depicted by the guilds added dialogue, and the end product was the creation of a massive biblical cycle. In Chambers's view this process began some fifteen years after the initiation of the Corpus Christi feast, and it was completed within fifty years, so that the great cycles came into existence in the latter third of the fourteenth century.

As usual, this kind of sweeping overview presents some attractive and, no doubt, accurate hypotheses. In general, it is probably true that a civic celebration of salvation history, geared to local interests, began with the celebration of the feast of Corpus Christi and that the procession acquired a quasi-dramatic character, one that suited the concept of journey or pilgrimage and expressed the Augustinian view of history. What is wrong with Chambers's conception, however, is that the facts do not provide us with such a neat pattern of development. It is now clear that the Chester cycle, Chambers's paradigm example, was not the earliest but the latest of the major cycles to develop. Moreover, not all popular drama developed from procession to pageant wagon. The York cycle, with its copious records (Johnston and Rogerson), represents only one performance model. The much more typical stage throughout Europe was an in-situ production at a specific location—sometimes a specially built theater, as at Valenciennes, or the site for the performance of the N-Town cycle; sometimes an established location like the marketplace at Lucerne. Finally and perhaps most important, the manuscripts of the cycles are all very late; they date from the latter part of the fifteenth through the sixteenth and even the early seventeenth centuries. The indication is that fully developed literary cycles did not develop until the age of the manuscripts or perhaps shortly before. Consequently, the drama as we know it from texts cannot be taken as the one that played in the streets during the fourteenth century and that supplied Chaucer with his allusions in the Miller's Tale (1.3124, 3384). Civic festival may well be considered an early form of the great cycles, and it no doubt influenced the iconography and the dramaturgy of the late stage, but it is not the drama that is preserved in our manuscripts. In short, the process took longer and followed a more diversified course than that presented in the early drama histories.

3. *The biblical cycles are basically constructed alike; one can study them as a piece through representative pageants.* The cycles do resemble each other, containing similar episodes, similar characterizations, and similar grand designs. Noah's wife is usually, though not inevitably, a shrew; there is always a scene of Abraham's sacrifice; Herod is a braggart. So too, Old Testament episodes serve as typological foreshadowing; the Crucifixion focuses on the brutality of the torturers and the suffering of Christ; the stage is a composite picture of the universe: Heaven, hell mouth, and middle earth are its component parts. These similarities may be there as a result of common tradition or of the direct influence of one cycle on another, as York, for example, provided the base text for Wakefield. They constitute the generic features of what we have come, somewhat inaccurately, to call the Corpus Christi cycle (the one at Chester was a Whitsun play).

But theater history has too often ignored the differences among the cycles, English and Continental. Typically, anthologies since the beginning of the study of the drama have pieced a cycle together from various sources, thus leading to the impression that the pageants are basically made up of interchangeable parts. The teaching of the medieval drama should recognize the existence of differences, a task that can well be accomplished by a comparative analysis of one episode (Hanning) or by isolating a single cycle and demonstrating its continuity and its overall coherence (Travis). The N-Town pageants of the early life of Mary form a single coherent whole, one that stands in direct parallelism with the infancy of Jesus. This pattern cannot be grasped if one reads the episode "The Conception of Mary" from N-Town followed by "The Annunciation" from Wakefield. Ideally, a course in the medieval drama should provide both a vertical (full-cycle) reading of a Corpus Christi play and a horizontal approach (the comparative study of a single episode). Only in that manner can the full literary dimension of the individual cycles be perceived.

4. *The medieval theater is amateur folk entertainment; it can at best provide only the rudiments for a serious, formal study of dramatic art.* This view prevailed for a long time in the study of medieval culture,

and it helps explain why literature survey courses until recently gave the drama short shrift. Yet the drama may well be the most composite of all the arts, not only providing an introduction to the theater but also drawing from art history, philosophy, theology, urban history, and the study of manuscripts to provide a window for the students' view of the Middle Ages. Work with medieval records, furthermore, has demonstrated that the productions, far from being amateurish, were often lavish and expensive. Most important, the plays themselves are complex expressions of the popular culture of their times. To account for the deprecatory view of the drama, one must look at the cultural framework within which earlier literary study was generally set. Perhaps the single most influential book concerned with the culture of the late Middle Ages was Johan Huizinga's *Waning of the Middle Ages*. Though first published in 1924, the book was introduced to most American readers as a hardback in 1949 and as a paperback in 1955. A pioneer work in cultural history, the book is an exciting and provocative account of a period that is often given short shrift by all but constitutional and political historians. For Huizinga what was interesting was the fact of the period's "waning," though that term was, in fact, a reinterpretation of the original title, *Herfsttij*, the Dutch word for "autumn," made in consultation with the author (Aston 1–2). Huizinga saw the fifteenth century as a violent and irritable age in which a great culture expired. What he admired about the time was its pulsebeat and its valiant effort to hang on to the politesse of its high art in the face of the onslaught of the ignorant populace and their values (it is surprising how often the word *ignorant* occurs to describe the folk). Buried in his approach is a strong belief in the idea of progress and the perfectability of humankind (38), and for him the expiring Middle Ages constitute essentially a time of pessimism and dislocation.

Recent revaluations present a new perspective on the fifteenth century. With the advent of Bakhtin, we have come to a new and fuller appreciation of what once was dismissed as folk literature, to see the importance of grotesque realism and of carnival in our understanding of popular culture. The plays, in this larger view, are not a primitive expression of folk ignorance but a focus for a new view of the fifteenth century. As part of the process of canon reformation, the drama can be seen as the birth of a bourgeois literature—the beginning, not the ending, of something important (significantly, Huizinga glosses over the drama almost entirely)—as an expression of a time of transition. The new literature comes during or after some of the most disruptive upheavals of the social order: a gigantic economic depression, the passing of the plague, one hundred years of war, a divided papacy. What it expresses is the growth of a new awareness and a new literacy, of which *heteroglossia*, an apt Bakhtinian term, is the earmark that allows the tyrant's rant with its alliterative pulse (the Wakefield Herod characterizes that form of speech as "French" [play 16, p. 513]) to stand against the "Southern tooth" used as a form of linguistic deception by Mak, the common man, in the *Second Shepherds' Play* (play 13, p. 215). It is also a reexamination of the values that should govern life; the ubiquitous movement toward popular piety, of which all forms of the medieval drama are an expression, teaches a new juxtaposition of the sacred and the profane, a movement that Huizinga saw as a threat to "serious divines" (152–53). The plays were able to redefine the social order on the basis of Christian precept. The act that led to intense self-examination, even self-flagellation, also led to contemporary reenactments of the Crucifixion in the city marketplace and the reliving of the lives and the sufferings of saints. The plays, in this new view of their context, lead to a reinvigorated sense of morality. At least in England, they are probably the most important literary works of their times, even if they are not the expression of the elite. They combine with the works of Thomas Malory, the other great literary accomplishment of fifteenth-century England, to define a new social order. Theirs is the matrix of the new; Malory's is the tragic-heroic reflection of the old.

## Approaches

In the foregoing discussion, I suggest approaches to the teaching of medieval drama. Since this book describes several specific approaches and courses, I confine this introductory discussion to a few general guidelines to the teaching of the medieval drama.

*Manuscripts and the Whole Text.* I have written elsewhere about the importance of manuscripts in interpreting drama (M. Stevens, *Cycles* 12–14, etc.). It is impossible in undergraduate courses, especially those that include the drama under larger headings, to examine a medieval manuscript whole. Yet at least some acquaintance with the format and the nature of the manuscript helps students understand the complexity of the texts as literary works. The plays emerge from such an examination as a folk literature that has been carefully compiled by unknown author-redactors to develop special insights into the interrelation of Scripture (sometimes Apocryphal) and society. A review of a manuscript page, now easily available for many of the major English plays in the facsimile series sponsored by Leeds Texts and Monographs, demonstrates the nature and the importance of rubrics, stage directions, cue lines, versification, and editorial interpretation. Most of the manuscripts are easily read, especially with the use of a good modern edition as a guide. The notion that individual pageants are parts of a coherent larger design can be underscored for survey classes by a table of contents of the whole cycle (using original titles where possible) to give some intimation of contexts. In classes

devoted entirely or largely to the cycle plays, I recommend concentration on one cycle, with select comparative analyses of crucial pageants
or clusters of pageants from other cycles.

*Iconography as a Guide to Staging.*   The visual arts are the hidden
correlative subject of any course in the medieval drama. Our understanding of dramatic form requires that we visualize the text on stage;
that is the work of the dramaturge and the director. The text, the stage
directions, and the records of the drama provide some specific
orientation toward dramatic scenes, but often we do not have a whole
visual image until we have looked closely at contemporary artistic
representations (as near as possible in time and place). How, for
example, was the Devil conceived in the individual plays? We know
that the records of the smiths at Coventry repeatedly refer to the
repairing and the "dressing" of the "devyls hede" (Craig 82–92),
indicating that the Devil wore a carefully prepared mask. Wall
paintings from medieval churches, illuminations in manuscripts,
church sculpture, and stained glass give us good illustrations and
highlight some common features in their representations and also
present some much individualized pictures. With this example in mind,
I urge the use of slides and other visual supports in the teaching of the
drama.

*Anachronism as an Aesthetic Principle.*   Medieval drama demonstrates the principle that great art and classic themes are, in fact, both
timeless and timely. As Erich Auerbach notes concerning the Anglo-
Norman *Ordo repraesentationis Adae*, "the everyday and real is . . . an
essential element of medieval Christian art and especially of the
Christian drama" (138). The study of that drama requires an imaginative transference of scriptural episodes to medieval times. Thus, Jesus
is born and eventually crucified in the medieval city of York. His
Advent and his Passion are experienced within the context of medieval
time and place; and so the sources of Christian belief are brought to
life as part of a deep spiritual interpretation and invigoration of
contemporary life. It may be anachronistic to have Caiaphas and Annas
appear in the garb of medieval bishops; but through such chronological
frame breaking, we come to realize that Jesus is being submitted anew
and constantly to the corrupt demands of a temporal society. In the
course of the play, if it works according to its established aesthetic
principles, the audience experiences a cultic renewal. It is directly
involved, through anachronistic representation, in the life of Christ;
therefore, when Jesus speaks his last plaintive speech from the Cross,
he addresses not a stage audience but a real audience, and that
audience for the moment becomes part of the play. Any consideration
of the medieval drama—cyclic, morality, or saints'—is timeless in this
sense; it is theater in the raw.

Anachronism is best tested in performance, and some performance aspects of the drama should be explored in any classroom concerned with the drama. Even an examination of the phenomenon of performance proper can add to our understanding of anachronism as a dramatic principle. When, for example, a company re-creates a medieval play in its historic setting—presenting the play on a pageant wagon, re-creating the medieval marketplace as a stage, using medieval costumes—does it defy the spirit of the play? Is not such a performance exactly what the play itself warns against? The original medieval productions did not re-create biblical settings, so why should modern performances re-create medieval settings (except perhaps as a classroom exercise)? Maybe the best medieval plays we have are attempts to bring the meaning of the play into our own time. For example, the National Theatre production *The Mysteries* (Harrison), a composite of several of the original mystery cycles, is played in modern dress and uses Yorkshire accents and devices like a forklift truck to transport God about the stage. The result is a play that is both timeless and timely. A sound reading of a medieval play should always have this principle of transferability in mind.

*Drama and Its Social Contexts.* In recent years, literary study, especially in the form of the new historicism, has brought new emphasis to the social contexts out of which texts arose. The concentration of such study has been on the Renaissance stage, but the principles also apply widely to the medieval drama. We have already noted that the religious plays of the Middle Ages, perhaps especially the Corpus Christi cycles, are a popular art form. The texts developed, at least at first, as a result of a process of accretion. Their intention is dictated by all sorts of circumstances, including the nature of the occasion; the community; the forms of worship, the liturgy, and the Scripture out of which they arose; and the general economic and civic temperaments that governed their performance. We must separate text from performance in the study of the drama, but the two were closely intertwined. Authorship, important as it is in the final product, nevertheless takes on a secondary role to the occasion in the overall development of the genre. We cannot understand the plays without understanding as well how they functioned in their communities. With what expectations did an audience come to view them? Who constituted that audience? What meaning did the play have for a city that sponsored it? What were the economic limitations imposed on the play? How did government, civic, and ecclesiastical leaders interact with the playmakers? What about the relation of the play with holiday and festival? To what extent is the Bakhtinian notion of carnival applicable to the performance and the text? My personal experience has taught me that I must rely on a wide spectrum of social history, especially such primary evidence as civic records, to teach the drama with full attention to its meaning and its implications.

*The Medieval Drama as Interdisciplinary Subject.*   Medieval drama is a composite form that is truly adaptable to interdisciplinary and even team teaching. I have on occasion taught the medieval drama on both the graduate and the undergraduate levels with an art historian and sometimes with a theologian. These classes added an enormous range of teaching possibilities to what would have been a much more restricted course. While team teaching is not always workable, the drama is the sort of subject that encourages guest lectures by experts and the use of audiovisual materials. It is, furthermore, one of the courses that fits naturally into a medieval studies curriculum. Such possibilities should be considered by all who wish the subject to come alive.

# CRITICAL AND THEORETICAL APPROACHES

## Teaching the Medieval Latin "Drama": Reflections Historical and Theoretical

### C. Clifford Flanigan

The study of the medieval drama has changed drastically in the last quarter century for two fundamental reasons. In the first place, historical scholarship has radically altered our understanding of these texts and their place in medieval life. But just as important, there has been a paradigm shift in the literary and, to a smaller extent, the historical studies that has left behind some of the concerns of the old scholarship and replaced them with new and different issues. Although the new historical perspectives on both Latin and vernacular medieval dramatic texts can be readily encountered in specialist books and journals, they have not filtered down to the public represented by general histories of the theater and nonspecialist undergraduate and even graduate classrooms. Often the supposed facts determined by outdated modes of inquiry are repeated as if they had never been called into question. Just as striking are those instances in which old terminology, with all its attendant connotations, is repeatedly used, even when the recent understanding of the medieval drama is presented. This essay is a response to this situation. I spell out some implications of the recent historical understanding of the medieval drama and of the new theoretical paradigms for the teaching of medieval Latin drama.

A generation ago, some mention was almost always made of medieval Latin plays in any consideration of the vernacular drama of the Middle Ages or even of the Shakespearean stage. Western drama was widely thought to have been "reborn" in the Latin liturgy of the tenth century and to have expanded from these humble beginnings, first into more elaborate Latin plays and then into the vernacular cycles of the late Middle Ages. In the study of English literature this elaborate and incremental growth was believed to lie behind the development of the Renaissance stage and its supposed culmination in the Shakespearean moment. Thus, one studied the "first" Latin "drama," the *Visitatio sepulchri* in the *Regularis concordia*, because it was the first modern drama, and it was the task of scholarship to show how from these humble and not wholly appealing beginnings the modern drama was born, apparently by a process of increased secularization that brought about significant improvements in aesthetic value. Emphasis was laid on a great line of continuity and on transformations within that line. Interest in the Latin drama was dominated by a profound belief in the importance of origins, a belief fostered both by a continuing fascination with Darwinism and by the influence of Platonic essentialism. Historical scholarship, including literary history, had unquestioning confidence in its ability to function objectively, to know the history of the drama, as it really happened, and to state the definitive results of its inquiry once and for all. Indeed, literary historians were so confident of these results—carefully built up and elaborated by several generations of scholars and, for the Latin drama at least, culminating in the monumental work of Karl Young—that for more than a generation after the publication of *The Drama of the Medieval Church* in 1933 innovative study of Latin church drama ceased. As late as the mid-1960s, the Latin drama was usually described in terms wholly derived from the model developed by Young and, before him, E. K. Chambers.

This state of affairs was decisively called into question with the publication of O. B. Hardison's *Christian Rite and Christian Drama in the Middle Ages* in 1965. Hardison's book offered a number of perspectives on the Latin drama, the most significant of which was his claim that the surviving textual evidence does not support the evolutionary model. Hardison argued that the scheme that had for nearly a century seemed convincing was the result of prevailing ideological presuppositions indigenous to the academic profession and of a general failure to understand the character of liturgical celebration. Hardison claimed that the vernacular dramatic traditions of the late Middle Ages are by no means the logical development of the earlier Latin Christmas and Easter offices; the two traditions, he suggested, have entirely different characteristics. The historical work on which Hardison based these assertions found support in the phenomenological description offered by scholars like Glynne Wickham, who had argued already in volume 1 of *Early English Stages* that

> we must admit the likelihood of two dramas of a single Christian origin but of independent motivation: the drama of the Real

Presence within the liturgy and the imitative drama of Christ's Humanity in the world outside. The one is a drama of adoration, praise, thanksgiving; the other is a drama of humour, suffering, and violence, of laughter and sorrow. Where the former remains ritualistic, the latter carries within it the germs of tragedy and comedy. (314)

It is significant that, while lip service is given to such claims, the study of the early English drama has, despite itself, persistently retreated from the implications to be drawn from the claims. Hardison and Wickham themselves fell back on alternative schemes of development in which the Latin "dramatic" texts are still seen as precursors of the vernacular cycle dramas. Similarly, David Bevington's anthology *Medieval Drama* repeats Hardison's arguments against an evolutionary view in a chapter paradoxically entitled "Liturgical Beginnings." Rather than retreat to the discredited claims of past scholarship in this way, we should, at least initially, take with utmost seriousness what Hardison, Wickham, and others have taught us about these Latin texts: that they seem to belong more to the world of ritual than to the world of the literary and that their relation to later vernacular texts is problematic.

Our concern is with the implications of these views for the teaching of medieval English vernacular drama. We must, first of all, bluntly admit that a teacher need not include any Latin drama in the curriculum. The old misunderstandings of the history of the drama are, in fact, most readily perpetuated by courses that consider Latin "liturgical beginnings" as a prelude to developed drama in the vernacular. Thus, at least on first consideration, historical scholarship seems to advocate the removal of texts like the *Visitatio sepulchri* from the English curriculum. But matters are not so simple. More than strictly historical issues are involved; that becomes clear when we shift our consideration from the revolution in historical scholarship about the liturgical drama to the revolution that at least equally determines, or should determine, what happens in the classroom: the revolution in critical theory. Here a radically different pedagogical perspective on the texts emerges. From the point of view of contemporary theory, why would one talk about medieval Latin dramatic texts at all? To historicists of previous generations and to their contemporary successors, the answer seemed simple: one taught the texts to describe what "really happened," to impart concrete knowledge about the early history of drama. But the human sciences and perhaps the natural sciences as well have rightly become suspicious about their ability to know or to teach facts and not only because previously prevailing neat models can easily be shot down by new sets of facts, though certainly that is a significant observation in the case of the Latin drama. A theoretically informed view of the purpose of teaching texts such as the ones under consideration here can be grounded neither in the imparting of facts about texts nor in close readings. Rather, drawing on several different approaches that take their points of departure from linguistic models, we see that pedagogy responsible to current literary theory is a highly self-reflexive activity. Its goal is to teach something about semiotic processes, about how communication takes place and fails to take place, and about what is ideologically at stake in various forms of discourse. Understood in this way, pedagogy concerns the ways that language involves us in endless chains of readings and misreadings, mystifications, demystifications, and remystifications.

What are the practical implications of such claims for the teacher confronted with the question of whether to include a unit on Latin liturgical drama in a course? The first implication is that such a decision need not be based on whether or not a chain of development links these texts with the later vernacular drama nor on whether or not these texts are genuinely dramatic or literary. Instead, one can begin with the indisputable observation that these texts have traditionally been identified as the beginnings of modern drama. Significant questions then arise about what is at stake in such a claim and about the criteria used to test its validity. The questions of what the assets and liabilities of this view are and who stands to gain and lose by its advocacy become major issues. What is under scrutiny is not so much the place of, for example, the *Quem quaeritis* in the history of drama as the place of the *Quem quaeritis* in the discourse about drama. This shift is not motivated by a love of theoretical issues for themselves. Rather, we are led to these concerns by historical scholarship that has questioned the place of these Latin texts in the history of drama, by the theoretical models prevailing in our discipline, and by contemporary pedagogy, which understands the ultimate subject of teaching about texts to be the communication process itself.

Perhaps this approach becomes clearer when we consider it in the light of the text most likely to be studied if the medieval Latin drama is taught at all, the *Visitatio sepulchri* from the *Regularis concordia*, as it appears in Bevington's anthology (27–28) and in Young's book (249–50). If we give attention to the way that Young laid out his text on the page (Bevington follows him in every detail and provides translations into modern English), with a division of parts for each of the actors, it seems apparent at first that a respectable case can be made for reading this example of the *Visitatio* as a primitive and highly stylized play. For Young the text shows all the marks of a drama that attempts to impersonate biblical characters and to give psychological motivations to their actions. Even examining the *Regularis concordia* text in this form is likely to leave a student slightly dissatisfied with Young's evocation of a dramatic model. How, for example, is one to account for the strange mixture of stylization and what Young regarded as physical and psychological realism? This question can lead us and our students to understand why the simplistic linear evolutionary model was an essential element in traditional attempts to read these texts as dramas: the most heavily stylized nondramatic features of the text could be explained away as vestigial elements surviving from a predramatic stage of *Visitatio* texts.

Texts of medieval English plays are almost always read in modern versions prepared by editors like Young. Yet these editions are often unintentionally deceptive. Young was such an honest scholar that, in addition to editing the *Regularis concordia* text, he included a photographic reproduction of the appropriate page of British Library manuscript Cotton Tiberius A.III (Young, facing p. 250) and thereby enabled his readers to compare his edition with its original. It is important to bring this readily available copy of the manuscript page into any classroom discussion of the *Regularis concordia* text. Even a student with no knowledge of Latin can discern that the arrangement of the tenth-century text is different from the one that Young provides. In the manuscript there is no division of parts between speakers. Furthermore, nothing in the manuscript suggests that the section of the text that begins *"Dum tertia recitatur lectio . . .* [while the third lesson is being sung . . .]" was regarded by the scribe as separate or different from what comes before it, the usual text of Easter matins. Yet Young apparently believed that he was justified in separating one part of the contents of the page from the other parts. Such a procedure can only be justified by Young's understanding of the manuscript as a dramatic text. This observation points to a central difficulty for those who defend the claim that *Visitatio sepulchri* texts like the one found in the *Regularis concordia* belong to dramatic history: nothing in the manuscripts in which they survive indicates that they were regarded as plays by their original audiences. On the contrary, even a casual scrutiny of the manuscripts containing these "dramas" suggests that they were understood as ordinary elements of the liturgical rites in which they were embedded. Thus, Young's reproduction of the crucial page from the *Regularis concordia* provides an excellent classroom example of how the creation of at least one "liturgical drama" is the product of editorial practices that, perhaps inadvertently, obscure the text's alterity as a record of liturgical action and bend it into the familiar modern genre of drama.

This significant claim can be made even more vivid to students once it is pointed out to them that Young's and Bevington's texts all but hide the fact that manuscript exemplars of the *Visitatio sepulchri* record not a spoken practice but a musical one chanted in exactly the same way as other pieces of the liturgy. If these Latin texts are taught at all, they should be accompanied by recordings that allow the students to hear a modern reconstruction of medieval liturgical chant, preferably a recording of a *Visitatio* office. By thus emphasizing yet another way in which *Visitatio* texts seem alien to modern dramatic sensibilities, the teacher enables the students without appropriate technical skills to encounter a medieval artifact directly and to gain insight into the ways that presuppositions necessarily and unavoidably govern the reconstructions of even the most meticulous scholars like Young, for whom, astonishingly, musical aspects did not belong to the essence of the texts he edited. Such insights have broad ramifications. By learning about early medieval texts, the students are forced to confront important semiotic and hermeneutical issues that are implicated in every act of interpretation and communication.

Viewing the earliest liturgical drama as at least partially the creation of its modern editors leads to other questions and other pedagogical possibilities. Foremost among them is the use of liturgical, rather than literary or dramatic, paradigms for interpreting these texts. If one follows this direction, classroom discussion may center on the ritual practices of the early Middle Ages. Works of liturgiological scholarship like René Hesbert's four-volume reference book on the medieval divine office can be used to reconstruct, for example, the liturgical cursus of Easter and to note how all the individual lines that constitute the *Visitatio sepulchri* can be found elsewhere in the paschal rites. Given our present resources, such a project requires some knowledge of Latin. But even if only the instructor carries out this project and shares the process and the results with the class, the gains are important: materials significant for the interpretation of *Visitatio* texts that have been neglected, even by most contemporary specialists, are made accessible for pedagogical appropriation. Original research and teaching fall together. And, more significant, students learn what it is to do research and discern that even acts of historical recovery of something as alien to modern culture as the medieval liturgy are largely determined by the horizons of expectations of researchers and the academic and other ideological communities in which they operate. The act of viewing these texts as liturgical in nature raises significant questions about the social function of medieval ritual, the institutions in which and for which it was fostered, and the appropriateness of discussing liturgy in a literature class.

These few suggestions by no means exhaust even an initial consideration of why and how those texts conventionally termed medieval Latin dramas can be used in the classroom. The complexity of the historical situation should be conveyed to students. For instance, some examples of the *Visitatio* show the kind of dramatic division into parts that is lacking in the *Regularis concordia* manuscript. Indeed, texts that offer considerable support for the dramatic claims advanced by early scholars are readily at hand in Bevington's anthology. And texts such as the Beauvais *Daniel* and those contained in the Fleury *Playbook* (a modern designation) are part of the tradition of the drama of the medieval church but have little in common with the example of the *Visitatio sepulchri* that we have considered here. I have elsewhere explored the historical significance of the traditions that constitute the medieval Latin drama and the manner in which its appreciation depends at least partially on current theoretical and critical modes ("Fleury *Playbook*"). Viewing these texts from such a perspective suggests that they can be used to confront students with the alterity of the past and with the unavoidable role that our individual and communal horizons of expectations play in our processing of historical artifacts.

What is in the end essential in any teaching about medieval Latin drama is not much different from what is essential in the teaching of any text, ancient or modern. First, we must be responsible to the existing scholarship, even if we disagree with it; it is astonishing how little the last quarter-century's work is reflected in what even our best anthologies and guidebooks say about these texts, and this situation needs to be remedied at once. It is time to stop talking unproblematically of these texts under such rubrics as the "liturgical beginnings" of the English drama, as if this were a self-evident conclusion validated by current scholarly opinion. Second, history must be given its due. We must let the past confront our students in all its alterity—its alien, alienating, and for us irrelevant aspects; what is most objectionable about the traditional treatment of these texts is the way that it has so easily assimilated them to postmedieval institutions without reflecting the hermeneutic process by which such an appropriation is possible. Finally, our teaching must be governed by some larger purpose than teaching the facts of literary history or the fostering of an appreciation of past practices. Most of our students will not become and do not wish to become experts in the medieval drama. But they need to see how the difficulties of interpreting these texts and the strategies by which these difficulties are tentatively but never definitively overcome are similar to the difficulties and strategies we use with all texts, including the texts of our own lives.

# Cultural Approaches to
# Medieval Drama

## Kathleen M. Ashley

It takes great imagination for an American today to appreciate how central theater was to the public life of medieval Europe. From the fourteenth through the sixteenth centuries, virtually every communal event was marked by costumed processions, mimed tableaux, and plays. Performances took place in public spaces like the streets, city squares, large churches, and guild halls and typically engaged actors who were members of the community. What we now call drama and read in a few surviving texts may more usefully be considered cultural performance, something to be studied as part of the ritual and the ceremony of late medieval society.

As the anthropologist Milton Singer points out, cultural performances are convenient and concrete units of a society to analyze, for each event has a time span, a program of activity, a set of performers, an audience, a place, and an occasion of performance (xiii). In medieval performances the circumstances may be largely unknown where a text exists (as with the Wakefield cycle), or the complete text may be lacking where we have copious production data (as with the Coventry Corpus Christi play). Nevertheless, partial reconstruction is often possible for medieval performances.

Beyond the considerable problem of missing data about medieval events lies the challenge of interpretation. A cultural approach to the drama assumes that it is more than just entertainment, that it literally performs social functions. Anthropologists have defined cultural performances as occasions on which a society dramatizes its collective myths, defines itself, and reflects on its practices and values, possibly considering alternative ways of behaving and believing (MacAloon 1). Typically, cultural performances belong to what Victor Turner has called a society's "subjunctive mood," one that expresses desire and possibility, rather than simply representing what is (20). Medieval society experienced its collective subjunctive mood on feast days and festival occasions, when almost all dramatic performances took place. Like the drama of ancient Greece, medieval drama is festive drama, which must be understood not as a simple reflection of its society but as a complex set of formal possibilities for playing out and playing with the structures and themes of the culture.

To speak of the culture of medieval society is somewhat misleading, however, since any performance is the product not of the whole society but of a specific community or subculture within it. The predominantly religious subject matter of medieval drama led early scholars to assume that most plays were produced by the church as part of its mission to indoctrinate the laity, but the production records published by the Records of Early English Drama project clearly show that the drama was produced under many auspices. As members of an educated elite in the community, the clergy may have helped write or revise scripts and may have acted in plays, but control over the performance was often non-ecclesiastical. Certainly by the fifteenth century lay appropriation of religious ritual was widespread, and the Christian myth provided the symbolic language for the whole society. If we regard drama as cultural performance, we must then ask how the language of the myth is being used by those responsible for producing and participating in the cultural event. The same biblical story may function quite differently in the drama of different communities or of subcultures within the same community.

## Village Festivity

Nothing but tantalizing allusion remains of the dramatic activities popular in the medieval village. We know from records that Robin Hood games and Saint George ridings were associated with the season from May to Midsummer, as were such activities as dancing around a maypole, sword fighting, wrestling, archery contests, morris dancing, and bonfires. (For a sixteenth-century Robin Hood text, see Blackston; for analysis of an ambitious Robin Hood game that drew an audience of 2,000, see MacLean's "King Games.") May Day and Midsummer folk rituals celebrated the season and in the fifteenth and sixteenth centuries often provided the occasion to raise money for parish church repairs with an annual fair and the selling of ale. Since much of our information about these seasonal village festivities comes from church-wardens' accounts, it's clear that folklore figures like Robin Hood, popular athletic contests, and church sponsorship could be combined within the festive frame. Distinctions between secular and sacred and between folk and elite were not important on these occasions of communal festivity.

Attempting to distinguish plays per se from other kinds of festive role-playing is probably futile where these activities were largely traditional, improvisatory, and unscripted. Even the chief characters— Robin Hood, Saint George, the Lord and the Lady of the May—were associated less with plots or stories than with conventional actions and episodes. Combat-play forms the basis of traditional drama among the pagan peoples of northern Europe, according to Richard Axton (33–34). In the absence of medieval texts, Axton has called attention to folk traditions in the mummers' plays recorded by antiquarians over the past two centuries. Combats and killings by the hero, the resurrection or the healing of the dead by a doctor, the wooing of a lady, the collection of money from the audience, the presence of the fool, and the use of disguises and formulaic and nonsense language— all characterized village mummers' plays. Axton notes the presence of similar motifs in a variety of medieval plays: farcical boasts by tyrants or their servants are common in medieval drama; quack doctors who promise cures appear in the Croxton *Play of the Sacrament* and many French plays; the beheading of a devil-monster occurs in *Mankind*, as does nonsense patter and buffoonery.

Common to popular festive actions, as Robert Weimann points out, is parodic inversion:

> There is a remarkable continuity of playfully inverted conceptions of the world which extends from the Roman Saturnalia down to the rural May games, the *episcopus puerorum* and *festum stultorum* of the lower clergy, the *sermon joyeux* and burlesque *sottie* in France, and the urban mummings and masques in England. . . . The nature of such mimetic topsy-turveydom and its inversive quality is neatly glossed in Archbishop Grindal's 1576 inquiry as to "whether the minister and churchwardens have suffered any lords of misrule or summer lords or ladies, or any disguised persons, or others, in Christmas or at May-games, or any morris dancers, or at any other times, to come unreverently into the church or churchyard, and there to dance, or to play unseemly parts, with scoffs, jests, wanton gestures, or ribald talk." (21–22)

As Weimann notes, "these late medieval modes of inversion were all associated with both 'dance' and the playing of 'unseemly parts,' " on an occasion at which verbal and physical action, "jests" and "gestures," were significantly linked. Typically, they invert or mock normal assumptions of age, sex, and rank through a kind of "licensed buffoonery" (Axton 38). Whether the playing out of these alternatives to the status quo through festive action served to stabilize or subvert the social structure has become a controversial issue among anthropologists and social historians. While many theorists argue that such festivities function as escape valves to preserve the norms, Marxist theorists have emphasized the subversive potential of popular festivals. A third position suggests that whether a festival undermines or reinforces the social structure depends on local conditions at a particular moment of history. Archbishop Grindal in the latter part of the sixteenth century expressed hostility to festive inversions, but their ubiquity in church-sponsored festivals of the previous century demonstrated that in the view of the local establishment they could also strengthen the social fabric.

## Civic Cycles

The seasonal improvisatory revels typical of the village community were echoed in large towns by neighborhood parishes, male youth groups, and other social organizations dedicated to festivity. On the Continent, urban guilds for dramatic production were common, but in England the cultural performances that made many cities famous were the cycle plays. Situated at the ritual center of the urban ceremonial year and crucial to civic mythmaking, the cycles performed the town's identity both for its citizens and to the nation at large.

The historian Charles Phythian-Adams has observed that ritual was a "living mirror of the city," dramatizing the community's image of itself through both idealization and distortion (*Desolation* 178). Despite the use of biblical history as the vehicle for social expression, the cycle play was firmly controlled by the civic authorities, whose council determined whether the play would be performed in a given year. Cities that established large cycles of plays needed strong secular governments; perhaps we should say that the plays only came into being when civic governments required symbolic vehicles to enact their power. As Lawrence Clopper suggests, there is a correlation between the enhancement of civic authority in cities like Norwich, Lincoln, Chester, and Beverly and the establishment or expansion of a cycle of plays ("Social Contexts").

In addition to their symbolic value in displaying the honor of the city, a cycle of plays offered the opportunity to involve the craft guilds in the urban cultural performance. As a number of scholars (James; Homan; and Beadle, *York Plays* 19–39) have shown, individual plays were allocated to different guilds, sometimes on the basis of affinity between the craft and the subject matter of the play (the goldsmiths were assigned the *Magi* play and the bakers the *Last Supper* at York) and sometimes matching the most prominent guilds with the most lavish plays (the York mercers produced the *Last Judgment* play). Mervyn James argues that, beyond a representation of the social and economic stratifications within the urban community, the production of the cycle play enabled the guilds to shift fortunes over time with minimal conflict. The cycle projected an idealized image of civic unity and also brought that unity into being out of diversity and flux. The performance of a cycle thus had crucial social functions within the late medieval town.

Other cultural theorists emphasize that cultural performances within the frame of a festival or game may be reflexive: they may question the society's accepted assignments of power, wealth, status, or value. Categories of people normally separated by social roles are often brought together in festivals, with the result that everyday structures are dissolved and values transcending the mundane are elevated. Thus, although control over the cycle plays was held by the urban oligarchy, made up of successful male citizens, the productions involved were from many socioeconomic levels and occupational groups. Furthermore, characters within individual plays voice sentiments at odds with the dominant urban ideologies. The shepherds and other lower-class characters who make impassioned social protests and Noah's wife, whose rebellious behavior challenges God's plan and society's model of ideal husband-wife relations—such liminal figures cannot be totally contained within authorized frameworks. Comic and evil characters in the cycle plays of York, Chester, and Towneley are allowed to express unorthodox and anomalous social and religious opinions. How can we understand this phenomenon?

The traditional argument of humanist criticism has been that evil and comic characters in the cycles demonstrate what not to say, think, or do and that their expressions of unorthodox opinions should not be taken seriously. Marxist critics like Anthony Gash do take the protests seriously, arguing that liminal characters express popular and controversial ideas suppressed by the authorities mounting the cycles (76). Only occasionally can an unorthodox writer smuggle some of these views into his drama, but they are the exception, rather than the rule. Recent cultural theorists, however, regard such liminal figures as central to ritual and festive events. The critique of society they engender is also seen as crucial to certain types of cultural performance, including festivals. The festival form itself, they point out, often erects mock models of society and encourages the active parody of the social order through satire, allegory, and buffoonery (Handelman 166). This is especially true of festivals in highly differentiated and hierarchical societies that have a strong sense of their communal identities, a category the late medieval urban societies of York and Chester certainly fit. Within such a society the people know their respective places in a world that is securely bounded and stratified—we might say restricted. On festival occasions, however, the self is released to play with the categories, assumptions, and norms of everyday life. The status quo can be examined, mocked, and challenged, and alternate possibilities can be playfully considered. This exploration of the limits of conventional existence is as much at the core of the urban festival as the obvious function of promoting an idealized image of town identity, according to cultural criticism.

The York and Chester cycles and to a smaller extent the Towneley cycle (about which many questions concerning location remain) fit the urban festival model that cultural theorists have proposed. These cycles were festive events, sponsored by civic elites, that celebrated religious and social myths fundamental to urban society. They also brought together categories of persons who in everyday life did not mingle, allowing within the festive structures of the drama both parody and a close critique of the social order. Thus, many scenes in Chester and York offer anatomies of political power and social organization, mirroring urban processes like trials and workplace dynamics. They model appropriate behaviors for husbands, wives, children, rulers and citizens, employers and employees, but they also display the antagonisms and the strains within such relationships. Some scenes appear to promote the bourgeois ideology of the cycle sponsors; others subject those values to critical scrutiny and propose alternative value systems. As a festive form, the cycle permits a complex and various representation of its society, one that paradoxically both reaffirms that society and allows for its transformation.

## Religious Guild Drama

The chief civic cycles were produced in cooperation with craft guilds, but religious guilds also offered plays in some towns. York, for example, had a *Creed* play produced by the Corpus Christi guild from the mid-fifteenth through the mid-sixteenth centuries, and other guilds put on a *Pater Noster* play; both play texts have been lost, although records of their performance remain (Johnston and Rogerson xv–xvi). In the absence of manuscripts, it is difficult to discuss the cultural performances of religious guilds in England; however, one of the surviving cycles—known as N-Town because its affiliation is obscure and the Banns suggest it was taken on tour—may have been the product of such a group. We know nothing concrete about the production of the text, since no external records link it with a place. It is a composite manuscript and may never have been performed as a cyclic whole, though sections show hard wear. Arguing deductively on the basis of its many differences from Chester, York, and Towneley, we can see N-Town as performed for and by a religious guild whose cosmology differed from that of large scale socioeconomic organizations.

The anthropologist Mary Douglas defines a cosmology as the ultimate justifying ideas that are invoked as part of the natural order of things but that are actually a product of social patterns of interaction ("Grid/Group Analysis"). Among the cosmologies she has defined is one typical of small groups or communities that separate themselves from the larger society. Such a cosmology, which is attentive to boundaries between the group and others, worries about issues of purity. Groups dominated by this cosmology (whether religious or political) perceive threats to the group from witches, subversives, traitors, and aliens and periodically mobilize the group machinery to root out these enemies to the purity of the group. Many of the distinctive features of the N-Town cycle fit this model strikingly and suggest that the manuscript was put together from plays performed by a religious guild. The exploration of group boundaries, with the pure included and the defiled excluded, is more elaborate in N-Town than in any other extant cycle. Purity is celebrated and epitomized in the figure of Mary, whose life receives fuller dramatization in N-Town than elsewhere. What is missing from the N-Town cycle is also significant; there is little parody, comedy, or buffoonery, and the representations of social processes and organizations are relatively undetailed. Unlike the civic cycles, whose social context is a minutely differentiated society that festival play parodies, small-group performances play down internal differences. All members of the guild are brothers or sisters, for example, rather than members of a status hierarchy. N-Town also emphasizes kinship and membership in the group as a whole, rather than being a critique of insiders. These deductions from internal evidence are hypotheses, but cultural theory does offer a coherent model of the types of performance to be expected from different social structures that makes some sense of N-Town cosmology.

## Traveling Troupes

Household and city records reveal the presence of other kinds of performance, too—namely, entertainments by traveling players and musicians. Typically, troupes of four or five men performed indoors during winter feasts, using available spaces, like the great hall or a manor house, and portable props. They might claim to be "Lord _____ 's players," although such an identity was often a hedge against being labeled vagabounds. In patterns of entertainment, large monastic establishments resembled aristocratic households; they received eminent visitors and required musical or dramatic entertainments, usually provided by itinerant troupes. The mayor and the aldermen might also see a play in their hall before granting a license for public performance in town. David Bevington's *From* Mankind *to Marlowe* provides the most convincing discussion of these troupes and their repertoires for the century between 1470 and 1570.

Although much intensive historical work has shown how the establishment of secular professional theater at the end of the sixteenth century can be traced to these troupes of itinerant, semiprofessional players, the seemingly crucial distinction between professional and amateur actor that such scholarship seeks to make is, from the point of view of cultural criticism, superficial. The local actors who performed in amateur town cycle plays were often paid, and it is likely that some of the principal roles were taken by people who supported themselves by acting. More crucial, culturally, is the relation between the actors or the acting company and the community in and for which they performed. The itinerant troupes of the late fifteenth and early sixteenth centuries were still performing within a festive and public frame, even when they collected money for their labors. Coming out of a different set of social and performance arrangements than village festivity, civic festival, or religious guild plays, the cultural performances of traveling troupes project a unique cosmology. They provide ambulatory allegorical guides to the individual conduct of a life. The world they portray is neither that of a socially differentiated political, economic, and family structure (like the civic cycles) nor that of a group whose boundaries are threatened (like the N-Town cycle); it is that of the individual moral psyche.

## Sixteenth-Century Developments: The Disruption of Festival Culture

The cultural conditions that gave dramatic performances their privileged position at the festive heart of medieval community life changed irrevocably by the end of the sixteenth century.

Perhaps the most crucial development in England was the centralizing of power in London in the monarchy. The cycle plays in particular had represented their provincial home towns to the nation. They may have been suppressed by authorities citing antipapist reasons, but they were defended by townsfolk, council members, and mayors who saw in their plays a performance of their political identity (Sanders). The extinguishing of most civic plays by 1580 is a reliable index to the loss of provincial town identity, which was undermined from within and without, and the correlative rise of London's political and cultural dominance.

A second major development was the ejection of drama from the community center. Once performed in city streets and squares or on tour around the countryside, plays came to occupy restricted locations. Beginning in 1576, Elizabethan and Jacobean playhouses were constructed outside the walls of London, a site that expressed the professional theater's ideological marginality to civic society, as Steven Mullaney has recently argued. Patronized and regulated by the court, prohibited by the Puritan city, this was a theater of ambivalent status that could comment on and contradict the body politic itself (Mullaney vii-ix). The cultural performances produced by the court and the city of London verged on spectacle, unambiguous displays of official ideology without the liminal freedom to criticize built into medieval festive performances of most types. Detached from ritual and polity, liminality occupied a separate and in many ways more vulnerable place in early modern culture.

A third major result of the alliance between political centralization and religious Reformation was the effective regulation of popular culture. Archbishop Grindal and his ilk all over Europe actively suppressed festivity (Burke 207–22). Both Catholic and Protestant reformers of the sixteenth century objected to popular religious forms like saints' feasts, pilgrimages, and plays, as well as secular activities like bearbaiting, charivaris, maypoles, and abbeys of misrule. The result of sustained repressive legislation was a clear distinction between sacred and mundane spheres and between popular and elite groups. The festival culture of medieval society that had brought different social groups together and had blurred the distinctions between play, worship, and socioeconomic function was fatally disrupted, and its characteristic performances ceased or were transmuted within their new contexts.

## Implications for Teaching

The classroom teaching of all drama tends to be text-based. Sometimes we make an explicit commitment to the play as literature, a commitment grounded in a notion that we should be teaching texts of literary masterpieces, with the corollary that we are proving these medieval dramatic texts are as exciting literarily as any others. At other times, we find it too onerous to recreate the drama as performance within the confines of a classroom not designed for performance. The additional challenge posed by a cultural approach to the drama is that of recreating a social context within which a particular dramatic text may have large cultural functions. In essence, the teacher of medieval drama must become a social historian or an anthropologist.

If this task seems overwhelming, given the data gaps about the texts we have, it need not be. A fruitful way to open a semester is to point out that medieval drama was popular culture, in many ways analogous to the entertainment media of the twentieth century. (One can also explore the differences.) Furthermore, the distinction between what the elite and the folk knew and did was far less rigid than it became in the early modern period. Popular culture was everyone's culture, especially in festive contexts.

A logical next step is to outline the festive calendar, for virtually all performances are tied to festival and feast occasions. Everyone shared a Christian liturgical calendar and folk seasons like midwinter and Midsummer. The two calendars can be analytically separated, then the overlaps shown and discussed. For example, the Christian calendar absorbed many of the traditional pagan festivals and continued to use the appropriated energy to fuel its own feast days.

A third step or organizing principle is to look at festive occasions within different social milieus. The monastery, for example, celebrated many of the same feast days as the village community or the town. Certain types of performance were common to all milieus (one thinks of Resurrection plays), but often a kind of performance is primarily associated with one milieu; the cycle plays were always located in towns of a certain size and political constitution. Locating each surviving text within a specific socioeconomic and cultural context and then connecting it to such production information as can be gleaned from the Records of Early English Drama series or other theater histories flesh out the text as cultural performance.

Finally, bearing in mind the rich cultural context should suggest ways of reading the dramatic text. Although most of our surviving plays use the language of the Christian myth, they do so in ways that would have been relevant to their particular audience and performance context. The assumption that medieval drama was produced by the church to instruct the laity is both too crude and too inaccurate to account for differences in the way the Christian myth is presented in different plays. The Passion sequences of the four cycles, for example, dramatize the ordeal of Christ in significantly distinctive ways. Chester's emphasis on his divine power minimizes his human vulnerability, while Towneley's interest in larger-than-life evil characters is quite different from York's complex portrayal of political and legal institutions.

Connecting text to context, showing how the mode of dramatization and the emphasized features of the story were communicated to particular types of audiences within particular festive structures in the interests of their producers, is the great challenge of cultural criticism. It is a process that is just beginning, and for that reason interpreters within the classroom setting are in the exciting position of being toe-to-toe with the scholars.

# The Semiotics of Christ's
# Body in the English Cycles

*Peter W. Travis*

Medieval plays are not easy to teach. Even in a course devoted to medieval drama, the problem of what I call the absence of a pedagogical middle distance persists. Students can immediately begin discussing these plays by using their second-nature critical approaches—appreciating characterization, exploring dramatic conflicts, analyzing the plays' propagandistic strategies, fleshing out the plays' power as theatrical spectacles, and articulating their sense of the plays' curious otherness as medieval cultural artifacts. But the next critical step is a major one, often requiring an undue amount of student research or professorial lecturing. How much of the Christian liturgy, for example, need a student know? (Selected chapters from Alan W. Watts's *Myth and Ritual in Christianity* provide a good deal of readable information.) How much medieval iconography or scriptural exegesis needs to be supplied to set a single dramatic moment into context? (Rosemary Woolf's lengthy but brilliant *English Mystery Plays* details the many interpretive options an educated playwright can exploit in dramatizing a single scriptural event.) How much urban history, late medieval aesthetics, and traditions of popular piety must a student absorb? The problem is one of diminishing returns: most areas of knowledge crucial to an in-depth appreciation of medieval drama are impressively resistant to short-order distillation. Since I prefer to teach medieval plays dialogically, with students' critical intuitions cross-pollinating with occasional supplements of scholarly information, I find that interpretive paradigms whose vocabulary is as much the students' as the scholar's are worth developing. The human body is one such paradigm.

Of all the images and metaphors of the human body, the physical body of Christ dominates medieval drama. Since the beginning of medieval drama (which is normally identified as that moment in the Eastertide liturgical celebrations when ritual figures first acted out the Marys' search for Christ's body) until its end (which is often represented by the banning of the English Corpus Christi cycles because the cycles had presumed to give human form to the Word of God), medieval drama is preoccupied with the body of Christ. The diachronic permutations of Christ's body as theatrical image are thus likely to be an important issue in any course tracing the development of medieval drama over the centuries. But Christ's body is such a powerful sign, incorporating codes on many levels, that many dialects of body language are speaking at once in a single play. Students of medieval drama can hardly be expected to read the host of recent studies of the body written across such divergent fields as anthropology (Blacking; Morris), sociology (Turner), psychology (Levin), and literary criticism and theory (Barker; Michie; Scarry, *Literature*). But a classroom discussion subtly influenced by selected paradigms of body symbolism should assist in developing interpretive models applicable to a wide variety of medieval plays. The imperfect fit between one scholarly model and another and between them and any play is often an educational boon in itself. These gaps may suggest not only the dissonance among different body sign systems but also the distance between medieval and modern readings of the body, both sacred and profane.

A neutral, nonmedieval place to begin is John O'Neill's *Five Bodies*, a 1985 sociological study of five levels at which the human body has served Western men and women as a symbolic medium through which they may apprehend their relation to the world. The first level is the world's body, wherein the world is seen as a human body writ large, a macrocosm whose individual elements are both similar and sympathetic to the working organs of the individual person. The second level is the social body, wherein society is perceived to be a structure designed like the human body, with head, hands, feet, sinews, and organs—all ideally working in balanced harmony. The third mode of embodied perception is the body politic, wherein the health and the harmony of the state is maintained through the coordination of its interdependent organs, such as the arts of commerce, law, and governance. The fourth level is the consumer body, the human body that needs such things as food, drink, clean air, rest, shelter, clothing, and standards of health and safety. The fifth level is the medical body, the body whose nature we are most aware of in its conception, birth, nurturing, sexual conduct, illness, pain, aging, and dying. O'Neill's fivefold taxonomy of the body is hardly a model of literary critical praxis, yet, if we force its constraints on the most often studied of medieval plays, the Wakefield *Second Shepherds' Play*, certain correspondences readily emerge. In this pageant the world body appears to be suffering from a cosmic disease; the social body of England is in disarray; political corruption and favoritism have sharpened the shepherds' unrest; their consumer bodies are woefully undernourished; and the plight of the medical body is a constant complaint, epitomized by Gill's mock labor and Mak's burlesque punishment.

Although O'Neill's schema coordinates a number of dominant motifs in the Wakefield *Second Shepherds' Play*, one of its most obvious limitations is the absence of any sacred metaphors to valorize these images of the body and to clarify their interconnections. In the Wakefield *Second Shepherds' Play*, the presence of the Christ child as *corpus Christi* is a dramatic reality that tests and redefines the existing relation between the social, the political, and the physical bodies and the world body into which Christ is born. Furthermore, serving as the pageant's cynosure of dramatic worship, Christ's body may suggest how medieval drama as a social act addresses the desires and the complaints of the social, political, and personal bodies of the culture for whom these plays were performed. Thus, any approach focusing on Christ's body as an interpretive paradigm must recognize that in the Middle Ages other images of the body not only contribute to the significance of his sacred body but also celebrate their own identities in ways that both seek and resist total incorporation into the semiotics of his physical person.

One virtue of the human body as a critical topos is that its relative novelty encourages the exploration of interpretive ideas that traditional medieval drama scholarship has kept at a distance. In the following outline I move from orthodox to experimental modes of interpretation, beginning with various artistic images of Christ's body and fairly standard ways of interpreting its significance. I proceed then to Christ's body as a social metaphor and to the structural principles that often underlie interpretations of the cycles as social acts. The next decoding of Christ's body is psychoanalytic. Since modern psychological readings of medieval plays are rare, I take some time to describe part of one theory and to apply it to one important dramatic moment in the cycles. I conclude by suggesting some of the possibilities of the body of festive resistance, the dramatic celebration of somatic images that challenge any unifying schemes of interpretation, including my own. As I parse out some features of the grammar of the body in medieval drama, I restrict my examples to the English cycles. But all forms of medieval drama—saint plays, moralities, folk plays, interludes—construct images of the body that are distinctly their own and that require their own mix of interpretive systems to decode them.

## The Body of Christ in Art and Theology

One effective way of introducing the power of Christ's body is with slides and plates of Christ's representation in medieval art. With little or no formal training in art history or in Christianity, students may readily perceive different aspects of Christ's person projected in different moments of his life. *The Holkham Bible Picture Book* (ed. Hassall) is an especially useful one-volume cycle of salvation history that illustrates Christ in his many roles: as architect of the universe, as incarnated deity at the nativity, as performer of miracles in his ministry, as the subject of the physical tortures and humiliations of the Passion, as resurrected Savior in wounded glory, and as justiciar at the Last Judgment. In addition to retracing the major events of Christ's life, *The Holkham Bible Picture Book* exploits the spectacle of Christ's body in its attitudes of dress and undress to project the nuances of his person, both human and divine: his power and regality, his humility and compassion, his pain and anguish. Whereas each of these qualities of his person tends naturally to be foregrounded at different moments of Christ's career, meditating on the ways each quality can be differently emphasized in a single scene begins to open up the range of Christological positions available to artists and dramatists in the Middle Ages.

An important complement to the interpretations of Christ's body realized by one artist in one brief span of time is a broad historical survey of several artistic interpretations of Christ's body in a single scene. The Crucifixion probably best illustrates the transformation of early medieval spiritual religiosity into the visceral piety characteristic of the late Middle Ages. Such a survey begins logically with venerated crosses of the tenth century, moves to crucifixions projecting a regal and unsuffering Christ standing on the Cross, progresses then through the increasingly realistic depictions of the suffering of his suspended body, and concludes with the Gothic horrors of the Isenheim altarpiece and of the fifteenth-century Netherlandish Christs represented in James H. Marrow's *Passion Iconography in Northern European Art of the Late Middle Ages and Early Renaissance.*

A heightened awareness of the variety of Christs represented in medieval art should lead not only to a more sensitive reading of the different Christs presented in individual pageants and cycles but also to a greater awareness of how Christ's flesh is deeply encoded, especially in its humanation, in its sacramentality, and in its violation. Leo Steinberg's *Sexuality of Christ in Renaissance Art and in Modern Oblivion* is an attention-grabbing study of the symbolism of Christ's naked body and specifically of the centrality of his penis in fifteenth- and sixteenth-century paintings. Steinberg's puckish delight, as he lifts the invisible veil of self-censorship that centuries of neo-Puritan viewers have draped between their own eyes and Christ's genitals, is balanced by a sober exegesis extrapolated from the arguments of late medieval incarnational theology: simply put, Christ would have been less than perfectly human if he had been sexually incomplete; his genitals thus symbolize his sexuality, and his sexuality in turn symbolizes his fully-taken-on humanity. In "The Body of Christ in the Later Middle Ages: A Reply to Leo Steinberg" Caroline Walker Bynum argues that, rather than his male sexuality, Christ's flesh embodies his feminine nature, especially in its wounded state. She agrees with Steinberg that Christ's circumcised penis, the first element of his body to feel pain, is a proleptic sign of his Passion (a connection often made in Crucifixion paintings by a bloody hyphen tracing from Christ's breast wound down under his loincloth). But that wound in Christ's side is feminine: in painting after painting, Christ is presented as the nurturing mother, the blood spouting from his lactating breast offering spiritual life to his suckling children. Christ's late medieval body, then, is a sign not so much of his male sexuality as of his painful, universal, and double-gendered human nature (Bynum, *Jesus* 110–69 and *Holy Feast*).

Both the questions and the underlying assumptions in this scholarly exchange between Steinberg and Bynum provide assistance in interpreting the significance of Christ's body in medieval drama. Christ's unique nakedness, in striking contrast to the fully clothed and often sumptuously dressed characters around him, asks to be interpreted in terms of both its gendered and its theological significance. His Passion, for example, is dramatized as if it were a protracted mugging or gang rape, the viewers of the play voyeuristically permitting four pronouncedly male figures (often dressed in the full armor of soldiers) to maul and bludgeon a naked, weak, and passive subject to the point of death. The maternal side of Christ's feminine nature is emphasized in those Resurrection and Last Judgment scenes in which he exposes the wound in his breast and beseeches his viewers to seek salvation in him. In other scenes, such as the harrowing of hell, Christ's masculine nature is brought to the fore; in yet other scenes both his words and his deeds emphasize his divinity. The overall impulse of the Corpus Christi plays, however, is toward the reification of his human nature, as his double-gendered body invites viewers, both male and female, to experience their mutual physical bonding with their savior.

This somatic bond leads to a second level of significance, one that medieval viewers perceived more readily than modern spectators do. Christ was understood to have entered the food chain on many levels: as vegetable (bread and wine), as animal (the lamb of God), and as man (this is my body, this is my blood). In the Mass, Christ is food, his body literally immolated and consumed in a ritual of canonized cannibalism. Similarly, in the cycles, Christ offers himself to his viewers in a rite of ocular communion, explicitly equating his body with the Eucharistic host, as in the Chester *Resurrection*:

> I am verey bread of liffe.
> From heaven I light and am send.
> Whoe eateth that bread, man or wiffe,
> shall lyve with me withowt end.
> (Lumiansky and Mills, lines 170–73)

As Leah Sinanoglou has shown in "The Christ Child as Sacrifice: A Medieval Tradition and the Corpus Christi Plays," the sacramental significance of Christ's body as *corpus Christi* is embedded less explicitly yet just as profoundly in other parts of the cycles in a host of gestures, images, and allusions. The cycles have been aptly named plays of Corpus Christi: the spectators beholding Christ's body are participating in something akin to the rite of communion.

A third feature of Christ's body, in addition to its double-gendered human nature and its sacramental identity, is the pain it suffers when in the Passion his naked flesh is gradually transformed into a pulpy mass of welts, lacerations, bruises, and open sores. The resistance of this pain to exegetical interpretation is part of the genius of late medieval Christian aesthetics, wherein rationality is well-nigh paralyzed by a surfeit of powerful sensations. Students need not read any of the recent studies of the phenomenology of human pain as it has been represented in history, art, scripture, and ritual (see, e.g., Foucault; Girard; Scarry), but they must attempt to articulate in their own words the importance of physical wounding and bodily fragmentation in the cycles. It is apparent in the Passion sequences of these cycles that only through Christ's violent dismemberment may one hope to achieve unity of being. Only through protracted physical disincorporation is one able to undo one's own separateness, to feel and to touch pain, to open up the channels of grace.

## The Social Body

Since the dynamic of physical unity and dismemberment is powerfully incorporated into the cycles, another important way of understanding these plays is as embodiments of the viewers' sense of themselves as living organisms made up of discrete, interdependent, and potentially rivalrous parts. One of the earliest and most influential deployments of this image is Paul's in 1 Corinthians 12, where the diverse congregation of the Corinthian church are described as members unified ultimately in the body of their Lord:

> For as the body is one and hath many members: and all the members of the body, whereas they are many, yet are one body: so also is Christ. . . . If the foot should say: Because I am not the hand, I am not of the body: Is it therefore not of the body? And if the ear should say: Because I am not the eye, I am not of the body: Is it therefore not of the body? . . . But now there are many members indeed, yet one body. . . . And if one member suffer any thing, all the members suffer with it: or if one member glory, all the members rejoice with it. Now you are the body of Christ and members of member. (Douay-Rheims version)

Recognizing the tendency of social bodies to break up into misaligned fragments yet appreciating the special importance of the most lowly organs, Paul's vision of Christ's body and the unifying and disunifying function of its discrete parts is a vision that ramifies throughout the Middle Ages. Not only was this living metaphor sacralized in peculiarly complicated ways in the idea of the king's two bodies, but it blended with various late medieval ways of conceiving the polis, the city or state perceived as a sacred human organism of interdependent economic, social, political, and geographic units (Kantorowicz; Barkan). The occasion that most fully dramatized the English medieval city's vision of itself as a version of Christ's body was the feast of Corpus Christi, as Mervyn James has shown in his essay "Ritual, Drama and Social Body in the Late Medieval English Town." For James, the Corpus Christi procession most clearly articulated the city's identity as a holy body: the individual guilds processing in order, the humbler followed by the more powerful, with the place of greatest honor, the procession's end, reserved for the mayor, his aldermen, and the clergy attending the Host displayed in a gilded monstrance. James notes that, on occasion, friction developed at the most vulnerable points in this hierarchically structured procession, in the joints and the opening between one guild and the next, and he suggests in passing that the cycles, because they are less rigidly designed, may have included implications for social change.

Without delving at length into the history and the social constructions of late medieval English cities—as studied, for example, in Phythian-Adams's *Desolation of a City*—one may read the English cycles as plays reflecting the urban population for whom they were performed. In large part the plays are flattering celebrations of the city's mythic wholeness: the ideal social body obliquely projected in their performance is unified, harmonious, healthy, and sacred. But other images and metaphors of the body, Christ's mutilated body being the most prominent, make available a less flattering, even at times dystopian image of the city and its members (Travis "Social Body"). It is not too extreme to ask the kinds of questions that anthropologists have asked about a culture's strictures and taboos relating to the body and its parts (see Douglas, *Natural Symbols;* Leach 61-62; Geertz 98-120). Christ's body tacitly queries its viewers: Are we complete? What parts of ourselves are sacred? What parts are profane? Why is nakedness a sign of weakness or cause for shame? Do we honor our humble members? Why shouldn't they revolt? How are we, as a social body, equivalent to *corpus Christi?* The self-reflexivity of these plays as social commentaries is partially inscribed in the body that the community has created, dramatized, and chosen to honor.

## The Body as an Image of the Self

Christ's body may also be seen as asking questions that pertain to the viewers as individual persons. In beholding Christ's body, spectators may be observing a mirror of their private selves, or—to use terms taken from modern psychoanalysis—they may be returning to a confrontation of rival self-images that have haunted them since early childhood. In his essay "The Mirror Stage as Formative of the Function of the I," Jacques Lacan contends that the formation of the ego commences at that moment in our development when we first see our own images reflected in a mirror and for the first time conceive of our bodies as totalities. The mirror image is the first organized form of the person, an exaggeratedly perfect and idealized form with which we fall narcissistically in love and through which our vision of the world is subsequently ordered and constituted. But because our subconscious fully acknowledges that it is only an image, a fictive reflection, we harbor this form as a distant and uncircumscribable ideal—a virtual, alienated, and perfect unity that cannot be touched. The mirror stage is life's first tragedy because it constructs not only an unattainable other but also a retroactive alter image of the subject's body, a fragmented body of misaligned and ravaged parts, *le corps morcelé* (the body in bits and pieces). The child repeatedly experiences a violent discord between two somatic images of the self, one fragmented and the other unified, as an aggressive disintegration of the body, conceived in images of "castration, mutilation, dismemberment, dislocation, devouring, [and] bursting open" (Lacan, "Aggressivity" 11).

The child thus finds a rival in the self before finding rivals in others, and each of these rival others in turn participates in varying degrees in that mirror image of the self. From early on, each of us is captured by the human form of that other image and is conditioned by the other's look—for example, by the face and the gaze of the mother—resulting in a primary conflict between one's identity with the other's image and one's rivalry with it. No resolution of this conflict is in sight: rather, the aggressive desire of the ego effects a succession of fantasies that progress from an image of the body in bits and pieces to an idealized form Lacan calls "orthopedic" in its totality and then to a third fantasy Lacan calls the "armor" of an alienating identity, which "will mark with its rigid structure the subject's entire mental development" ("Mirror Stage" 4).

The corollaries between Lacan's scenario of the drama of the mirror stage and the Corpus Christi drama's projection of the human body are especially pronounced in the Passion sequence, where Lacan's three images—the fragmented body, the ideal body, and the armored body—are superimposed one on the other. That Christ is the perfect human being all medieval viewers believe: they have just seen his body in the Corpus Christi procession, a circular and pure white wafer offering salvation to those who, perfectly shriven, commune and become unified with him. And they have beheld an image of that body, an idealized human form of an actor dressed in white skintights, being violently transformed to its antithesis, the fragmented body in bits and pieces, *le corps morcelé*. The agents of this transformation, the torturers, play what Lacan would call a transitivist role, whether or not they are dressed as soldiers or as generic English urban craftsmen. Exercised by a sense of insufficiency before the ideal imago of the other, they articulate and effect the aggressive disintegration of the individual. Their rigidity is a sign of their authority, for the brutalities they enact are, ironically, lawful and necessary, sanctioned and ordered by the Father. And if their aggressive rivalry is nevertheless cause for guilt or shame, they are apparently to be forgiven, for, like the ego in Lacan's theory of the self, they know not what they do. That is, rather than a "perception-consciousness system," Lacan sees the ego as constituted of *méconaissances*, misreadings, misprisions—a host of stratagems designed to ward off the truth. Only the unconscious is apparently able to speak the truth, which the ego in turn distorts and denies. In Lacanian terms, it is appropriate that the torturers dominate the action of the Passion, subtly yet crudely maneuvering between Christ and his spectators, manipulating their field of vision, reviling and misreading his body, transforming the shape of that body while effecting in the onlookers an emotional decentering, both desired and resisted, homologous to Christ's physical fragmentation.

The arresting moment of this drama—when Christ fixes his eyes on his viewers and beseeches them to behold the mutilated parts of his body—is a moment that appears to offer light, insight, and self-knowledge. "O thou side-piercing sight!"— Edgar's exclamation in *King Lear* (4.6.85)—is appropriately addressed to Lear's archetype, Christ, whose unaccommodated body effects in the viewer an anxiety analogous to the pain of the wound felt in his side. It is not only the sight of Christ but Christ's own sight (the power of his eyes to see) that is side-piercing, for what Christ may see in his viewer's eyes is the image of an embodied self as fragmented as his own. Christ's "side-piercing sight" is thus a sight-piercing sight, challenging the viewer to look into his eyes and to discover there a somatic image of himself analogous to the Savior's mutilated body. At some level of this specular exchange, the emboldened viewer may be persuaded that he is experiencing the painful privilege of observing his own consciousness seeing itself seeing itself. For Lacan, however, this experience is an illusion: fullness of vision is never granted. But in this illusion, he contends, one finds the basis for the enigma of the Gaze, where an unnamable and elusive It imagined by the subject to exist in the field of the Other determines, by its absence, the identity of the subject as existing in the world of the visible ("Of the Gaze").

Because Lacan's theories are essentialist, ahistorical, and centered on the male subject, a number of important questions concerning the propriety of applying his models to medieval drama need to be explored. (One question is whether any interpretive models are entirely free of the presumed limitations of a Lacanian approach.) However, in a number of ways the dialectic that a Lacanian reading discovers in this dramatic exchange between Christ and his viewer, each seeking in the other something he lacks and provoking in the other a desire to be fulfilled, is a dialectic that Christianity glosses similarly, although with a more traditional vocabulary. Christ's body in these plays serves as a polyvalent sign, one layer of which is that of the sought-for maternal Other. It can be argued that the desire to become unified with a sacred Other created in one's own image is the collective desire that compelled medieval townspeople to reenact their mirror-stage drama, like a ritual abreaction, year after year.

## The Body of Festive Resistance

Performed year after year inside that zone of playful inversion that characterizes the liminal status of many festive celebrations, the cycles might be expected to embrace, at least marginally, an image of the flesh comically at odds with the ideal human torso. But the carnival body that Bakhtin made his central concern—fragmented, gross, driven by its animal appetites—is a body granted little space in the cycles (in contrast to the morality plays). Instead, the festive body is displaced into images of the flesh that both participate in the semiotics of Christ's body and consistently undermine any attempt at determining their ultimate meaning. I am thinking specifically of the fabulous feasts of the shepherds in the Chester cycle and in the Wakefield *First Shepherds' Play*. In Wakefield (the Chester play is similar but hardly identical), the down-at-the-heels shepherds have the wherewithal for a prodigious meal, an eclectic mess of aristocratic and peasant fare: a "browne" (flesh) of a boar, with mustard sauce; a cow's foot; the "pestell" (leg) of a sow that has been seasoned ("powdered"); two blood puddings ("blodyngys") and a "leueryng" (a liver pudding in the form of a sausage); a beef; mutton from "an ewe that was roton"; an oxtail; a pie; two "swyne-gronys" (pig snouts); an entire hare except for the loins; a goose leg; "chekyns endorde" (chickens glazed with egg yolk); a pork; a "tart for a lorde"; a calf liver garnished with crab-apple juice ("veryose"); and, finally, ale (England and Pollard, *Towneley Plays* 107).

Although numerous scholars have tried to make sense out of all this food, one wonders if it isn't a futile undertaking (see the opposed readings in Lepow; Adams). It is a cornucopian feast out of the pages of Rabelais, conceived in the spirit of Bakhtin's prandial libertinism, celebrating (if nothing else) excess for the sake of excess. The problem is that these articles of food carry with them a troublesome amount of conflicting semiotic baggage. For example, the Wakefield list contains several foods forbidden in the Old Testament as "abominations" against the Lord: the hare ("it chews the cud but does not part the hoof" [Lev. 11.5]); the swine ("it parts the hoof and is cloven-footed, but does not chew the cud" [Lev. 11.3]); liver and oxtail, food reserved for God alone; any meat with blood still in it (such as the blood puddings), for blood was considered in the Old Testament to be the soul of life. But it is not clear if any of these proscriptions matter: the shepherds are quasi-Christian Englishmen, and Christ in his ministry will erase these dietary taboos and transcend the social boundaries they expressed. Second, in a general way all this foodstuff typologically anticipates the Eucharist and the Passion of Christ's body: the ale a reminder that wine accompanies the Host; the blood puddings a reminder of Christ's blood shed on the Cross; the slaughtered animals a collective reminder of Christ as sacrificial victim. But if auguring the Passion is the sole point of all this food, there is an inexplicable overkill, a surplus of signs. Third, whether or not this comic meal on the heath was actually real has been the subject of long debate. Cawley is convinced no actual food appeared on stage, whereas Weimann (95) believes the food was both produced and shared with the audience. This may be an irresolvable problem, forced on us by the scarcity of stage directions and performance records. It may also be an ambiguity central to the unstable meaning of the feasts themselves.

The significance of this composite of foodstuffs is torn in many directions. In a rough-hewn way the banquet is akin to the paschal meal of Christ's body. But—disjointed, detotalized, showing the effects of their butchery—these pieces of meat are also crudely analogous to the maladroit and decentered lives of the shepherds. Like the street language that Bakhtin identifies with carnival, the food is loose and impromptu, a mix of registers both sacred and profane, socially both high and low. If there is a social tension implicit in this varied fare between an official culture and a potentially emergent one, it is a tension, like the myriad other semiotic issues, played out in hermeneutical space. The rapid ocular parade of these meaty parts— leg, liver, snout, and so on—gives a sense of corporeal chaos and rampant slaughter. This, too, points in many directions, one being the fact that, for a society never far from the threat of famine, the slaughter of animals was cause for deep, if short-lived, delight and joy. But the only certainty is that there is no concluding certainty, other than that these pieces of animal flesh are part of a complex system of signs— ranging from the mystical to the quotidian, the economic to the biological, the social to the psychological, the political to the pro- fane—which in its totality renders the English cycles a rich spectacle of images and metaphors for the human body.

To explore medieval plays as the site of various modelings of the body is one way of encouraging students to think dialogically inside those two critical poles that Susan Noakes has called the exegesis of historical reconstruction and the interpretation of contemporary thought. Since the human body is a phenomenon that provokes a variety of contradictory feelings (fascination and inadequacy, attraction and distrust), it should be able to serve in future criticism as a ground metaphor for a variety of interrelated but never perfectly complementary paradigms. The relative novelty of the body as an interpretive matrix may even begin to attract some graduate students back to the study of medieval drama, a field that the present generation has by and large dismissed as being unworthy of sustained theoretical attention. Combined with other interpretive approaches, some outlined in this volume and others not yet dreamed of, the semiotics of the body could help resituate the field of medieval drama nearer the center of the canon as a subject worthy of rigorous critical thought and sustained classroom attention.

# A Feminist Approach to
# The Corpus Christi Cycles

## Theresa Coletti

At this moment in the history of literary studies, we hardly need to provide any rationale for a feminist approach to medieval drama, either in scholarship or in pedagogy. A drama that commandeered the attention and the resources of many medieval people for a long period of time and that was deeply embedded in the culture's prevailing modes of social organization, in its dominant myths, and in its ceremonial and festive life must surely bear important relations to medieval thinking about gender. Yet a feminist criticism of medieval drama remains largely unrealized. This state of affairs influences the present possibilities for a feminist pedagogy of medieval drama.

A feminist approach to medieval drama has thus far assumed a low profile because of the prevailing trends in medieval drama scholarship. After the ground swell of critical and interpretative studies that appeared in the years following the publication of the important books by O. B. Hardison and V. A. Kolve, medieval drama scholarship in the past decade has largely been given over to the exhaustive recovery of dramatic records, to the historical study of performance, and to modern production—activities whose major ambitions do not call for the privileging of gender as a category of analysis. These trends are the reflection, in part, of the disabling lack of knowledge about many features of the drama that are crucial to the interpretation of its texts. Both the scholar and the teacher must confront these gaps in knowledge. We do not know who wrote the cycles; we must speculate about the composition of their audiences; we cannot be certain of the places of origin of Wakefield and N-Town. Apart from a tantalizing bit of evidence suggesting that the wives of Chester were instrumental in putting on that cycle's *Assumption* play, we know little about the possible contributions of women to these dramatic endeavors, either as producers or as members of the audience (Martin Stevens, *Four Middle English Mystery Cycles* 260–61; Clopper, "History and Development" 226–27).

The teacher may find an even greater obstacle to the advancement of a feminist approach to medieval drama in the way that women do or do not figure in the texts. For example, the possibilities for a gender-oriented consideration of the Corpus Christi cycles are ostensibly inhibited by the limitations that dramatic form and biblical story imposed on the characterization of women. With the exception of the Virgin Mary and Mary Magdalene, the biblical narrative that the cycles present is a narrative largely dominated by males and male roles; it is a story of heroes and villains, of Christ and his Old Testament types and his spiritual and earthly opponents. The women who people the Corpus Christi cycles' texts and stages are helpmates and servants; they attest to events more often than they participate in them; they are, in many instances, marginal to the central action.

To be sure, characterization in the cycles—both male and female—is generally problematic, since, as several critics have written, many aspects of character are prescribed by biblical roles and by notions of the scriptural or moral type (Clopper, "Tyrants and Villains"; Mills, "Characterisation"). But these difficulties are compounded in the drama's treatment of gender roles and behaviors by the inevitable incorporation of the tension, virtually ubiquitous in the Middle Ages, between misogyny and idealization of women, a tension customarily registered in the familiar dichotomy of Eve and the Virgin Mary. If much medieval thinking about women can be subsumed within the typology inherent in this dichotomy, the Corpus Christi cycles may already provide the terms for a feminist approach, since they include as actual characters these famous *genetrices* of female stereotyping in the Christian West. But pinpointing stereotypes, which does not make for inspiring classroom teaching, constitutes a feminist approach only in the narrowest sense, for it risks mistaking the perception of a type for an understanding of the dramatic text's representation of gender.

Given these circumstances, it is hardly surprising that medieval-drama scholarship has not produced any sustained, focused feminist analysis of the Corpus Christi cycles or even a significant piece of one. Formulating a clear methodology for a feminist approach to medieval drama is no easy task. Many aspects of the cycle plays' composition, sponsorship, and enactment preclude the adoption of the kind of approach that has dominated much of Anglo-American feminist literary scholarship, which privileges women as writers and readers, as the critical points of origin and reception for textual production. Yet the absence of women in the textual production of medieval drama or the silence about their possible presence does not mean we must resort to a feminist reading of what Toril Moi calls the "images of women" variety (42–49). Rather, what is needed, as Elaine Showalter has suggested in a different context, is an approach to the dramatic representation of women that aims for "a maximum interdisciplinary contextualism, in which the complexity of attitudes towards the feminine can be analyzed in their fullest cultural and historical frame" (91). Such an approach must also be attentive to the complexity of any possible relationship between dramatic representation and social reality. There are no easy mimetic correspondences between the two. Natalie Zemon Davis's caveat for the women's historian is useful here: while "sexual symbols and symbolic behavior based on sex" certainly make statements about nature and human experience, they do not necessarily "reflect and prescribe the position and behavior of the sexes" ("Women's History" 91).

Feminist critics of Shakespeare such as Lisa Jardine have confronted this methodological problem head-on in recent years, providing helpful directives for the feminist reading of medieval drama because many of their basic observations about the cultural construction of the meaning of women in the late sixteenth century are equally true for the late Middle Ages (*Still Harping* 6–7; "Cultural Confusion" 1–5). Kathleen McLuskie urges us to

> acknowledge that the issues of sex, sexuality, sexual relations and sexual division were areas of conflict of which the contradictions of writing about women were only one manifestation alongside the complexity of . . . forms of social control of sex and the family. (91)

Whatever use the critic may make of historical knowledge to "speculate about the possible creation of meaning in the light of past institutions and ideologies," McLuskie stresses, "the gap between textual meaning and social meaning can never be completely filled" (93).

Within the general framework provided by these observations, we can begin to make sense of medieval drama's problematic representation of women, which does not easily break down into positive and negative but is intensely qualified, remarkably diverse, and frequently ambiguous. In this essay I examine aspects of these representations that are particularly germane to the exploration of drama in the classroom, either because of their centrality as issues or because of the likelihood of their engaging student interest. I consider ways of rethinking our understanding of some of the drama's most powerful stereotypes, looking first at the figure of the unruly woman and then at the Virgin Mary. Then I question what medieval dramatic representations of women may indicate about the larger context of the institutional religion in which the drama was situated. Since the cycle drama flourished in the period that witnessed changes in recognized dogma and religious practice, if not in actual matters of belief, it is worth considering the extent to which these changes were registered in the patterns and the emphases of the cycles' representation of women.

A feminist approach to medieval drama profitably directs student attention to the cycles' frequent use of the unruly woman, who emerges as a commanding figure in the plays regularly anthologized and taught. In this company are Uxor Noah in the Wakefield, Chester, and York cycles, Mak's wife Gyl in the *Secunda pastorum*, and the mothers of the Innocents in Wakefield and Chester. These dramatic figurations of female disorder are informed by festive traditions of early modern Europe that foregrounded the unruly woman, the vigorous, outrageous, garrulous creature featured in literary, pictorial, and social manifestations of misrule directed at marriage and the hierarchies of sex and gender (Davis, *Society and Culture* 124-51). The unruly woman is often armed with a distaff, the symbol of woman's labor and woman's fallen morals (Eve's postlapsarian labor was spinning). She represents woman's physical, verbal, and sexual power. In the cycle plays these "women on top," as they have come to be known, bear all the characteristics of their type: they do battle with their male opponents, the Noahs and the soldiers of Herod, often striking them with their distaffs or giving every indication of doing so; they engage in derisive repartee, fighting a battle of words as well as of limbs. The mothers of the Chester *Innocents* play are especially foulmouthed: "Saye, rotten hunter with thy gode, / stytton stallon, styck-tode" (Lumiansky and Mills 197, lines 313–14). This linguistic abuse or, as in the *Noah* plays of Chester and Wakefield, the identification of the unruly woman with excessive talk is also linked to her sexuality (Brooke-Rose 14–15; Patterson 660–66). Though the cycle plays are relatively quiet about the sexuality of their women on top, the identification of the women as sexual beings is implicit in their roles as wives and mothers. The cycles reserve explicit comment on woman's sexuality for the dramatization of Mary's virginal conception.

Though the unruly women of the English cycles can be traced back to ancient and ubiquitous folk plays and folk customs, the impulse to posit a connection between the ritualized hostilities of dramatic and other festive representations and actual social and sexual arrangements of early modern Europe must be recognized (Axton 36–40, 42–43). The social aims of the festive inversions of the unruly woman are often disputed: some evidence suggests both that they widened the options for women and critiqued existing familial and social orders and that they afforded only a temporary carnivallike release from values already in place (Davis, *Society and Culture* 142–45). The possibilities are rendered more problematic and provocative—and this is a fruitful topic for classroom discussion—when we consider that these festive inversions involved the donning of female garb by men who played the female roles. This theatrical cross-dressing or cross-playing, as it has been termed, has already received attention from the perspective of contemporary performance (Twycross, " 'Transvestism' in the Mystery Plays"; Rastall, "Female Roles"). It is an aspect of medieval dramatic representation that a feminist approach can scarcely overlook, though an analysis along these lines does not have at its disposal the same wealth of material that has enabled the recent study of cross-dressing in Renaissance drama (Marcus; Rackin).

Aspects of the cycles' representations of the unruly woman can provide challenging topics for student discussion and research. The cycles incorporate this figure for various purposes, purposes that are not always easy to determine. Similarly, the absence of the figure in places where she customarily appears may also be telling: the N-Town plays include neither a termagant Uxor Noah nor raucous mothers for the Innocents, omissions that are noteworthy in light of N-Town's preoccupation not only with the Virgin Mary but also with the female presence in religious myth and practice.

But the cycles augment their appropriation of this familiar festive type with plays in which the usual features of woman's unruliness are engaged to subvert male points of view. The Coventry Weavers' play *Presentation and Disputation in the Temple*, for example, presents a highly unusual episode featuring Joseph and Mary preparing for Mary's purification (Craig 33–71). Gabriel has just appeared to Mary and told her to present her son and two "whyt turtuls" at the temple (line 376). Returning to Joseph, who claims his willingness to serve his wife ("You neuer cawll but I am reddy" [line 417]), Mary tells him he must procure the turtle doves. But Joseph launches into a diatribe in which he insists that he is too old to go prying into birds' nests, that Mary is inconsiderate of the infirmities of his age, and that, if she wants turtle doves, she should get them herself or find a "new page" to get them for her (line 449). In a conflict that basically reverses the gender roles in the disputes of the Noah plays, here Mary assures Joseph that God will not only provide for but reward the man who willingly fulfills his commands, but her spouse remains intractable. He adopts the stance that more frequently appears in the plays of Joseph's Doubt, where his reluctance to believe his wife is understandably supported by the evidence of his own eyes and his own ignorance. But in the Weavers' pageant, Joseph can claim no such ignorance of either the purity of his wife's intentions or the divinity of her son. Thus, when he laments the situation of the old man who has taken a young wife, his words are startlingly incongruous with the nature of the wife they are meant to describe. Sounding like one of the Wife of Bath's first three husbands or Chaucer's Merchant, Joseph proclaims:

> How sey ye all this cumpany
> Thatt be weddid asse well asse I?
> I wene that ye suffur moche woo;
> For he thatt weddyth a yonge thyng
> Must fullfyl all hir byddyng,
> Or els ma he his handis wryng,
> Or watur his iis when he wold syng;
> And thatt all you do knoo.
>
> . . . . . . . . . . . . . . . . . . . . . . . . . . . .
>
> Dame, all this cumpany wyll sey the same.
> Ys itt not soo? Speyke, men, for schame!

> Tell you the trothe ase you well con!
> For the that woll nott there wyffis plese
> Ofte-tymis schall suffur moche dysees;
> Therefore I holde hym well at es
> Thatt hathe to doo with non.   (lines 463–78)

Joseph's lament about the constraints of the May-December marriage—about the suffering, tears, and handwringing of the man so
unfortunate as to be under the domination of a powerful young wife—
form part of an address to the audience obviously meant to invoke
familiar antifeminist sympathies. But the force of his words is
undermined by their referent herself: Mary calmly endures his tantrum
and is proved correct by the angel who eventually appears to Joseph
with consoling words and two turtle doves.

A similar undermining of a male who comes into conflict with a
female authority figure occurs in the Wakefield play *Thomas of India*
(England and Pollard 337–52). Here, as told in Scripture, Mary
Magdalene proclaims the news of Christ's Resurrection to the apostles.
Though Mary is not herself unruly in the festive, combative sense, the
apostles challenge her announcement in language that invokes the
medieval antifeminist criticism of woman's speech. Despite the
Magdalene's assertion that she saw what she saw and that the apostles'
disbelief is a "heresy," Paul, who does not even belong in this scene,
offers this observation:

> And it is wretyn in oure law
> 'Ther is no trust in womans saw,
> No trust faith to belefe;
> ffor with thare quayntyse and thare gyle
> Can thay laghe and wepe som while,
> And yit nothyng theym grefe.'
>
> In oure bookes thus fynde we wretyn,
> All manere of men well it wyttyn,
> Of women on this wyse;
> Till an appyll she is lyke—
> Withoutten faill ther is none slyke—
> In horde ther it lyse,
>
> Bot if a man assay it wittely,
> It is full roten inwardly
> At the colke within;
> Wherfor in woman is no laghe,
> ffor she is withoutten aghe,
> As crist me lowse of syn.

Therfor trast we not trystely,
Bot if we sagh it witterly
Then wold we trastly trow;
In womans saw affy we noght,
ffor thay are fekill in word and thoght,
This make I myne avowe.   (lines 29–52)

However familiar Paul's negative stereotyping of woman's speech
may be, its interjection at this moment departs so much from the
Scripture's account that it calls attention to the play's subtle manipula-
tion of gender roles and definitions. For here the introduction of the
misogynistic stereotyping for which Paul became famous is, quite
simply, wrong. His condemnation of woman's deceptiveness and
unreliability, her rottenness to the core, and her lawlessness jars with
the occasion in which these words are uttered. The play of *Thomas of
India* has been preceded by the play of the *Resurrection*, in which Mary
Magdalene had met the risen Christ. Mary speaks the truth to the
apostles; their contestation of her word only reveals the shakiness of
their own faith. Paul's antifeminist challenge to the authenticity of
Mary's good news is further undermined only a few stanzas later when
Christ himself appears. The discourse against women is both put in its
erroneous place and displaced by the living proof that the male
apostles insist on seeing for themselves.

The examples furnished by these two plays suggest the degree to
which medieval dramatic texts self-consciously appropriate the reign-
ing female stereotypes toward distinctive ends. They also point up how
a feminist approach to medieval drama can direct student inquiry to
exploring the sources of the language in which women are discussed
and addressed or through which they present themselves. In the two
cases discussed here the gender-specific, highly oppositional dis-
courses of Joseph and Paul are exposed for their limitations. Their
challenges to women's power and women's language are rendered
ambiguous by the instability of their own positions.

The Virgin Mary provides another character, figure, or type that a
feminist approach to medieval drama needs to examine. She is, as Julia
Kristeva aptly puts it, "one of the most potent imaginary constructs
known to any civilization," and much of that potency is due to the
many roles and meanings attributed to her during the Middle Ages
(135). The Virgin Mary has posed a significant problem to contemporary feminism, both in the realms of theory and in traditional scholarly
pursuits. She represents an ideal whose value has been assessed in
relation to historical women and to contemporary attitudes toward sex
and the body, criteria that have led to evaluations of the "exacerbated
masochism" she offers and the "sadistic invention" she represents
(Kristeva 149; Bal 39). Similarly, for historians of Christian theology

and religion, the Virgin Mary has inspired much debate between those who find in her feminizing of Christianity a positive valuation of women and those who see in her cult the continuation of efforts by a male-dominated religion to underline "the weakness, inferiority, and the subordination of real females" (McLaughlin 246).

There is some truth in all these positions. Since these points of view are likely to parallel the reactions of students unfamiliar with the Middle Ages or with medieval Christianity, they are well worth interrogating in the classroom. Such an interrogation should yield the insight that a feminist reading of the concept of the Virgin Mary in the Middle Ages and in medieval drama particularly is not well served by an approach that polarizes her probable connections to the valorizing or the oppression of women. Rather, it is the very construction of Mary that merits attention. Created virtually ex nihilo from scattered references in the Synoptic Gospels, the Virgin Mary is a cultural construction whose richness and range of meanings and symbols is of central importance to Christian theology at all its crucial points of development because of her special relationship to Christ and her unique status among human beings. The connections between Mariolatry and Christology and the multiple valences accorded to Mary by the intricate teachings of Christian theology and spirituality are beautifully illustrated by the English cycle plays. These are matters that a feminist approach may profitably explore, matters that, in fact, point up the perspective that ought to inform feminist literary practice. To study the diversity of roles and behaviors of the Virgin Mary in medieval drama is to uncover elements of contingency in religious and theological concepts; it requires the historicizing of what other perspectives may deem timeless and absolute. The cultural creation of the Virgin Mary reflected in medieval drama is an important chapter in the cultural construction of the female in the West.

The English cycle plays illustrate that there is no one Virgin Mary; there are only Virgin Marys. This is a powerful and essential point to make for students whose tendencies to generalize are often greater than their urges to make distinctions. The representation of Mary varies not only between cycles but also within a single cycle. This variety is partly a function of the serial and collaborative composition of the cycle texts themselves; but it is just as much an indication of the distinctive and potentially competing interpretive and symbolic traditions associated with the mother of Christ. The Mary of the English cycles is a chaste virgin and a humble wife; but she is not consistently the perfect wife, or, as we have seen, this is what Joseph in the Coventry Weavers' play would have the audience believe. The York *Flight into Egypt* offers another unusual twist on the relation of Mary and Joseph, this time one in which Joseph stands on slightly firmer ground as he struggles to get an untypical Mary to stay calm long enough to get on the road to Egypt. But the potential for disharmony in the relation of Joseph and Mary in the cycles is regularly overshadowed by Mary's other pious, elevated, or emotive roles. She is the Queen assumed to Heaven to sit at her Son's right hand; the Mother of Mercy whose intercessory powers are available to the sinner; the vessel, temple, and tabernacle of God's incarnate Son. In N-Town, as Martin Stevens points out, Mary is a figure of learning and cloistered contemplation (*Four Middle English Mystery Cycles* 218–20). In all the cycles, York and Wakefield especially, Mary is meticulously represented in one of her most famous late medieval roles, the *mater dolorosa* who laments the death of her son at the foot of the cross.

One important dimension of the cycles' representation of Mary involves the ways they come to terms with the problem of Mary's body. Though the cycles follow medieval theology and popular tradition in emphasizing Mary's virginal conception, her own freedom from sin, and her assumption into Heaven, they make dramatic capital out of the contradictions and the paradoxes that result from the idea of a virginal maternity and a perfect woman who is also fully human. Perhaps, as the Coventry Weavers' play and the York *Flight into Egypt* suggest, the playwrights' efforts to link Mary with flawed womanly behaviors, for all their humor, reflect a discomfort with the ideal she represents. The least that can be said is that the plays share, along with medieval medicotheological theories and popular pieties, a fascination with the Virgin Mary's reproductive processes (Wood 717–27). The seeming impossibility of a virginal maternity provides the foundation for the plays of Joseph's Doubt, in which the puzzled old carpenter can only interpret the pregnant wife he sees as evidence that she has taken a young lover. Simeon in the Chester *Purification* exhibits a variation on the same incredulity, insisting on changing the words of Isaiah to read that "a good woman," not a "virgin," would conceive without man's help (lines 33-95, in Lumiansky and Mills). The doubting midwives of N-Town and Chester partake of this same interrogating company, which also includes, perhaps in the most interesting form, the false accusors of the N-Town *Trial of Joseph and Mary* (Block 123–35). Though the play is intended in part as a satire on the ecclesiastical court (it includes a false, bribing Summoner), it also offers a unique twist on the problem of Mary's maternity by connecting the false charges of adultery to the problems of the husband who must suffer the economic hardship of feeding another man's child with his own "swynk" (line 68).

The N-Town *Trial of Joseph and Mary* richly suggests the ways that dramatic representations of Mary's maternity can comment on legal aspects of domestic and marital arrangements. A feminist reading seeking a larger framework for the cycles' preoccupation with the physical dimensions of Mary's maternity and childbearing might ask students to consider the theological interest in Marian physiology that was occasioned by belief in her Immaculate Conception, an interest that must be seen in the context of prevailing views of women's bodies and sexuality and a problematic misogyny (Wood 710–17). Dramatic representations interrogating the nature of Mary's childbearing participate in the larger medieval gesture that sought to link Mary to the rules governing ordinary mortals (Gold). The cycles' instances of this gesture are frequently the locus for their best comic energies. The general relation between the cycles' association of female issues with comic elements is a rich subject for classroom consideration because of the drama's general ambiguity on this score. The plays provide a humor that cuts several ways, celebrating the miracle of Christ's divine Incarnation in a totally human mother, yet registering nonetheless the dis-ease and ambivalence that may result from embracing a notion so palpably difficult to fathom.

A feminist approach to medieval drama in the classroom needs to come to terms with the many valences of that drama's representations of Mary. A comparison of plays within and between cycles shows that the plays' preoccupation with Mary's miraculous maternity is simply the sacred component of their general portrayal of women as fundamentally corporeal creatures. The unruly women who assault with their words and their distaffs are also identified as fleshly beings, as are many of the female characters who have significant roles: Mary Magdalene, the woman taken in adultery, Pilate's wife. In this regard the Virgin Mary joins an unusual sisterhood, one based on the idea that, whatever her role in the Christian story, woman is preeminently a physical body, an identity whose significance is shared by the cycles' major character, Jesus Christ (Bynum, *Holy* 265–69).

The figure of the Virgin Mary in medieval drama opens still another avenue for a feminist approach to explore by directing students to look at patterns of representation that distinguish individual cycles. The N-Town cycle, for example, gives such a prominent role to Mary that Martin Stevens has noted that the cycle's Marian episodes contribute to a multiple plot in which the life of Mary parallels the life of Christ (*Four Middle English Mystery Cycles* 244–45). In contrast, the Chester cycle is distinguished by a neglect of Mary, a feature whose complement may be the cycle's emphasis on a triumphant Christ, a powerful God, and what Stevens calls a virulent antifeminism (276–77). These basic characteristics are supported by still other features of each cycle. N-Town's attention, through the life of Mary, to aspects of female experience—to contemplative enclosure and to marriage—corresponds to its interest in a feminized religion in which the intercessory powers of the Virgin play a crucial role. Chester's neglect of the Virgin Mary and its foregrounding of the dramatic metaphor of the throne contribute to its focus on a patriarchal God known more through his power than through his humanity (301).

It is a mistake to see in these differences any simple, clear-cut representation of these cycles' specific affiliations with either institutional religion or theological positions, Protestant or Catholic. The cycles are not easily susceptible to that kind of analysis; they are more aptly characterized by hybrid theologies, by the tensions between Protestant and Catholic sympathies that they may represent. Nonetheless it is impossible to overlook the fact that the extant cycle texts (and as best as we can surmise, their actual production) date from a period when England experienced religious turmoil, and it is reasonable to assume that some of that is registered in the cycles. It is in this light that the gender differences between N-Town and Chester are significant. For the emphases of N-Town, filtered through its focus on the Virgin Mary—her roles, her devotions, and her powers—are fundamentally Catholic in orientation, while the emphases of Chester—with its miracle-working, all-powerful God in Heaven—are significantly Protestant in their orientation. Though the reformist movements of England, both Lollard and Protestant, are customarily attributed with correcting a "medieval" misogyny by valorizing the efficacious roles of women in religion and in the home, the religion that these movements promoted was one in which the feminine had little place in doctrine or observance (Davis 78–94; Cross; McLuskie 90).

Thus, a feminist approach to teaching medieval drama has much to consider. My attention here has been devoted exclusively to the English cycle plays, but an equally rich territory for the exploration of a feminist reading is furnished by the noncyclic texts—for example, the Digby plays *Mary Magdalene* and *Killing of the Children of Israel* and the devotional dramas of Christ's *Burial* and *Resurrection* in Bodleian Library MS e Museo 160 (Baker, Murphy, and Hall). A feminist approach to medieval drama in the classroom should have as its goal the elucidation of the primacy of gender roles and definitions in the texts under consideration, and it should undertake to illuminate these in light of the religious, social, and festive contexts in which the texts originated. A feminist approach to these texts should further cultivate the perception of differences among works that may too hastily be homogeneously grouped together. It should aim to question the ideological and social constructions that may inform dramatic representations of gender, remaining attentive to the drama's kinship with other forms of cultural representation. Its contribution to the study of medieval drama and to early modern literature will be in illuminating the role of dramatic texts in the efforts to recuperate historically the understanding of sex and gender roles in the distant past.

# Typology and the Teaching
# of Medieval Drama

## Pamela Sheingorn

Nothing is easier than to dismiss the highly elaborated typological system of the Middle Ages as an intellectual construct having little to do with popular culture or with the experience of a genre, like medieval drama, that was aimed at a large audience. The view that typology had little relevance for the drama was expressed, in fact, in Arnold Williams's essay "Typology and the Cycle Plays." Underlying the present essay is the view that Williams narrows his focus too much by considering only the stage picture, rather than the whole repertory of images in the minds of medieval audiences. In fact, medieval drama can be taught effectively, perhaps most effectively, when students learn how to reconstruct that repertory through the principles of typological interpretation. This conclusion is based on team-teaching courses at both the graduate and the undergraduate levels in which typology served as an important point of departure for the teaching of drama.[1] The ease with which our students grasped a range of issues, from the liturgical reverberations in such drama to its inherently visual nature, convinced us not only that our exposition of typology was time well-spent but also that our students had found their way closer to the world view of much medieval art and literature: they had mastered a methodology with wide applications.

A basic definition of typology or figural interpretation may be found in Erich Auerbach's classic essay "Figura": "Figural interpretation establishes a connection between two events or persons, the first of which signifies not only itself but also the second, while the second encompasses or fulfills the first" (53). Typology, in effect, subsumes the Old Testament in the New Testament, insisting that from the divine perspective—and, therefore, the only correct perspective— events in the Hebrew Bible point toward and foreshadow events in the life of Christ. A number of essays have moved toward the rehabilitation of typology in its application to the study of drama: the articles by Walter Meyers, Robert E. Reiter, and Thomas Rendall and chapter 3 of Martin Stevens's *Four Middle English Mystery Cycles* are especially useful. The goals of this essay are to demonstrate typological approaches to the drama that help students understand both individual plays and their relation to the cycles of which they are a part. Such approaches also provide avenues for the introduction of recent critical theory. Thus, we have no better way to communicate the intertextuality of medieval literature than to introduce a method grounded in the way early Christians read the Hebrew Bible, elaborated in the liturgy and the theology of the Middle Ages and incorporated into innumerable works of medieval art and literature. As W. H. Beuken puts it, "The *Concordantia Veteris et Novi Testamenti* was, for the man of the Middle Ages, a simply given fact" (Beuken and Marrow 46).

In this essay a variety of ways of introducing typology into the study of drama are described by means of extended examples based on the typological relationship of Isaac to Christ, beginning with an individual play and proceeding to the structure of a cycle. No matter which approach is adopted, introducing the typological method does not take much time and can effectively be done through example, although literature majors ought, at some point, to become familiar with Auerbach's essay. The typological method can be taught from a variety of starting points: the narrative of the type in the Hebrew Bible, its fulfilling antitype in the New Testament, a text like a play that assumes knowledge of typology, and works of art that juxtapose types and antitype. From any of these points, connecting threads lead to other points that tie together a complex of ideas. Fullest understanding may be gained by beginning with a narrative in the Hebrew Bible; demonstrating its typological meaning for Christians as they read back from the New Testament antitype; tracing the history of the two juxtaposed incidents in medieval liturgy, art, and literature up to the time of the play; and then reading the play or by reversing the process. In either case the student is provided with the means of coming close to the reception of the text, to its full effect on a medieval audience.

The inclusion of the Brome *Sacrifice of Isaac* in several anthologies means that the Abraham and Isaac play is frequently taught, so the focus here is on that text. As students read the play, they should be encouraged to read visually, not only constructing a sequence of stage pictures but also searching for one or more central images that effectively summarize the action of the play. Once these images have been identified, assignments or examples introduced in class can be used to assist students in discovering that these central images are usually elements in a typological system. In this way students reconstruct for themselves the position of an individual episode within the medieval view of world history.

Since V. A. Kolve argues persuasively for the existence and the effectiveness of such central visual images in Chaucer, his assertion that these narrative images are "affiliated with other images in other texts" (*Chaucer* 361) provides a handy bridge for the teacher introducing the drama after Chaucer has been taught. Kolve identifies one or two images for each of the *Canterbury Tales* that both carry the weight of an iconographic tradition and are "characteristically assimilated to the verisimilar and mimetic texture of the whole" (*Chaucer* 60). For biblical drama such scenes are easily identified, sometimes as those that correspond to feasts of the Church, and examples from the pictorial arts of the Middle Ages are readily available. After a careful reading of the Brome *Sacrifice of Isaac*, most students select two central images: first, the journey, because it summarizes all that went before, communicates Isaac's cheerful obedience to his father's commands, and in psychological terms allows the audience to empathize with Abraham's mental state—we know what he must yet tell his beloved son. Second and even more frequently selected, the moment when the angel stops Abraham's sword; here one image recapitulates the entire narrative while effectively communicating the difficult lesson of obedience to God.

At this point the teacher may either introduce or direct the students to find works of art representing these scenes that function as memorial centers—if possible, from the time and the place of the drama's writing and performance history. Since pictorial representations of the major events in Christian world history occur in many examples in both the public and the private arts of the Middle Ages, the teacher is on safe ground in declaring that these are images with which the writers, the producers, and the audience would have been familiar and in suggesting that a production would deliberately have evoked a particular image in the mind of the audience, as has been demonstrated for the Man of Sorrows and Resurrection images in the plays of the Resurrection (Sheingorn, "Moment of Resurrection").

Once students have accepted the idea of a memorial center and have identified some examples in the plays they have read (and asking students to do this as an out-of-class assignment, bringing an example of a work of art to the class and presenting it along with an argument that it does capture the memorial center of the play is one effective way to incorporate the pictorial arts into the teaching of literature), the teacher can either make use of the typological context of the images introduced by the students or supply additional images that introduce typology. Especially effective are illustrated typological compilations like the *Speculum humanae salvationis* and the *Biblia pauperum*, and both are readily available in modern editions that should be in college libraries (A. Henry, *Mirour;* Wilson and Wilson, *Medieval Mirror*; A. Henry, *Biblia*). The recently published facsimile and edition of the *Biblia pauperum* by Avril Henry makes the book easily accessible to students because each page is accompanied by a translation of its Latin textual commentary. The *Biblia pauperum* was probably created in the first half of the thirteenth century and survives in many manuscripts and printed editions, for it was one of the most popular of all medieval books. Each page of the *Biblia pauperum* juxtaposes the antitype, placed in the center, with two types that flank it and includes four prophets for each antitype. The text of the *Speculum humanae salvationis* was written about 1324, possibly by Ludolf of Saxony, a

Dominican, and was an extremely popular book in the late Middle Ages. Here each antitype is accompanied by three types.

Both in the *Biblia pauperum* and in the *Speculum* the scene of Isaac's journey, the first of our memorial centers, is juxtaposed with the scene of Christ's journey to Calvary. More specifically, both Isaac and Christ carry the wood that is linked to their sacrifice, as in an early fifteenth-century *Speculum humanae salvationis*, probably made in Yorkshire (Morgan Library MS M. 766, fol. 43 verso; see Wilson and Wilson 47). After concluding that the visual tradition clearly considers Isaac to be a type of Christ and shapes the visual image to underscore that relationship, the students should be encouraged to return to the play text to determine whether this typology also underlies the Brome *Sacrifice of Isaac*. They note Abraham's directive to Isaac: "Hold this fagot upon thy ba[c]ke" (line 116), but they should also be encouraged to consult the biblical text to discover whether this is an invention of fifteenth-century Englishmen or is inherent in the tradition. In the Douay-Reims Bible (which should be used, because, as a translation of the Vulgate, it is closest to the text of the Bible read in the Middle Ages) they read Genesis 22.1–8:

> After these things, God tempted Abraham, and said to him: Abraham, Abraham. And he answered: Here I am. He said to him: Take thy only begotten son Isaac, whom thou lovest, and go into the land of vision: and there thou shalt offer him for an holocaust upon one of the mountains which I will shew thee. So Abraham rising up in the night, saddled his ass: and took with him two young men, and Isaac his son: and when he had cut wood for the holocaust he went his way to the place which God had commanded him. And on the third day, lifting up his eyes, he saw the place afar off. And he said to his young men: Stay you here with the ass: I and the boy will go with speed as far as yonder, and after we have worshipped, will return to you. And he took the wood for the holocaust, and laid it upon Isaac his son: and he himself carried in his hands fire and a sword. And as they two went on together, Isaac said to his father: My father. And he answered: What wilt thou, son? Behold saith he, fire and wood: where is the victim for the holocaust? And Abraham said: God will provide himself a victim for an holocaust, my son. So they went on together.

Handouts for the students may lead from the biblical text to the exegetical tradition, which firmly establishes Isaac as a type of Christ. For specifically English evidence there is no better authority than the Venerable Bede. In his *History of the Abbots of Wearmouth and Jarrow*

Bede describes paintings brought from Rome to Jarrow by Benedict Biscop:

> [H]e also displayed, for the adorning of the monastery and church of the blessed apostle Paul, paintings shewing the agreement of the Old and New Testaments, most cunningly ordered: for example, a picture of Isaac carrying the wood on which he was to be slain, was joined (in the next space answerable above) to one of the Lord carrying the cross on which He likewise was to suffer. (Davis-Weyer 75)

The value of this exercise for students (and a whole sequence of passages can be distributed for reading outside class) is that they conclude for themselves that typological reading coincides with early Christianity, that it is embedded in the understanding of these texts, and that it is at work in the plays. This is clearly demonstrated by Shalom Spiegel, who provides examples of Christian borrowings from Judaism in the interpretation of this story:

> Already in the Epistle of Barnabas [c. AD 130], Isaac is referred to as the prototype for the sufferings and trials of Jesus. Irenaeus exhorts Christians that in their faith they too must be on the alert to *bear the cross* just as Isaac bore the wood for the burnt-offering wood-pile. The Church Fathers were especially fond of this image of bearing his own cross—which occurs in midrashic-talmudic sources, as does the phrase, "Like one going out to be burned and carrying on his own shoulders the wood for his pyre."
> (84)

Spiegel goes on to discuss other epithets associated with Isaac that were borrowed by Christians for Christ, such as the notion of Isaac as the sheep or lamb for the sacrifice.

Whereas the first memorial center underscores the conservative nature of this play in the way it uses traditional Christian exegesis, typological study of the second memorial center, the scene of Isaac's sacrifice with the angel's stopping the motion of Abraham's sword, can underscore the liturgical function of this episode and introduce a discussion of the Brome *Sacrifice of Isaac* as an embodiment of late medieval popular piety.

An examination of contexts in which their second memorial image appears easily leads students to the conclusion that medieval artists presented this scene as a type of the Crucifixion of Christ, as is seen on a page from the *Biblia pauperum*. Again the text of the Brome *Isaac* supports this interpretation, specifically when Isaac says:

A, Fader of Heuyn, to the[e] I crye:
Lord, reseive me into thy hand!   (Davis, lines 295–96)

This should be compared with Jesus's cry from the Cross: "Father, into thy hands I commend my spirit" (Luke 23.46). The students may then read the Canon of the Mass, focusing on the passage that connects the offerings of the altar, the Eucharist, with episodes of sacrifice in the Hebrew Bible:

> Be pleased to look upon these offerings with a favourable and gracious countenance; accept them as you were pleased to accept the offerings of your servant Abel the righteous, the sacrifice of our father Abraham, and that of Melchisedech, your high priest, a holy sacrifice, a blameless victim.

From this passage it is clear that the typological juxtaposition incorporated in the Brome *Isaac* immediately reminded the play's audience of the sacrifice of the Mass. Effective visual illustrations of this juxtaposition may be drawn from the mosaic decoration in the choir of the sixth-century Church of San Vitale in Ravenna and from a liturgical book like the *Drogo Sacramentary*. The mosaics in Ravenna put into visual form the typological relationship in which the sacrifice of Isaac is understood to be a type of the sacrifice of Christ and the renewal of that sacrifice in the Eucharist, for the celebration of the Eucharist took place at the altar just below the mosaics. Liturgical books, crosses, and objects used in the performance of the liturgy were frequently decorated with the scene of the sacrifice of Isaac and illustrate how often the typological relationship of Isaac and Christ was portrayed on these functional objects. For example, the *Drogo Sacramentary*, a Carolingian manuscript made in the mid-ninth century in Metz, devotes a full page to the first initial of the Canon of the Mass, the "T" of "Te igitur" (fol. 15 verso, illustrated in color on plate 28 of Mütherich and Gaehde and in black and white on plate 88 of Calkins). The four fields of the initial refer to the Old Testament types of sacrifice mentioned in the Canon of the Mass as types of the sacrifice of Christ:

1. Melchisidek, priest-king of Salem, in the center
2. Abel offering a lamb on the left
3. Abraham with a lamb on the right
4. Two bullocks at the foot of the initial

The "T" shape of the initial is itself the Cross, and each of the episodes alluded to foreshadows the event that the Eucharist celebrates.
Although the typological relationship of Isaac and Christ as illus-

trated by the liturgy certainly underlies the Brome *Isaac*, students should not be left with the superficial conclusion that medieval works of literature are simply illustrations of medieval doctrine. They should be urged to return again to the play text and to consider the message it leaves with its audience as explicitly stated by the interpreter within the play, the doctor:

> For this story scho[w]it[h] yowe [here]
> How we schuld kepe, to owre po[we]re,
> Goddys commaw[nd]mentys withowt groching.
> (Davis, lines 440–42)

The biblical narrative readily supports this lesson:

> And they came to the place which God had shewn him, where he built an altar, and laid the wood in order upon it: and when he had bound Isaac his son, he laid him on the altar upon the pile of wood. And he put forth his hand and took the sword, to sacrifice his son. And behold an angel of the Lord from heaven called to him, saying: Abraham, Abraham. And he answered: Here I am. And he said to him: Lay not thy hand upon the boy, neither do thou any thing to him: now I know that thou fearest God, and hast not spared thy only begotten son for my sake. Abraham lifted up his eyes, and saw behind his back a ram amongst the briers sticking fast by the horns, which he took and offered for a holocaust instead of his son. And he called the name of that place, The Lord seeth. Whereupon even to this day it is said: In the mountain the Lord will see. And the angel of the Lord called to Abraham a second time from heaven, saying: By my own self have I sworn, saith the Lord: because thou hast done this thing, and hast not spared thy only begotten son for my sake: I will bless thee, and I will multiply thy seed as the stars of heaven, and as the sand that is by the sea shore: thy seed shall possess the gates of their enemies. And in thy seed shall all the nations of the earth be blessed, because thou hast obeyed my voice. And Abraham returned to his young men, and they went to Bersabee together, and he dwelt there.   (Gen. 22.9–19)

In contrast to this fast-paced narrative, the Brome *Isaac* has Abraham do considerable "groching," and the resultant emotional intensity is, in fact, a key characteristic of this play. How are students to understand this departure from the biblical text? Again, typology helps explain how the play shapes its material, but with this example, if there is time, the teacher may introduce some critical theory as a means of reaching the typological interpretation.

Since critical theory has recently focused on the biblical text, this is an excellent place to introduce students to some theory of narrative. If students become aware of what they are doing when they read a text as compressed as this one, they relate more positively to the interpretations of medieval exegetes. Especially insightful is Meir Sternberg's "Literary Work as a System of Gaps."

> The world of situations and dramas constructed by the reader—causal sequence and all—is far from identical with what he encounters in the form of overt statement. From the viewpoint of what is directly given in the language, the literary work consists of bits and fragments to be linked and pieced together in the process of reading: it establishes a system of gaps that must be filled in.  (186)

Sternberg applies this theory to the story of Abraham and Isaac, and his analysis of that episode may well be given to students to read. Basically, Sternberg points to a gap in the biblical narrative: its complete neglect of Abraham's state of mind in this situation of extreme stress. In Sternberg's view, this gap functions to "foreground" Abraham's obedience; it is a deliberate or "systematic" omission that underscores Abraham's willingness to "sacrifice thought to action" (192).

Those actively engaged in interpreting such a narrative—writers of sermons, artists, and authors of plays—must directly encounter such systematic omissions and either make sense of them or fill the gaps. From this point of view the most usual representation of this narrative in the pictorial arts, that showing Abraham with sword upraised over the bound body of his son, responds sensitively to the omission. Such an interpretation gives visual expression to Abraham's obedience and is, therefore, faithful to the biblical text. But, as students notice, the Brome *Isaac* fills this gap by allowing Abraham to express his all-too-human anguish with such words as, "A, Lord, my hart brekith on twain" (Davis, line 127), leading the reader to ask why the playwright seems to undercut the notion of Abraham's unquestioning obedience. The answer to the question lies in the typological pairing of Abraham with God the Father. In the late Middle Ages, when much of the human ability to suffer had been attributed to the divine, God the Father was portrayed as suffering along with the Son as a result of the decision to undergo the Passion. This suffering, called the copassion of the Father, the playwright projects back onto Abraham to underscore the relationship of type and antitype (Woolf, "Effect of Typology").

Exegesis contemporary with the plays buttresses this explanation. For example, in the model sermon he provides for *Dominica in Quinquagesima*, Mirk quickly summarizes salvation history from the

Incarnation to the Last Judgment and moves on to retell the story of Isaac with the transition, "This was fygurt by Isaake" (Erbe 77). After describing the sacrifice of the substituted animal, Mirk glosses the story:

> Then by Abraham ye schull vnderstonde the Fadyr of Heuen, and by Isaac his sonne Ihesu Crist. The whech he sparyd not for no loue that he had to hym; but suffered the Iewes to lay the wode apon hym, that was the crosse apon hys schuldres, and ladden hym to the mount of Caluary, and ther dydyn hym on the autre of wode, that was the crosse. (77)

Thus, a medieval Christian method of filling gaps is to turn to the typological interpretation of the narrative. The view of Abraham as a type of God the Father leads to a de-emphasis of Abraham's obedience and, thus, to a tension between the text of the Brome *Isaac* and its moral, which gives the play much of its depth and satisfying complexity. The pictorial arts did not respond to this shift in the view of Abraham by altering the established imagery for the sacrifice of Isaac but invented a new image of God the Father presenting the crucified Christ (called the Throne of Grace Trinity) partly to express the idea of the copassion of the Father.

If a specific play is to be read as part of the study of an entire cycle, typological compilations such as the *Biblia pauperum* and the *Speculum humanae salvationis* can be used to introduce to students the basic concepts of Christian world history. Both *Biblia pauperum* and *Speculum humanae salvationis* supply collections of types grouped with antitypes that cover the same time span as the cycle plays. Thus, an especially effective assignment is to ask each student to study a different chapter or set of images from one or the other of these books and to explicate it to the class, explaining the relations between the scenes depicted. Students may also be assigned to compare and contrast the cyclical structure of plays and typological books, remembering to take into account both the verbal and the visual aspects of each. Or each student can be asked to propose staging an individual play or episode in a way that maximizes its typological effect on the viewer, illustrating these suggestions with examples from the visual arts. Not only does this assignment remind students that drama is one of the visual arts, but it reminds them of the necessity to expose themselves to a range of pictorial interpretations of the texts they have been reading.

Because the organizing narrative thread is the life of Christ, both the *Biblia pauperum* and the *Speculum* present events from the Hebrew Bible completely out of chronological sequence but juxtaposed with their New Testament antitypes, demonstrating that, from the medieval perspective, an episode from the Hebrew Bible is likely to call to mind its antitype, rather than its narrative context. Conversely, an episode from the life of Christ contains within itself the episodes that foreshadow it. Looking at these juxtapositions of visual images convinces the viewer that they could exist in the mind of the medieval audience as a sequence, not only with one recalling to mind all the others but also with the antitype serving as a cumulative pattern within which the outlines of chronologically earlier images are seen. Thus, behind the image of the Annunciation one sees the burning bush, and behind the harrowing of hell one sees Moses freeing the Israelites from Egypt.

This point can be made quickly and forcefully through the use of a fifteenth-century typological *Mirror of the Life of Our Lord* (Beuken and Marrow; Morgan Library MS M. 868). After the Passion sequence in a cycle has been read, miniatures in this manuscript can be shown to give students an idea of the stage picture. For example, the miniature on fol. 41 recto, which shows Christ carrying his Cross, contains many visual details worthy of comment, such as a soldier tugging on the rope around Christ's waist. But the miniature comes after the text it illustrates, and the biblical quotations written above and below the miniature are drawn from the Hebrew Bible and refer not to Christ but to a lamb. The text reads:

> *How Jesus carried his Cross himself to Calvary: A figure.*

> It stands described in Genesis how that Isaac carried a heap of wood up a hill, where he was to be killed and offered by his father Abraham according to God's command. . . . Just like Isaac, our Lord carried that wood of the Cross on his shoulders himself, where he was offered to his heavenly Father for the love of us and for our sins, in order that we might become his children.

A type from Maccabees is also described, after which a relevant passage from each of the four Gospels is cited. The chapter ends with a prayer:

> *Prayer*: Lord Jesus Christ, grant to me that I may follow after you in the sweet-smelling odor of your Passion and suffering, in order that the heaviness and burden of your Cross that you have commanded me to carry after you might be light and pleasant for my shoulders to carry. And lay down on me that sweet Cross, which is the tree of life to all who embrace it, whose breadth is the love that extends itself out over all creatures, whose length is

eternity, whose height is omnipotence, and its depth is inscruta-
ble wisdom. Amen.[2]

Opposite this prayer is the illustration, with a text adapted from Isaiah
57.3 above it: "I am led to death like a sheep and like a lamb who
keeps silent before the one who will shear it." Below the illustration is
the text of Jeremiah 11.19, similarly adapted so that the prophecy
becomes the fulfillment: "I am like a gentle lamb that is led to be an
offering."

The picture itself, separated from its context, has no typological
character whatever. Yet it must be understood in terms of the book of
which it forms a part. In that book each chapter begins with a type,
creating a picture in the mind, and, through a devotional prayer, brings
about a mental fadeover technique, so that the type has superimposed
on it an image from the life of Christ, which, in its turn, has
implications for the spiritual life of the reader. Yet resonances from the
type remain, shaping the interpretation of the picture. Such a process
suggests what took place in the mind of a medieval audience steeped in
typology while watching, for example, a play of the Passion. And an
understanding of medieval typology enables the modern reader to
construct a repertory of appropriate visual images and to recreate the
experience of the medieval audience.

For the teaching of medieval drama, typology offers an approach
that incorporates an important aspect of the medieval view of world
history, integrates the visual arts in a meaningful way—not just as
enrichment or illustration—and actively engages the reader in the
process of interpretation. It is worth the effort.


## Notes

[1]Throughout, this essay reflects how much I have learned from my
coteachers, Martin Stevens and Michael Plekon.

[2]For her authoritative assistance with the translation of the *Mirror of the Life
of Our Lord* from Middle Dutch, I am grateful to Johanna C. Prins of the
Department of Germanic Languages, Columbia University.

# COURSES AND STRATEGIES

## Faith and Prosperity:
## Cultural Values in Medieval Drama

### Peter H. Greenfield

In 1531–32 the Chester city council proclaimed that the cycle was to be played in Whitsun week

> not only for the Augmentacion & incres of the holy & Catholick faith of our Sauiour iesu Crist & to exort the myndes of the common people to good deuotion & holsome doctryne therof but also for the commenwelth & prosperitie of this Citie. . . . (Clopper, *Chester* 27)

Faith and prosperity. The recognition that the play's purpose is to increase both underlies my approach in the medieval drama section of my course Drama and Society: Medieval Chester, Elizabethan London, and Contemporary America. The course treats the plays' religious and social functions as linked. For instance, the plays following the Crucifixion not only enact the creation of a new Christian community but also, as Peter W. Travis has pointed out, use techniques intended to involve the audience in reaffirming its own membership in that community. Furthermore, as Mervyn James has shown, the efforts of the civic authorities and the guilds to produce the plays involve both the performers and the audience in a parallel reaffirmation of the urban social community.

Like all courses that fulfill the comparative values requirement of our university core, this course brings together seniors from a variety of majors to develop a critical understanding of the value systems of different cultures. In the first section we focus on the Chester cycle. In the second section we investigate the drama of Elizabethan and Jacobean London to discover how English values and the ways that plays reveal them have changed as we move forward in time and from provincial city to urban capital. In the final section we look at the plays, films, and television programs most familiar to students to become conscious and analytical about the values bombarding us from large and small screens.

The medieval section combines an analysis of representative plays from the Chester cycle with an examination of selected records from Lawrence Clopper's *Records of Early English Drama: Chester*, culminating in student performances of some of the plays. Examining a mystery cycle in its particular local context allows me to integrate literary study and intellectual history with social history in an effort to understand how the texts and performances of the plays express and reflect the linked values of faith and prosperity. The records help make the connection, for, as Theresa Coletti suggested,

> One way the records may appropriately be read . . . is as an expression of a symbolic system that articulates for specific kinds of medieval English towns the meaning of the cult of Corpus Christi, a cult that through an elaborate program of festive activities and an highly developed public mythology served to link the governmental structure with an idealized theological concept of social organization and identity. ("Records")

Focusing on a particular place limits the choice of cycles to Chester and York. I have so far resisted the attractions of the York texts, principally because of two books, F. M. Salter's *Medieval Drama in Chester* and Peter W. Travis's *Dramatic Design in the Chester Cycle*. Salter shares the course's interest in both the drama and the people who performed it, and his readable style and missionary zeal for medieval drama make the book valuable supplementary reading, even if many of its points must be amplified or challenged on the basis of more recent scholarship. Travis's book has shaped many of my ideas about the Chester cycle and the course as a whole, so, while I do not require it—many of the non-English majors find it heavy going—I like to have it available for sophisticated students.

My approach relies principally on a discussion of the primary sources, augmented by student research reports and occasional minilectures when needed to understand the plays and the records. The medieval section of the course begins with a lecture that gives a bare sketch of the late medieval period and then concentrates on the economic and social structure of the sixteenth-century town. The students read the appropriate chapters from Colin Platt's *English Mediaeval Town*, which is entertaining yet scholarly and has excellent illustrations. (Further material for this lecture and for student reports comes from Peter Clark and Paul Slack's *English Towns in Transition, 1500–1700,* and Peter Clark's *Early Modern Town.*) At the end of the class session I focus on Chester by showing slides of the town walls, the cathedral, and the processional route of the plays.

A second lecture traces the development of medieval drama and the cycle form in the cultural context established by the first lecture. Rogers's Breviary and other descriptions of the Chester cycle and its origins furnish an introduction both to the cycle and to the records. I caution students about taking these descriptions at face value but leave interpretation for later.

We start the cycle with the first three pageants, initially collecting impressions of what the students think of the plays and what they imagine it would be like to see them performed and to perform in them. Then we consider what these impressions suggest about the society that produced the plays and what values the plays reveal. That the plays are Christian is obvious, so the real questions become: Which Christian values do the plays emphasize? Do those values manifest themselves differently in sixteenth-century England than in contemporary Christianity? And do those values have importance for living in Chester, as well as for the individual Christian's pursuit of salvation?

The first three plays stress humility and obedience before God, but in this urban context what God values in Christian souls also has value for the stability and the prosperity of earthly society. To save themselves, Noah and his family must, as Travis points out, engage in communal hard work (*Dramatic Design*). That work reflects the cooperative effort within and between guilds necessary to produce the cycle, the effort that itself served as an example of the communal hard work required to maintain the continued prosperity of those guilds and their city. This last point sets up the class examination of a specific guild's participation.

I often leave the Abraham pageant for later, to show how individual plays fit into the overall pattern. Instead, we turn to the *Shepherds' Play.* This pageant makes an effective centerpiece for the course, since the effect of the Nativity on the shepherds mirrors the intended effect of Corpus Christi on the audience: through communal celebration, discord gives way to harmony within both the spiritual and the social bodies. That harmony is good not only for the shepherds' souls but also, one presumes, for the future prosperity of their sheepherding.

Concern with prosperity leads naturally to discussing excerpts from the accounts (especially for 1568, 1572, and 1575) of the painters, glaziers, embroiderers, and stationers guild, which put on the *Shepherds' Play* (Clopper, *Chester* 81–84, 91–94, 106–08). I point out the amounts spent on props, costumes, food and drink, and wages for the players, and I ask the students to consider the implications of the size of these expenditures. (I augment Salter's discussion of the relative value of the guilds' expenses with Ann Jennalie Cook's treatment of wages and prices in that period, based on more recent studies, in *The Privileged Playgoers of Shakespeare's London: 1576–1642*.) What value does producing the play have for the guild as a whole and for its individual members? Are the rehearsals and the performance entirely pious exercises, or do they also have social and commercial value? A number of other records add usefully to the discussion, including the Smiths' accounts of 1560–61 and 1566–67 (Clopper, *Chester* 65–67, 77–79), which indicate the amount each member paid to support their play, and the saddlers' charter of 1471–72 (Clopper, *Chester* 13–15), which seems to make support of the play the crucial element of membership. (Half the fine for illegally practicing the trade goes to the guild for its play.) The 1534–35 charter of the painters, glaziers, embroiderers, and stationers shows one way in which the drama created community within the city: the four guilds incorporated "into one body" by this charter note that they have been "tyme out of minde one Brotherhood for the costs & Expences of the plae of the shepperds Wach with the Angells hyme & likewayes for otherr layinge out conserninge the wellferr & prosperetie of the saide citty . . . " (Clopper, *Chester* 29–30).

We continue with a sampling of plays from the rest of the cycle, giving emphasis to the community-creating strategies of the post-*Resurrection* plays mentioned earlier. The *Judgment* play makes an especially apt conclusion, for Christ's address to the audience makes explicit the values that the individual audience members must act on if they are to gain salvation. The stress on each Christian's obligation to perform acts of corporal mercy links individual salvation to participation in the community, which is, theologically, the Corpus Christi but is in practical, day-to-day terms the city of Chester.

Once we have finished the *Shepherds' Play*, discussion of play texts and records is interspersed with rehearsals for the performance and research reports. Each student chooses a topic to research and present in a ten-minute oral report. Topics include interpretation of individual pageants (comparing critical treatments or the Chester version with another), discussion of a particular figure (Herod, Antichrist), interpretation of a set of records, the development of the cycle, the Reformation and the suppression of the plays, civic and religious functions of guilds, civic government, and economics. The students prepare a one-page outline or summary of their findings with bibliographical citations and quoted passages for duplication and distribution to the rest of the class.

Rehearsing and performing some of the plays from the cycle becomes an effort to experience imaginatively what we have learned. The first week the students form themselves into a guild or guilds, depending on the size of the class. At the "fyrste reherse," which generally occurs during class time, they read through the play, assign roles, and determine what set pieces, costumes, and props the play will require. Some students perform with quite elaborate costumes and props, others with none, but I ask each group to submit a list of what they would ideally use and some kind of design for their pageant wagon. The master of each guild keeps an account of real and imagined expenses, including food and drink at the rehearsals.

On the last day of the medieval section, the students perform (sometimes just for themselves, sometimes for a larger audience), and we discuss what they have discovered in the rehearsal and performance process. We discuss, for instance, how seeing Christ played by many different men, all known to the audience members, moves us away from the realistic aesthetic of most film and television portrayals toward the recognition that the plays present Christ's life less as a reenactment of historical events than as a physical realization of the spiritual journey each Christian must take to salvation. At the same time, this same experience of many Christs makes us more truly aware that, as Christ tells the saved in the *Judgment* play, we feed, clothe, and shelter him by doing these things for the less fortunate members of our own human community. We discuss, too, the sense of community the performance creates in us: individuals who may view each other as competitors develop a sense of shared purpose and values with those in their "guilds" and in the class as a whole.

By studying the drama of medieval Chester and Elizabethan London, students become conscious of the range of social functions drama can serve and sensitive to the subtle ways drama can express and shape the values of the society that creates it. They can then turn a critical eye on the present, especially on the electronic drama that holds great power to communicate but also to manipulate our values. This concentration on values, combined with a participatory approach, can make medieval drama accessible not only to advanced English majors and graduate students but also to the broad spectrum of undergraduates.

# Middle English Drama
# and Middle English Lyrics

## Mark Allen

One helpful way to combine several units of a Middle English literary survey course is to link drama with lyric poetry by means of subject matter. Some of the best-known plays match nicely with the arrangement of lyrics in several popular collections, enabling a class to consider, for example, the *Second Shepherds' Play* in the light of Nativity lyrics, the York *Crucifixion* with Passion lyrics, and *Everyman* with lyrics about death and worldly transience.

My undergraduate survey of medieval English literature studies these three plays for several reasons, the most emphatic being availability. The three are included in the first volume of the *Norton Anthology of English Literature* (gen. ed. Abrams), presented there in moderately normalized texts with judicious glossing. The Norton anthology does not include enough lyrics, though, so I supplement it with, among other books, Brian Stone's *Medieval English Verse. Middle English Lyrics*, edited by Maxwell S. Luria and Richard L. Hoffman, has the advantage over Stone's book of being in the original language, but it is more expensive and lacks materials studied in other units of the course, especially *Pearl*. Nevertheless, both collections arrange representative lyrics topically, allowing the course syllabus to be arranged in similar fashion, crossing genres and using the lyrics to discover nuances in the plays and vice versa. Because of time limitations, the York *Crucifixion* is slighted, but the other two plays are central to two two-week units in my fifteen-week semester.

The *Second Shepherds' Play* makes evident to the students the significance of the Nativity to the medieval audience. Through discussion of the comedic structure of the play and its contribution to the comedic structure of the Towneley cycle (indeed, all extant cycles), the students come to appreciate the ritual significance of the Nativity in the annual liturgical cycle and in the broad cycle of human history. More specific analysis of the play discovers its anachronisms and spatial impossibilities, leading to an awareness of the timeless universality of the event that the play celebrates. Consideration of the characterization of Mak and the shepherds clarifies the pathos-ridden *contemptus mundi* (contempt for the world) theme of the first half of the play and, by contrast, the comedic peripeteia that leads to the final rejuvenating scene in Bethlehem. Class discussion throughout is punctuated by an awareness of the humor and the realism for which the Wakefield Master is well known.

These perspectives produce considerable excitement among the

106

students when they carry them to the lyrics. Especially in translation and when confronted as a unit for the first time, Nativity lyrics run the danger of simulating a Sunday-school drone—familiar scene, conventional imagery, and placid, serene tone. "Where's the art?" asked one of my students before we read the parallel drama. The art, we discovered retrospectively through the play, lies in the various perspectives on the event that the play and the lyrics encourage, even demand. In each, verbal and structural devices enforce a shift or a series of shifts in perspective that encourage the audience to recognize the spiritual analogy between the mundane and the sublime. The lyrics, in effect, suggest their own dramas—thematically, even structurally, related to the rejuvenating comedy of the *Second Shepherds' Play* but focused on different moments in the traditional action of the Nativity. Stone's "Poems on the Nativity" in *Medieval English Verse* includes two Annunciation poems, two macaronic celebrations of Mary that emphasize *contemptus mundi*, two balladic celebrations of rejuvenation, a tender address from Mary to the child Jesus, and a dream vision in which Joseph visits the narrator to explain the birth. In each case and in the *Second Shepherds' Play*, the work confronts the mystery of virgin birth or the Incarnation in a way that focuses attention on rejuvenation or theophany, at once thematic and structural devices. In particular, the vision in which Joseph appears encourages the students to recognize that the lyrics present exemplary perspectives on the Nativity—in this case, a confrontation with the enigma of virgin birth that Joseph must take personally and then transcend in the sublimity of the mystery. Similarly, the poem that depicts Mary's address to the child Jesus emphasizes his humanity and, by omission, exalts the mystery of the Incarnation. The *Second Shepherds' Play* asserts the same mystery in parallel fashion: the play's radical shift in geography and in tone encourages us to recognize how magnificent the rejuvenation of fallen England in Bethlehem is.

The ironic juxtaposition of the Bethlehem scene with the scene at Gill's bedside asserts to audiences both medieval and modern that the disguising of Mak's lamb as a child has been transcended majestically in the Incarnation of the Lamb of God. The rough humor and the slapstick of the first part of the play are transcended by the higher comedy of the childbirth. Indeed, human comedy becomes divine comedy. Such interplay between the two portions of the play produces a rich discussion of cacophony versus harmony, the two opposed dreams of the play, Gill's false birth pangs (recalling Eve's punishment) versus Mary's serenity, and the contrast between the shepherds' world-weary complaints that open the play and the closing reward they receive for their just though charitable treatment of Mak. With such concerns in mind, the students see that the harmonious meter and refrains of the lyrics take on thematic value, the epistemology of the dream about Joseph makes more sense, the Eva-Ave puns gain dimension, and the variations on the *contemptus mundi* theme come into sharper focus. The play and the lyrics evoke the spiritual through the worldly and vice versa, exploring the essential paradox of the Nativity—the coming together of divinity and humanity in one being.

More important than a discussion of any single theme or device is the students' willingness to pursue signals to irony among the works. In the lyrics the students recognize puns, enigmas, paradoxes, and conventional iconography as poetic devices similar to the juxtaposition basic to the play; they confront technique, as well as meaning, and willingly carry such concerns back to the play. Just as the structure of the play makes evident the poetic devices in the poetry, the lyrics highlight the play's verbal niceties—for example, the iconography of the ironic double reference to "day-starn" (lines 577, 727), the dialectical pun on "sin" (520), even the Eucharistic echo in Gill's threat to eat her lamb (537). The discussion can then lead from some sense of the medieval distance between the mundane and the sublime to the bridging of this distance in poetic expression and the structure of drama and ritual.

*Everyman* and lyrics about death interact in ways similar to the interplay between the *Second Shepherds' Play* and Nativity lyrics. Since the realism and the comedy of the *Second Shepherds' Play* appeal more immediately than anything in *Everyman*, some other encouragement is necessary to help students approach the death literature. Like the Nativity lyrics, the death literature strikes students as cliché-ridden, conventional to a fault, and overly obvious in the light of recurrences of the plague in the Middle Ages. Here, too, the art can be approached as a matter of perspective—this time, the difference between medieval and modern perspectives, an easy step from our previous discussions of poetic technique. On the basis of their readings of *Everyman* and the "Poems on Sin and Death" (Stone), students compare and contrast medieval and modern attitudes toward death. Usually, they recognize that the modern tendency to consider death socially (students most often consider death when they hear of others' dying) contrasts with the medieval presentation of death as a personal, subjective concern, less a result of witnessing the death of another than of considering the death of oneself. The first third of *Everyman* helps clarify the relative insignificance of the social aspects of death in medieval literature. The rejections of Everyman by Fellowship, Kindred and Cousin, and Goods are barely touched by their mourning, since the emphasis is on the ephemeral nature of worldly attachments, provoking further discussion of *contemptus mundi*.

Inevitably, someone questions why the medieval presentation of death is not celebrative, a good question when prompted by a familiarity with the *contemptus mundi* tradition and the medieval opposition of the worldly and the heavenly. Why does medieval death literature not focus on the entry into Heaven, rather than the departure from earth? Why is it presented from the perspective of the one who is dying, rather than from that of the loved ones? Indeed, why is the tone anxious, rather than sorrowful or horrified?

The answers to such questions seem to lie most clearly in the theme of reckoning worked out in *Everyman*, which emphasizes, along with the medieval fear of infernal punishment, awareness of human moral failures and accomplishments, rather than heavenly potential or temporal loss. The reckoning of Everyman, prompted by the summons of Death, leads him to recognize worldly transience and heavenly potential, but the play centers on his growing awareness of his moral accomplishments, manifested in the sisterhood of Knowledge and Good Deeds and the support he derives from them.

Behind their apparent morbidity, the lyrics on death can be seen to reflect similar concerns, because Stone's selection clarifies the cyclic imagery associated with death. The poetry reminds the students of the notion of ritual cycle developed in their discussion of the Nativity and allows them to locate within this cycle human responsibility to meet theophany halfway. The theology of merit versus grace is briefly considered here (and is discussed more thoroughly when students read *Pearl*); the theme of human accountability associated with death nicely balances the theme of divine salvation evident in the Nativity literature. Students recognize the individual lyrics to be model tallies or reckonings that urge medieval Christians to make account of their moral state in the face of death. The clearest model tallies among Stone's lyrics are the address of the soul to the body (no. 27), the ten ages of humankind (no. 30), and the use of the traditional *ubi sunt* motif (no. 32). In each of the poems, however, rhetorical listing, repetition, or some kind of circularity establishes a frame that structures the imagery of decay or transience, not only recalling the pains of death but formally encouraging contemplation or reckoning.

Such frames parallel Everyman's exemplary reckoning and help students recognize a cyclic pattern in the play: the reduplicative pattern of the opening summons by Death is fulfilled in the concluding descent into the grave. Perhaps I strain the text of the play slightly in doing so, but I ask the students whether the summons of Death cannot be seen as the birth of Everyman, as well as the more obvious end of his life—whether all birth is not a call to death and all death a rebirth. The play is remarkably flexible in this respect, allowing if not encouraging us to see Everyman's reckoning as a beginning, as well as an ending. The concern with cycle in the lyrics and drama alike enables the students to correlate the cycle of individual human life with the regenerative cycle we discussed earlier with the Nativity, leading to a further discussion of medieval concepts of exemplarism, reduplication, typology, and tropology.

Such concepts and labels for concepts may not be ends in themselves, but they are happy results of pursuing the interplay between drama and lyric. More substantial benefits include a surprising number of the kind of echoic details and themes mentioned above (life as cycle, *contemptus mundi*, ephemeral value of Fortune's gifts). Most important, this approach encourages students to read the text aggressively and to compare medieval and modern sensibilities without privileging one or the other. Class time is also spent reading the lyrics closely and considering such topics as the stage history of both mystery and morality plays. Nevertheless, the central concerns of the course are the correlations of theme, technique, and mind-set discovered by paying close attention to the similarities between medieval plays and medieval poems.

# *Jesus Christ, Superstar* and Medieval Drama: Anachronism and Humor

## Michael L. Hall

The idea of using *Jesus Christ, Superstar* in a course on medieval drama came from my students, though not directly. They suggested to me that the Monty Python *Life of Brian* seemed to have elements of medieval pageants. I could see some slight validity to their claim. The Monty Python film does, in fact, present a purposefully distorted and satiric Passion play, and it even includes elements of the anachronism that students find fascinating in medieval English drama. The tone and the attitude of *The Life of Brian*, however, are completely wrong. Medieval drama was in earnest and presented its vision of Christian history from the inside out, rather than from the outside in. Medieval drama has examples of parody but not satire, at least none directed at Christ, though satiric barbs are aimed at certain social targets, such as landowners in the Wakefield *Second Shepherds' Play*. For that reason I suggested that *Jesus Christ, Superstar* is closer in substance and spirit to the medieval plays.

Using *Jesus Christ, Superstar* as a modern analogue of medieval drama has a number of virtues. First, it is a fine and accessible film that takes its subject seriously. Second, its contemporary setting is disorienting in ways that work on modern viewers the way many contemporary references worked on medieval audiences; both the cycle plays and the film make the familiar Christian story live with present meaning. Third, both the cycle plays and the film mix the serious and comic in ways that move and entertain at the same time.

I could go on with virtues, but I would be remiss if I failed to mention the dangers of such a comparison as a way of teaching medieval drama. One is that, to today's students, the film itself may seem somewhat historical, with its references to a 1960s counterculture that now sometimes appears distant and peculiar. Some of the language and visual allusions, particularly the costumes and sets, require glossing for students who have grown up after the film was made in 1973, but both the music and the staging remain up to date and are familiar to students who have grown up with MTV and rock and roll on television and in movies. A more serious problem is the film's agnosticism. The plot, particularly in the role of Judas, questions the divinity of Christ in ways that are alien to medieval drama. The romantic treatment of Mary Magdalene also poses a problem. These differences, however, can provide material for serious discussion: Why does a late twentieth-century Passion play focus on our questions and doubts? Why were these doubts not a central concern in the medieval drama?

Because of these dangers and perhaps others as well, some instructors feel that using *Jesus Christ, Superstar* in a study of medieval drama is distracting. But this problem can be minimized by scheduling the film for a special viewing, preferably at an evening session during which nothing else is planned. Doing so allows students an opportunity to view the entire film at one sitting and to discuss the film without feeling the necessity to make quick or facile comparisons with the medieval plays they have been reading. At the next regular class meeting, students can discuss the film in the context of the drama.

Some appropriate reading assignments to accompany the discussion are the *Second Shepherds' Play*, *The Offering of the Magi*, and *Herod the Great* from the Wakefield pageant and the York *Crucifixion*. (All of these are in Bevington's *Medieval Drama*, and all except *The Offering of the Magi* are also in Cawley's *Everyman and Medieval Miracle Plays*.) These plays read well themselves and include the mixture of serious Christian material with humor and contemporary settings and references. The use of anachronism in the plays corresponds aesthetically and sometimes even thematically to similar uses in *Jesus Christ, Superstar*, and the differences provide the occasion for a discussion of contrasts as well as comparisons.

The teacher need not insist that the film is based in any significant way on specific English mystery plays, though anyone familiar with English medieval drama finds numerous parallels in the motion picture. The point I try to make by using the film is that we can still create drama from the biblical stories in ways similar to those used by medieval dramatists.

To focus the discussion, I look at several discrete parts of the movie. The best way to do this is with an edited videotape and a television monitor in the classroom. (Skillful use of the fast-forward on a video cassette recorder also works but is distracting and can damage the tape.) A good place to begin is with the opening sequence, when the actors arrive in the Holy Land and assume the costumes and characters of their roles. Next, I focus on the scene in which Judas is alone in the desert as tanks loom up behind him before he runs to betray Christ to Caiaphas. Then I show the scenes in which Jesus is sent before Herod and returned to Pilate to be flogged. Finally, I show the Crucifixion and the final scene of the actors boarding the bus and leaving.

Other scenes would work just as well. Those who are using Bevington's *Medieval Drama* may want to compare and contrast the scourging scene in the film and *The Buffeting* and *The Scourging* from the Wakefield pageant. This also provides an opportunity to discuss the film's portrayal of Pontius Pilate. The object is not to show that the movie is the same as the plays but to show ways in which it can be seen as an analogue. The two elements of the film and the drama that I emphasize are the treatment of time and history—the purposeful use of anachronism—and the use of humor.

The opening sequence in the film introduces the subject of anachronism. Briefly, the film begins with a group of youthful actors and actresses driving into the desert in an old bus. A cross is protruding from the luggage on its roof. The bus comes to a stop, and the actors begin unloading their costumes and props, garbing themselves in the emblems of their roles—the soldiers putting on shiny chrome helmets, cracking whips, and shouldering pikes and automatic rifles; the Jewish priests putting on their tall black peaked caps. Having already seen the film, students notice that the actor who plays the part of Judas slips away from the rest of the group, looking back as the dancers begin rehearsing, dancing in a close circle. Jesus, in the center of the circle, is helped on with his white robe, the most historically accurate or, at least, historically suggestive costume.

When students discuss the costumes and the effect of this changing scene, questions come to mind: Why does the film begin here, rather than at a later point? What does it say to us as viewers? Strangely, a theatrical trick that might have destroyed the dramatic illusion has a different effect: it draws the viewer into the world of the film and emphasizes that the film takes place both now and then. The fact that the costumes are not historical but a blend of past and present reinforces this collapsing of time and history, an important element both of the medieval drama and of the film. In *Early English Stages*, Glynne Wickham concludes that for medieval stagings "contemporary costume was used to dress all historical characters including figures from Biblical history" (1: 103).

The scenes of the betrayal by Judas carry this discussion further. Just before Judas betrays Christ to Caiaphas, we see Judas alone in the desert. Suddenly, behind him three armored tanks appear and rumble over the dunes. Judas, running in front of the tanks, flees to tell Caiaphas and Annas where they can find Jesus. After the betrayal, a formation of jet fighters passes overhead. These scenes are not only anachronistic but also place the events of the Passion story in a contemporary context of Middle Eastern tensions. The film collapses biblical time and the present in ways that recall the references to medieval settings in the Corpus Christi plays—the local references in the Wakefield pageant and the references to the city and the guilds of York. Set in the Holy Land, the film becomes both historical and contemporary, with the tanks and the jet fighters helping us link in our own minds the similarities between the troubles then and the troubles now in and around Jerusalem. The tanks become the symbol of an occupying army, even if they are Israeli tanks, because they represent the threats to peace and love that Christ and the Christian story must face and ultimately come to terms with.

Another excellent exercise is a comparison of the film's portrayal of Herod with the Herod of the Wakefield plays. The discussion should bring out the differences, as well as the similarities, and should include some consideration of what those differences suggest about our own reading of Herod as villain compared with the medieval reading of Herod. In the film Herod is at first a wonderfully comic character, and the lavish production number in which he challenges Christ to "walk across my swimming pool" is one of the highlights of the movie. But in the scenes that follow, Herod appears cruel and finally weak and cowardly. The scenes involving Herod provide the best occasion for a discussion of the use of comedy in the film and in the medieval plays. In either case we must see the use of humor in context. Herod's mockery and ranting in the film and in the Corpus Christi drama may deceive us at first, may even attract us through its humor, but, as we observe it in context as part of the torturing of Christ, we draw back and recognize the horror. The film emphasizes this by cutting to Herod's face during the scourging scene. At first, he is convulsed with delighted laughter; then he begins to shrink in horror as the beating becomes more and more brutal. The humor in the Corpus Christi plays is different, and the students should be asked to consider the ways the medieval drama invites the audience to laugh at evil characters and often makes them appear ridiculous. The humor in the film does not work in the same way.

The last scenes I suggest for discussion are the Crucifixion and the conclusion of the film. (The York *Crucifixion* presents an interesting comparison: in both the film and the play the soldiers are cruelly efficient, but the business of the Crucifixion is drawn out in much more detail in the play.) When the Crucifixion is done and Christ has given up his spirit, the crowd begins to depart, and the camera cuts to the actors, now back in their own clothes, boarding the bus. We see the actor who played Pilate pause and look back in the direction of the Cross, and then Mary Magdalene does the same. Judas is the last to board, and the bus drives away with him still hanging out the door and looking into the desert. We have seen the entire cast board the bus, all except the actor who played Jesus Christ. The film concludes with a shot of the Cross silhouetted in the setting sun.

The story stops short of a Resurrection, or an Ascension, or a Last Judgment. The questions raised by the film, particularly by Judas, remain unanswered. *Jesus Christ, Superstar* is not a filmed mystery play or even a modern version of a medieval Passion play, but it can help show modern students that what they may at first find either alien or quaint in medieval drama was not so different from what a modern version of the story might look like.

Finally, I want to add a word about the film's use of music and dance. Staging the Passion play as a modern musical certainly goes far beyond anything we can document or realistically imagine about medieval drama. But it is worth noting that the medieval plays used music and song, that they were written in verse, and that sometimes they were sung. I would not push this comparison much further, but it is a way of introducing a discussion of the musical elements of medieval drama and of reminding students of the musical qualities of poetic drama.

# A Theater of Domestication and Entrapment:
## The Cycle Plays

*Robert W. Hanning*

I have for many years taught a course entitled English Literature from Its Beginnings to 1500, which devotes two or three weeks to the study of plays drawn from all the major Middle English cycles. (At present, readings are assigned from Peter Happé's *English Mystery Plays*.) This essay describes a strategy to introduce undergraduates to the cycle plays within the constraints of such a survey of medieval literature. After a brief summary of current theories concerning the origins and the staging conventions of the plays, the course addresses three basic topics: (1) how the cycle drama understands and articulates the powers, the limits, and the dangers of its dramatic medium; (2) how it domesticates its cosmic subject; and (3) how it addresses, involves, and manipulates (in order to move) its Christian audience.

The first task is to consider whether the cycle plays offer evidence of self-conscious meditation on the implications of their status as religious drama. The students focus on the Chester *Fall of Lucifer* (no. 1 in Happé), exploring how it both dramatizes the origin of sin in the universe and defines the peculiar enterprise of the Christian playwright. The discussion centers on two stage directions that mark key subdivisions in the play: *"Tunc cantabunt [angeli] et recedet Deus"* ("then the angels sing and God leaves"), following line 104; and *"et sedet [Lucifer]"* ("and Lucifer sits in God's throne"), following line 192. We examine the didactic and celebratory (quasiliturgical) nature of the play's words and actions before the first direction—that is, before God withdraws from the playing area—and contrast them with the tense, dramatic confrontation between the protosinners Lucifer and Lightburne on the one side and the obedient angels on the other that occurs between the first and the second direction—that is, between God's vacating his throne and Lucifer's occupying it in defiance of the divine prohibition.

The departure of God—a concept that makes no sense theologically, since God is by definition everywhere—can thus be understood to signify, "and God said, 'Let there be drama.'" But in the *Fall of Lucifer* it also signifies the opportunity for Lucifer to rebel against God's command and thus bring sin into the universe. Here is the central paradox of Christian drama: the birth of sin and the birth of drama coincide, which means the Christian play must embrace sin dramatically, while obviously (if it is to be a Christian play) rejecting it doctrinally. Students must understand that the *Fall of Lucifer* confronts this paradox head on—indeed, makes it its subject. The center of the play's translation of a theological notion—the origin of sin in the universe—into a dramatic action is the moment when Lucifer sits in God's throne, and this is an act of imitation by which the rebellious angel impersonates God. That is, Lucifer is the first actor, and his sitting in God's throne is not only the first sin but the first "play." In the biblical passage (Isa. 14.12–15) on which the medieval story of Lucifer's fall is primarily based, Lucifer sets up his own throne; only in the plays does he sit in God's throne.

We then discuss the significance of what happens after God returns and banishes Lucifer from Heaven to hell. The dialogue of wailing lament and angry recrimination between the fallen angels in their new habitat defines both their transformed, diabolical status and a new theatrical mode that frequently reappears in the succeeding plays of the cycle: the theater of uproar, disorder, scatology, and chaos. Evidence from other plays and documents illustrative of the disruptive antics and scatological language of stage devils throughout the cycle drama is considered here. (Allusion to the Vice of the morality play and even to Falstaff, as legatee of the cycle plays' diabolic uproar, is also appropriate.) The depiction of the devils is frequently at or over the edge of farce; the exigencies of plotted drama here give way to the impulses of improvisatory slapstick and to the disruptive, comic routines that, even on today's stage, bring dramatic momentum to a halt. (Evocation of the word and the concept "pandemonium" helps here.) In other words, diabolic uproar simultaneously threatens the providential plot of universal history—as the devils attempt to avenge themselves on God for their banishment by luring humanity from God's camp to theirs—and the orderly process of a drama that seeks to reproduce that divine plot. Yet the religious drama must include that uproar if it is to fulfill its function of warning Christians of the consequences of wrong, Luciferian moral choices.

The danger is that the immediate attractiveness of farcical uproar will, like the immediate attractiveness of the sin it represents, seduce both the playwright and the audience of the cycle drama from the complex and demanding task of giving and receiving salutary instruction to the infinitely easier task of purveying and deriving vulgar enjoyment under the guise of edification. The *Fall of Lucifer* playwright's recognition of this danger and of the need to contain the impulse to comic uproar finds structural expression in the containment of the diabolic exchange by a final scene in Heaven, where God establishes the ultimately moral intent of what has gone before, warning the angels and, by extension, the play's external audience of the dangers of pride.

Our next concern is to analyze the strategies by which the cycle plays domesticate the cosmic, the ways they bridge the gap between the experience of their audience and biblical or Apocryphal events and characters immensely remote in time, in space, and (perhaps most important) in the assumption of direct, palpable interaction between humanity and God. The class deals first with the cycle plays' most notorious domestication of the cosmic: their pervasive vein of anachronism. The double anachronism of the Wakefield shepherds' plays—Christian oaths and English (indeed, local Yorkshire) geographical and topical references put in the mouths of shepherds living in Palestine before the Incarnation—provides the most obvious entree to a dramatic strategy designed to eliminate temporal, spatial, and doctrinal alienation between the audience and the play situation. The discussion of the *Second Shepherds' Play* (no. 14 in Happé) considers how the audience is drawn first to identify with the diction, the location, and the sociopolitical perspective of the actors (who are, after all, their real-life neighbors) and then, in consequence, to experience empathically with them the joy of the angels' message and the discovery of the Christ child as a welcome contrast to the play's antecedent and brilliant evocation of natural and human discomforts (including the deceptions of Mak and Gyl). The play's ultimate aim is thus not simply to make the shepherds real but to endow the Christmas message—in theological terms, the historical fact of God's Incarnation—with existential significance for a late medieval audience.

A second strategy for domesticating the cosmic assimilates the behavior of biblical husbands and wives to stereotypical jokes at the expense of nagging or otherwise troublesome wives and their beleaguered husbands. Using the discourse of Chaucer's Wife of Bath (whose Prologue and Tale the students have already studied in the course) to establish the widespread medieval exploitation—both clerical and popular—of marital and gender stereotypes, we examine their presence and function within the otherwise divergent dramatic treatments of the Genesis flood narrative in the Wakefield *Processus Noe cum filiis* and the Chester *De Deluvio Noe* (nos. 4 and 5 in Happé). Analysis concentrates on speeches in both plays (Chester 105–12; Wakefield 388–400) that break the theatrical frame to instruct the audience by admonition or proverbial wisdom on parallels between antediluvian and modern perceptions of marital strife. Having thus established gender stereotypes, especially those directed against women, as available and convenient instruments of dramatic consensus and having adduced television's domestic situation comedies of the 1950s and 1960s as a cultural analogue, I direct attention to the Chester *Creation, and Adam and Eve* (no. 2 in Happé) to show how the Chester playwright evokes such stereotypes to explain and literally domesticate the Fall. For example, Eve's diabolic tempter bases his plan to "beguile" her on the "fact" (expressed in a proverbial form worthy of Chaucer's sententious Wife of Bath) that

That [what] woman is forbyd to doe
For any thinge therto will shooe [she]. . . .
For [because] women are full liccoris [desirous of pleasures],
That [eating the apple] she will not forsake. (185–86, 199–200)

Adam's sententious comment on his sin affirms the continuity between Eden then and England now:

Now all my kinde by me is kent [taught]
To flee woman's intisement;
That trustes them in anye intent
Truly he is decayved. (349-52)

These sentiments dovetail perfectly with those expressed by Sir Gawain when he attempts to exculpate himself for his sin (accepting the green girdle from Bercilak's wife) in the last fitt of *Sir Gawain and the Green Knight*, a text that in this course immediately precedes the drama. Gawain places himself in a lineage of men deceived by women that begins, in fact, with Adam, and thereby closes the circle of gender stereotyping.

The last topic identifies within the plays' strategy of domesticating the cosmic a counterstrategy of tropological entrapment—that is, a method of impelling the audience toward right moral choices by first seducing them into wrong ones. The theatrical experience thus creates within its spectators an unwilled confrontation with their own sinfulness—the necessary prelude to any attempt at reform. There are two types of tropological entrampment. In the first, a play presents characters or situations that, by Christian moral and theological standards, deserve only condemnation and then draws the audience into imaginative sympathy with them. The Wakefield *Mactatio Abel* (no. 3 in Happé) embodies this approach. The class can easily grasp this play's techniques for portraying Cain as a sinner: scatological diction, farcical bluster, and the fatal attack on Abel. Further discussion, however, elucidates how the play also presents Cain as a subsistence farmer with whose tribulations the Wakefield audience could readily sympathize and identify, thereby justifying Garcio's remark, in his opening harangue to the onlookers, "Bot I trow, bi God on life, / Som of you are his [Cain's] men" (19–20).

Cain is first seen attempting to plough the land but thwarted by the recalcitrance of his team. His boy, instead of feeding the horses, has placed stones in the feeding trough and put their food "behynd thare ars" (45), where the tied animals cannot reach it. Then Abel arrives, bringing not help in solving Cain's problems but a reminder that their father has instructed them to offer a sacrifice to the Lord and an admonition that they should now go "Gif [God] parte of oure fee, / Corne or catall, wheder it be" (76–77). Cain's frustration and anger at this point was all too understandable to a rural community. Abel refers to the proposed offering as a "tend" (73)—that is, a tithe. The students must understand the medieval system of tithing and the hostility it often prompted, especially among poor farmers. The students thus become aware of how the play assimilates the biblical sacrifice to an institution the audience knew well and doubtless grumbled about. Cain's angry, anticlerical comment, "My farthyng is in the preest hand / Syn last tyme I offyrd" (104–05), invites the audience to sympathize further with him as a farmer, down on his luck, but still obliged to pay tithes to a greedy ecclesiastical authority. The comic tour de force of Cain's choosing the ears of grain for his offering makes him doubly attractive—as the purveyor of effective stage business (which, we can assume, involves a good deal of slapstick movement and gesture) and as the trickster seeking to salvage what he can from a situation in which the odds and the establishment are definitely against him. By contrast, Abel's priggishness and passivity make him difficult to identify with. Hence, as spectators, we side viscerally with Cain and, in doing so, become "his men" and implicate ourselves in his fratricide and rebellion against our Creator.

The second type of tropological entrapment depends on the dramatization of a single action, so carefully prepared in language and gesture or movement as to generate a good deal of tension within the audience as they wait for the action to happen. The tension mounts to the point at which we become kinetically involved, straining both physically and mentally in empathy with the actors as they move toward the climax. We are irresistably invited to become, in effect, the coperformers of the action. (This is the kind of kinetic involvement generated in movies by situations in which the protagonist must perform a difficult physical task—for example, uncoupling the railroad car in which he is riding from the runaway train to which it is attached—within a short span of time, in the process bringing us to the edge of our seats as we empathically mime his actions while watching them.) But when the action is sinful, we, by our kinetic participation, are entrapped and implicated in actions that defy God's law or reject his love.

One of the best examples of entrapment is the York *Crucifixion* (no. 30 in Happé), a play that centers on the raising of the Cross by the soldiers—and, in effect, by us—once they have affixed Jesus to it. Students examine and characterize the different registers of language in this play and become aware of the presence of three distinct types of discourse: (1) the soldiers' jeering speeches of antagonism and unfeeling cruelty toward Jesus; (2) Jesus's only two utterances, spoken past his tormentors and with a sublime calm in contrast to the uproar of the torturers; and (3) a different language for the soldiers, related in tone to the first, but centered on expressions of effort and strain, exhortations to cooperative effort, and articulations of a macho thirst for honor and of its converse, a fear of shame. This last discourse occurs whenever the soldiers become engaged with the Crucifixion and induces us to become engaged with it as a set of interrelated physical problems—the need to stretch Jesus's limbs to accommodate the holes bored in the Cross for the nails, the difficulty of lifting the large Cross with a man on it—to be solved by usually collective exertion.

A Christian audience easily recoils from the soldiers' language of hate and responds affectively to the words and even more to the mute presence, of Jesus, but the language and the accompanying actions of cooperative physical effort considerably complicate audience response to the York *Crucifixion*. As the soldiers struggle, first to attach Jesus to the Cross made too large for his body and then to carry him on that Cross to the hill where the Cross is to be set into a hole prepared for it, their exertions create a kinetic perspective on the deed—an amoral, empathic tightening of the muscles and straining of the limbs. The students are asked to imagine their own responses to an effective performance of the raising of the Cross—to realize how much they, too, would find themselves straining with the actors and, in effect, committing themselves to the success of the physical actions qua actions that result in the death of the Son of God. Such irresistible theatrical entrapment offered its late medieval victims irrefutable evidence of their sinful participation in the sufferings of Jesus— participation stressed also in the contemporaneous, frequently grue-some "Meditations on the Passion," which, like the cycle plays, had as their ultimate goal the inducement of repentance and the reformation of the faithful.

It is impossible within a few weeks to give students much more than a hint of the rich variety of medieval drama. The advantage of the strategy outlined above for a course that can only study a few cycle plays is that—by focusing on its theatrical self-consciousness, its domestication of its cosmic subject, and its entrapment of the medieval audience—students are introduced to the essential nature of medieval drama. This approach, furthermore, requires careful attention to the language of the plays, considers their effective staging, and highlights certain recurring dramatic devices, such as the use of the comic, the anachronistic, and the stereotypical. Finally, it touches on various characteristic features of medieval culture that link the plays to the other literature under consideration and that provide coherence to the course. With this introduction, students can proceed to a more profound study of English medieval religious drama imbued with an appropriate sense of its sophistication and complexity.

# Medieval Drama through the Cycle Plays: Problems and Possibilities

## John C. Coldewey

Students coming to medieval drama for the first time face some daunting problems. To begin with, there is the sheer *mass* of material confronting them, much of it—the entire body of surviving cycle plays—of apparently similar inspiration, construction, and production. Yet the most cursory inspection makes clear that these plays, as individual pageants and as fully articulated sequences, present tremendously varied dramatic techniques, theatrical conventions, and poetic accomplishments. Moreover, the literary interactions between the cycles and with their kissing cousins on the Continent or with the other forms of medieval drama—the liturgical plays, the morality plays, the folk plays—remain puzzling and are only now beginning to be explored. Likewise, the texts, despite their deceptive metaphorical simplicity, offer difficulties of interpretation deriving from theatrical considerations, from sociological contexts, and from indistinct critical notions of their form and content. The play texts remain tissues of verbal complexity and, as scripts for performance, they register a further measure of iconographic, gestic, and musical ambivalence. And since these plays often present transparent examples of crass guild self-promotion and civic showmanship, the occasions of composition, revision, and performance of the medieval cycle plays cannot easily be divorced from any attempt to interpret them.

All this is not good news for the teacher who relishes a simple body of material or straightforward subject guidelines. In the course I teach introducing advanced undergraduate and graduate students to medieval drama, these problems are encountered naturally enough during the term, but the students' chief task is to master the Chester plays as best they can in ten weeks. The course has been successful, perhaps because it pares the multitude of texts down to one cycle, allowing the students to focus ever more closely on how that cycle works; this establishes some firm ground from which to survey the other medieval plays. I have found that, when the students come to terms with one of the mystery cycles, they also gain a natural intellectual vantage point providing access to medieval culture itself. And depending on the tone and the structure of the course, the students can come away from it with useful tools for further study in the genre and the period. In what follows I map out the direction my course takes and indicate not only the advantages but also some of the limitations of using the Chester cycle as the basis for a course in medieval drama.

If one has to choose a cycle of medieval plays to study, one that can represent the dramatic strengths and strategies of cycle plays as a subgenre, the obvious choice is Chester, for either by accident or by design a far greater range of supplementary resources is available for its study than for any of the other cycles. The recent Early English Text Society edition by Robert Lumiansky and David Mills is still in print, though it has to be specially ordered from an English bookseller and supplied to students privately. Once the text, which is the one book required for the course, is in hand, the wealth of supporting materials can be made accessible on limited loan periods in the library. The Lumiansky and Mills volume of essays and documents—with its valuable observations on textual, musical, and other matters—is one of the most important secondary texts. The older Herman Deimling and Dr. Matthews Early English Text Society edition offers some helpful lessons in textual editing, and its notes complement those of Lumiansky and Mills. The *Antichrist* is handled separately by W. W. Greg. For those interested in learning about the manuscript tradition of the Chester plays or in tracing editorial methods behind the printed text, facsimiles of the Bodleian and Huntington manuscripts are available (also edited by Lumiansky and Mills). Students interested in civic and guild roles in producing the Chester plays, in their long history of performance, or in any other aspects that may be illuminated by documentary evidence can consult Lawrence Clopper's Records of Early English Drama edition of the relevant Chester records. Good critical approaches to the cycle are not hard to find; they range from F. M. Salter's 1955 *Medieval Drama in Chester* to Peter W. Travis's *Dramatic Design in the Chester Cycle*. Jean D. Pfleiderer and Michael J. Preston's concordance gives a word-by-word gathering and sifting. And beyond these book-length resources lie many articles and chapters in books that investigate scholarly aspects and critical patterns, the most recent being Martin Stevens's appraisal of the cycle in *Four Middle English Mystery Cycles*. All these resources provide secure anchors for the study of the Chester plays, no matter which direction students want to explore.

I let the plays themselves organize the course, simply following the text pageant by pageant as the story unfolds. Typically, the class meets in two-hour sessions twice a week, and the learning curve is steep from the start. In the first week I give background lecture discussions and help the students develop some facility in Middle English. Many students have no previous experience with it, and I provide a handout four or five pages long that takes them backward through the great vowel shift. In class discussions I encourage them to give examples from the text and to present them orally. The ultimate uncertainty of Middle English pronunciation often receives its true test at these early moments in the term. Meanwhile, we consider some of the large cultural structures in place during the two hundred years these plays flourished, focusing mainly on political, ecclesiastical, and social history. Then I offer a thumbnail sketch of how various types of drama fit into this large scheme. The rest of the course is spent concentrating on the Chester cycle itself.

We address the textual issues right away, noting the late dates of the manuscripts and the evidence for revision; we compare the Lumiansky and Mills text with that of Deimling and Matthews; then we begin working our way through the pageants. The first part of each class period is devoted to one pageant, chosen earlier by a student guide scheduled to lead the discussion. With more pageants than class periods or students, not all pageants receive the same treatment, and each student usually has to make two presentations. During the second half of each period we consider the pageants that come in between those focused on by the presentations, and so the entire cycle can be covered in some depth. In their presentations the students are expected to take into account any other versions of the dramatized biblical episode from the other cycle plays; beyond that they are free to develop any approach that seems congenial. This provides the whole class with large theatrical and thematic contexts while ensuring that each student has special preparation for one individual pageant or two. Ordinarily, the students use one of the preparations as groundwork for the paper that is due at the end of the term. From the beginning of the course a student with computer skills acts as class bibliographer, compiling a current bibliography, including library call numbers whenever possible, of all the references used or alluded to by the class during the term. This has always turned out to be an extensive, valuable, continually updated list of resources that reflects the ongoing concerns of the students, however far afield they may have ranged.

As this last feature of the course—the bibliography generated by the entire class—indicates, perhaps the most important lesson to be learned here concerns the spirit of scholarly cooperation rather than cutthroat competition. Like the original performances of the cycle plays, the study of these dramatic works can be a group enterprise, coordinated and produced for the pleasure and the profit of the commonweal. Such an ethic also lies behind the rotation of class leadership; the stability of the framework allows for—in fact, encourages—fruitful unpredictability in performance. Thus, the guiding notion for this course on the Chester plays, the one that acts as its structuring principle, is an echo of the cycle's own history of production, with separate parties sharing the responsibilities of providing a means for instruction and delight.

However satisfying, enjoyable, and rewarding the experience of teaching this course is, I return to the question of limitations, a question that is tied intimately to the focus of the course on cycle plays, particularly the Chester cycle. It is true that studying a single cycle offers a vantage point from which to survey other forms of medieval drama, but it is also true that not all vantage points are of equal value, and neither are the cycles. The Chester cycle, for all its magic, is generally conceded to come nowhere near rivaling the inspired poetic conceptions of character or the theatrical brilliance of the Wakefield Master; for all its well-documented examples of coordination among the civic and guild authorities, the Chester cycle offers nothing like the labyrinthine financial and social complexities of production found at York; for all its rootedness in its own age, it does not compare well with the glittering and showy self-reflective qualities of the Coventry plays. Yet the Chester plays, the obvious choice, is the cycle most frequently taught. Scholarly paraphernalia for it abounds; studies of it continue to appear. It is, although modest in accomplishment, convenient. Is this enough?

A larger question lurks here, one that concerns the use of the cycle plays as the basis for a course on medieval drama. The cycle plays are arguably the best-known form of dramatic activity during the late Middle Ages in England and on the Continent and certainly the most monolithic form of drama at the time, but recent research—notably that coming out of the Records of Early English Drama project—indicates that cycle plays represent only the tip of the iceberg of medieval drama, that villages and parishes in hundreds of places all over the country put on single and group enterprises with astonishing frequency and zeal. Could not a course using the noncycle play offer a more historically accurate representation of medieval playing?

Moreover, in our desperate attempts to rescue medieval drama from its dreaded earlier characterization as pre-Shakespearean (an unusually remote description of cycle plays in any case), we may have sacrificed an important principle of continuity, cutting off our plays from what becomes the mainstream English tradition. By the 1590s, at the time the Chester play manuscripts were being copied, the native tradition of guild performance and sponsorship was seen as completely outmoded, not simply obsolescent but obsolete. This attitude applied not only to the doctrine, dogma, ritual echoes, and satiric possibilities embodied in the plays but to virtually all their theatrical conventions. The rude mechanicals of *A Midsummer Night's Dream*, clearly send-ups of apparent theatrical innocence now cast in the harsher light and expectations of professional productions in London, appear on the public stage without a trace of nostalgia. The break is complete, and the mode of theatrical experience that the cycle plays represented is for all practical purposes dead until our own century and Bertolt Brecht. But other English traditions provide obvious bridges to the Elizabethan and Jacobean theatrical habits and beyond. The morality plays in particular, as they shade into interludes, provide characters and character types, thematic resonance, emphases on internal moral struggles—all of which show up in the next generation of theater. In contrast to the indulgent and dismissive treatment of the rude mechanicals, the Good and Bad Angels in Christopher Marlowe's *Dr. Faustus*, also obvious figures from an earlier tradition, have been taken seriously and integrated into the play without losing any of their potency. If in our medieval drama courses we insist on using the cycle plays as its main representative form (as I have done), we may be teaching only the dead language of the medieval theater.

Meanwhile, as teachers of medieval drama, we are faced with the challenge of making critical sense of plays that resist many modern theories and sensibilities. The problems alluded to at the beginning of this essay need mediating, and it may be that we should start there, helping the students approach these plays through a grounding in specifics. The course I have outlined here works well in this regard, but it will be undergoing some changes the next time around. I look forward to developing a more critically ambitious course, one in which the emphasis can fall as much on the reader's resources as on the library's, one in which more of the aesthetic sensibilities informing both the composition of these plays and our responses to them are explored. I envision a framework for the study of selected dramatic texts that includes secondary readings in the lay piety movement, in cultural anthropology, in economic models of town and countryside, and in the semiotics of theater. A few studies have already pointed outside the bounds of past scholarship, and they can act as resources: for example, Charles Phythian-Adams's work on Coventry's ceremonial year, Mervyn James's and Peter Borsay's considerations of cultic celebration in the medieval town, Anthony Gash's analysis of carnival spirit and theatrical ambivalence, and Keir Elam's attempt to set forth a system of stage code and discourse.

In the end, we have many questions to answer about the late medieval drama in all its varieties, and the cycle plays alone cannot offer a sound basis for many answers. In all likelihood, whoever in the next generation of scholars continues the work of formulating questions and attempting answers will have received training as one of our own students. If we plan our courses well, we can teach them not only how to deal with problems inherent in the material but also how to communicate the delights, the literary craftmanship, and the theatrical exuberance that set these plays apart from theater of the ordinary sort.

# STAGING AND PERFORMANCE

## Escaping from English Literature: Dramatic Approaches to Medieval Drama

### Robert Potter

One major barrier to the understanding of English medieval drama is that traditionally it belongs, academically speaking, to English medieval literature, despite the fact that it is neither English nor medieval nor literature. This historic genre of performance is as native to Tuscany, Catalonia, and Flanders as it is to Yorkshire; many of its best texts are postmedieval, dating from well into the sixteenth century; and its plays, with the exception of *Everyman*, were never intended for reading, let alone literary analysis. Nevertheless, tradition has remanded it to the sonorous corridors of departments of English, somewhere beyond (but firmly below) Chaucer and before (yet infinitely beneath) Shakespeare. In such an environment it should have withered away from indifference or have been crushed under the weight of invidious literary historicity long ago. But despite the fact that medieval drama has remained virtually impervious to the scrutiny of literary criticism—being too irregular for the Augustans, too anonymous for the Romantics, too vulgar for the Victorians, too religious for the Marxists, too unambiguous for the New Critics, too formless for the structuralists, and too indestructible for the deconstructionists—despite all these odds, medieval drama has survived and grown steadily in scholarly reputation and in public esteem.

This success is primarily the result of its periodic and spectacular escapes from academic confinement, which began as early as 1901 with William Poel's production of *Everyman* and have become frequent in the years since World War II. Emerging on the stage, medieval drama gained a new sense of its freedom and its identity in rediscovering the originating context in which it was born, the medium of theatrical performance. Here in this twentieth and least medieval of centuries, what had seemed to be inert and minor emerged as living and significant. This process reached its climax in the 1980s with Bill Bryden's triumphant three-part production of *The Mysteries* at Britain's National Theatre and with the impressive and authentically staged revivals of whole cycles in Toronto.

Few teachers of these plays, whatever their views on the validity of particular productions, would wish to see English medieval drama returned to its cell of unperformance and locked up in solitary "pre-Shakespearean" confinement. But my own experience as an advocate of liberation theology in this context is somewhat out of the ordinary. I spent the first third of my academic career as a drama specialist in an English department, trying to explain to literature students my belief in the then slightly heretical notion that the reality and the intention of a play lies in its performance—particularly if it is a medieval play. At a crucial juncture in my career, I leaped the departmental barriers, and I have spent my subsequent years as a literature specialist in a drama department, trying to convince theater students that there is a medieval drama. In one sense this has simply involved exchanging one set of frustrations for another. But I believe I have gained some useful insights along the way about the variety of approaches one may take to the study and the enjoyment of medieval dramatic texts, or medieval playscripts if you prefer. This is particularly true because the teaching of drama in drama departments is also in a state of transition.

In drama and theater arts departments, medieval drama is traditionally encountered as a part of theater history. Like the art historian or the musicologist, the theater historian may have a special area of expertise within a particular culture, nation, or century but, as a generalist, must survey a field that is international, intercultural, and multilingual. This orientation is notably helpful in approaching medieval drama, which is so vividly a trans-European phenomenon. Moreover, theater history is of necessity cross-disciplinary. The goal of research and teaching is to document a wide diversity of ephemeral theatrical acts, every mode of the performance process from scenery to music to lighting to dance, with a particular emphasis on the evolution of acting styles and the rise of the director. Eschewing literary judgments, the traditional theater historian attempts to reconstruct and evaluate *what was done*.

Some of the achievements of theater history in increasing our understanding of medieval drama, and also some of its real limitations, may be seen in Alois M. Nagler's *Medieval Religious Stage*. Nagler, an acerbic and magisterial theater historian of the old school, led a theater history graduate seminar for many years in the Yale Drama School, and the book is an extended report on what resulted. Nagler records a painstaking search for documentary factual detail in reconstructing the circumstances of various medieval performances, but he conveys almost no sense of what the plays may have been like as human experiences or what they may have conveyed or meant to their original auditors, much less how they may have been expressive of the needs of the society, the city, the guild, or any other group that chose to perform them. It was a hunger for richer cultural insights that lured critics and scholars in theater studies into wider and more complex investigations of theater events and texts. The career of Glynne Wickham, the pathfinding first professor of drama in a British university, exemplifies the dynamic movement of theater scholars into new areas of concern. His major, multivolume work of scholarship, *Early English Stages*, is a herculean effort (not always initially successful but never halfhearted) to turn the vast, fragmentary, and complex factuality of medieval theater history to cultural and even literary account. As a result of the pioneering efforts of Wickham and like-minded scholars, progressive drama departments today take a much wider view of their academic discipline. Echoing Clemenceau's opinion of war and generals, they have concluded that dramatic literature is too important to be left to English departments.

I regularly teach two courses, one undergraduate and one graduate in alternate years, in which medieval drama is a major part of the curriculum. The undergraduate course, one of a sequence of seven courses tracing the development of dramatic art from the Greeks to the present day, covers the Middle Ages and the Renaissance, excluding Shakespeare, who is accorded a course in his own right. Approximately five weeks of the ten-week term are devoted to medieval theater and drama. Typically, the syllabus includes two church dramas (the *Quem quaeritis* and the Beauvais *Play of Daniel*), an early French farce (for example, *The Boy and the Blind Man* or *Pierre Pathelin*), examples of folk drama (such as *Robin Hood and the Friar*), some eight or nine plays from the English Corpus Christi cycles, and two moralities (one English, one Continental). Links to the visual arts and iconography are explored through slides; the problems of performance are investigated through lectures on staging and staged readings in class. When the students act out the Annunciation scene in the Coventry *Nativity*, for example, they discover a crucial visual event implicit in the text but invisible to the reader's eye: the highly comic moment in which Joseph (and the audience) see for the first time that Mary is pregnant. The students have an option, furthermore, of doing practical performance work on the plays for part of their grade, acting in scenes and then contributing essays following up on their discoveries and choices made in the course of the scene work.

The graduate seminar, in which most of the participants are doctoral candidates and the entire quarter is devoted to medieval drama, affords a much fuller and more wide-ranging study of medieval drama and theater. Using Bevington's *Medieval Drama* as a primary text, supplemented by much duplicated material, the students read widely in liturgical drama and its sources, study the *Jeu d'Adam*, the plays of Hrotsvitha, and the music drama of Hildegard of Bingen. One way in which the course differs significantly from similar graduate seminars in English departments is that it also considers in some depth the profane context of medieval performance, from seasonal ritual through the minstrelsy of Adam de la Halle to the dramatic innovations of the Dutch Rhetoricians. As many as twenty pageants from the Corpus Christi cycles may be considered, along with *Mankind, Everyman*, and *The Castle of Perseverance*, on which we do some in-class scene work. For example, we move class to a wide grassy area of the campus and stake out the various locations of the scaffolds noted in the *Perseverance* manuscript, creating a spacious circular playing area. We then take parts and read and act our way through the opening sequences of this epic play. No amount of lecturing on the inbuilt performance style of this play can demonstrate its special qualities and its theatrical viability as vividly and as convincingly as this practical work. Doctoral students who take this course (and most of them do) should develop a full and immediate sense of the range, the complexity, and the achievement of medieval drama and should be ready to direct productions with some knowledge of the state of the art, if occasion demands, in an academic or community context.

Performance is the test of whether the play's lessons have been comprehended. The true educational opportunity for medieval drama students and teachers comes when they combine forces and talents to produce the plays. When accompanied by a rigorous reinvestigation of the staging requirements and potentialities of the scripts, these productions can be acts of research in the best sense of the term. In this process, not merely the original text and stage directions but also the attempts of critics, scholars, and editors to clarify or to interpret medieval plays become crucial resources for actors and directors in staging the plays effectively. Future years should see concerted research and production in medieval drama more comprehensively integrated, for their goals are not antithetical but intimately related. It was a happy coincidence that led V. A. Kolve to see a revival of the York plays in 1957, en route to writing his landmark critical study, *The Play Called Corpus Christi*. We need to plan for such breakthroughs, rather than merely hope that they will turn up in the future.

A number of successful academic initiatives offer good examples of what can be done. Glynne Wickham's impetus brought about a sequence of remarkable medieval performances at the University of Bristol in the 1960s, culminating in the superb production by Neville Denny of the Cornish *Ordinalia* in 1969 in the vast original round arena in Cornwall. The University of Toronto, by complementing the archival research of the Records of Early English Drama project with the productive imagination of the Poculi Ludique Societas players, has brought this idea to its highest fruition in North America. Two recent achievements in the United States that combine research and production show that the example may be spreading: Trinity College's performance of and symposium on *Wisdom* in 1985 and the three-year (1985–87) production and research project at the University of California, Irvine, a joint effort of the English and drama departments that is funded by the university's Focused Research Project in Medieval Theater Studies. This project was masterminded by Edgar Schell, the editor and dramaturge for the productions. His scholarly expertise complemented the skills of Robert Cohen, a professional director, and his cast of masters-level actors, who together investigated and responded to the demands of the text. Organized in conjunction with the performances were a series of scholarly symposia notable for the well-prepared papers and informed discussions of the productions.

Behind all these performances and projects has been the energy of a now-validated educational idea. These robust and ambitious medieval plays can live again in the freedom that is created by knowledge, talent, and commitment, transcending pedantry and outwitting ignorance.

# The Harlotry Players:
# Teaching Medieval Drama through Performance

*Martin W. Walsh*

The Residential College at the University of Michigan was founded in 1967 to combine the advantages of a small liberal arts college with the resources of a major research university. Since its inception the college has supported a drama concentration within its humanities division. Initiated by J. L. Styan, the drama concentration developed a curriculum according to Styan's text-into-performance pedagogy, reflected in such works as *The Elements of Drama* and *Drama, Stage and Audience*. Scene work and other practical involvements with performance became essential ingredients of drama courses, placing them in a fertile middle ground between ordinary dramatic literature courses and specifically theater-training classes. Many theatrical experiments developed out of these innovative drama courses. A professional theater troupe—the Brecht Company, now in residence at the Residential College—was a direct outgrowth of the concentration and so was a more loosely defined group dedicated to medieval popular drama, the Harlotry Players.

The concentration had on at least one occasion in its early years offered the course Comparative Medieval Drama. Medieval drama was not, however, a major focus until I began to follow the work of the Poculi Ludique Societas troupe at the University of Toronto. Contact was made with the troupe's artistic director, David Parry, during their production of the Toronto (N-Town) Passion play in May 1981. The Poculi Ludique Societas was brought to the Residential College the following spring to conduct several workshops and present a varied program, including their celebrated *Mankind* production. Enthusiasm ran high, and soon after we contracted to do a play in the troupe's mounting of the Chester cycle in Toronto for May 1983. We were fortunate to get our first choice, *The Coming of Antichrist*. A play of such magnitude and complexity demanded a lengthy period of preparation, and so a course was scheduled, devoted exclusively to the project and modeled on the concentration's Play Production Seminar. This course is designed to take upper-level drama students through the various stages of conceptualization, planning, and execution of a stage production, giving them some first-hand experience of the roles of director, dramaturge, and designer. Each student is involved in extensive background research; beat-by-beat analyses of the play in question, including realization of the key scenes in varying interpretations; and various forms of problem solving in a site-specific staging. Each student, moreover, is required to discharge some role in the production, whether on stage or behind the scenes. In previous years the seminar had prepared productions of Luigi Pirandello, Anton Chekhov, Ben Jonson, and John Millington Synge.

The work on *Antichrist* was only a minor departure from the model. The scholarship on the Chester cycle and the Antichrist tradition was canvassed, heavy reliance being placed on the work of Robert Lumiansky and David Mills and of Peter W. Travis for the Chester cycle and on Richard K. Emmerson for the Antichrist tradition. Character groups within the play (prophets, kings, devils, zombies, archangels) were then divided up among teams for seminar presentations. The charge was to exhaust the typological and iconographic possibilities inherent in the characters and to locate significant visual and literary sources as close as possible to the sixteenth-century west England environment while following Clifford Davidson's guidelines on the interplay of medieval art and drama. This work required constant supervision and much pump priming, but the results were valuable. In particular, we located facsimiles of several German and English illustrated lives of Antichrist. These popular block books became our principal guides in conceptualization and design. Wynkyn de Worde's version, for example, gave us the authority to cast one of the princes of the earth as Queen of the Amazons. More important, the block books helped solve the major problem of just who and what Antichrist is in the dramatic text. Not a horned monster or even a demonically possessed person, our Antichrist developed along the lines of the popular tradition, a deluded messiah unaware of his total dependence on the demonic. In portraying this all-too-plausible charlatan, our actor had the advantage of some exposure to Bertolt Brecht. Indeed, a generally Brechtian approach began to manifest itself spontaneously through the work. Our actors never asked, "What's my motivation?" but, rather, "How can we best convey the inner contradiction here?"

As the course proceeded, a production team was also assembled. Mark Pilkington, the University of Michigan's leading medieval drama specialist at the time, was instrumental in raising funds and directing theater graduate students our way. We soon had a costumer, a mask builder, a set designer, a pyrotechnist, and a stage-combat coach working directly in and with the production seminar. Our production was lavish, and since part of the overall experiment was to re-create the Chester cycle in its last decade, the 1570s, while maintaining the cycle's apparently original pageant-wagon staging, we began to see *Antichrist* as a near precursor of Elizabethan epic dramas. We therefore elaborated sword fights, explosions, and shock effects and burst out of the confines of a single pageant wagon to make much more use of the ground level, although this was viewed as a violation in some quarters. Given the many episodes in *The Coming of Antichrist* and our many attempts at simulating the Toronto conditions (including, eventually, the use of a local hay wagon), we were led to view our Toronto wagon, no doubt smaller than its medieval predecessor, as forming only the high altar-throne of an imaginary cathedral. Antichrist's wonder-working sarcophagus was placed on the ground in front of the wagon at a right angle, thus forming another focal point for action. A lot took place, therefore, in the stage nave and off the wagon, though Antichrist's canopied seat remained the visual focal point. The large cast and nearly one-hour playing time seemed to warrant this, independent of our charge to explore the possibilities of Elizabethan cycle drama. The playing area, for example, needs to be littered with corpses—four kings, two prophets, and, eventually, Antichrist himself—a field of slaughter surpassing act 5 of *Hamlet*. It was hard even to imagine this all crammed onto one wagon. Enoch and Elias's preaching, moreover, seemed directed as much to the audience as to the kings, and our deliberately expansive staging allowed the two prophet actors to rivet the crowd with their deadly serious admonitions. Since this was not a send-up, many persons in the crowd experienced some real unease. Our possible liberties with the staging reopened the question of how many ways the pageant-wagon format could have been adopted, even within the same cycle. From the experience of *Antichrist* the venerable model of one wagon-one play seemed almost a scholarly fiction. If it still holds for York, for Chester it proved woefully inadequate.

Along the way we encountered innumerable instances of how production brings new insights to the text. One of the devils claims to have snatched Antichrist's soul and this immediately cried out for a prop, a black silk handkerchief-doll yanked from Antichrist's mouth and played with in the air. Antichrist puts himself to death in the course of the play to impress his followers with his subsequent resurrection. How this was done never occurred to the scholars but became a crucial question in production. One cannot simply claim that one is dying and expect everyone to believe it. We solved the problem by appropriating an earlier motif, the sacrifice of a lamb, having Antichrist slash his own throat upstage, pop a bunch of bright red ribbons from the top of his cassock, and turn, slumped dead on the arms of his doctor, like the crucified Son lifted up by the hands of the Father. To give another example, the prophets destroy Antichrist's zombie creatures by exposing them to the Eucharistic bread. A large white wafer might have sufficed, but we opted for a round loaf with a mirror attached to its flat bottom to flash the rays of the sun. It was another example of going for more theater, rather than less, when legitimate opportunities arose. Chester certainly seemed miles beyond the relatively static icons of liturgical drama, hence the technically enhanced holy bread. These are only a few of the highlights that made the *Antichrist* project a notable learning and theater experience for all concerned. Our appreciation of the complexities of medieval drama, not only on the technical level but on the psychological and the audience perceptual levels as well, expanded exponentially. My subsequent article, "Demon or Deluded Messiah? The Characterization of Antichrist in the Chester Cycle," was just one of the results of our experiencing an ancient text complexly.

One of the last touches to our Toronto production was to create a name for the group. Mistress Quickly's reactions to Falstaff's play extempore sprang readily to mind, "He doth it as like one of the harlotry players as ever I saw" (*1 Henry IV* 2.4 395–96). Our success in Toronto led many of us to believe that the Harlotry Players might have a future in Ann Arbor.

The Harlotry Players appeared again in the fall of 1984 with an original translation of Niklaus Manuel's *The Pardon Peddler* (*Der Ablasskrämer*) as part of a local Luther quincentennial conference. Although not attached to a course, as the *Antichrist* project was, the play required a similar, if more condensed, process of research and experimentation to realize its peculiar blend of violent farce and Reformation propaganda. With these two projects a pattern was established for the players that obtains to the present: theater productions resulting from specific academic courses and productions geared to scholarly conferences or other local venues. Two summer connections with the Harlaxton symposium in Lincolnshire, for example, led to experiments with performances in Middle English. One project set out to prove that a thirteenth-century fabliau, *Dame Sirith*, was a fully articulated three-character farce, and the other project was a production of the York *Joseph's Troubles about Mary*, a sacred cuckold play. Extensive work was done with cassette recordings of the original texts made for us by Middle English specialists. The cassettes proved to be an effective way of isolating enough of the key sounds to convey the essential flavor of the original without unduly hampering the acting. As with earlier Poculi Ludique Societas experiments, the original language often proved more playable and expressive than the available modernizations.

In 1984 I introduced the course Folk Drama and Calendar Performance under a Special Topics number in the drama concentration. Harvest rituals and performance events surrounding Halloween, Martinmas, and Yuletide were studied with emphasis on the traditions of the British Isles. The students were introduced to folkloric methods by an in-the-field experience with our East Quadrangle's then-notorious Halloween party. They were also engaged in a reconstruction of a traditional mummers' play. A hybrid script was created out of the text collections of R. J. E. Tiddy and Alex Helm, with props and costumes similarly developed from visual and photographic records. The perambulation proved to be a grueling affair on a raw December day as the play wound its way through Ann Arbor from the farmer's market to an old shopping arcade to the steps of the graduate library to the side door of the president's mansion, the equivalent, certainly, of the local manor house. Emphasis was placed on the economic underpinnings of such a practice. We were not allowed, for example, to finance our refreshments other than with the proceeds gathered in the event.

A similar course in performance traditions for the Twelfth Night to Maytide span is also planned, and it is hoped that the two courses will continue in a four-semester rotation. Anchoring medieval drama concerns in the primitive performances of the yearly cycle, some of which remain intact, proved to be of great interest and value to undergraduates. It attuned them to an organic sense of the seasons, all but lost in our electronic America, thus laying the foundation for the better understanding of a liturgical calendar. It also provided an almost budgetless theater-making that was immediate and topical (most celebratory performances lend themselves to satirical accretions) and at the same time established continuity with the remote past.

The drama concentration's popular commedia dell'arte workshops were also grounded in a broad notion of medieval comic tradition and the carnivalesque, and a general concern for extending the comic horizons of medieval drama led to a collaboration with Therese Decker of Lehigh University. Working with her literal translations, the players produced acting versions of the farcical afterpieces (*sotterniën*) in the Middle Dutch Hultheim manuscript that premiered at the Ann Arbor Medieval Festival in 1986 and 1987.

As with much else in our work, the process of concrete physicalization of an ancient play text has resulted in much more satisfying solutions to textual obscurities than a strictly literary approach might yield. Topical references always require the efforts of the scholarly specialist, but in the archaeology of jokes, as we now call it, in the art of finding the implied stage direction, nothing surpasses the actor in rehearsal, particularly if the actor is attuned to archaic and elemental modes of the comic.

The Harlotry Players' orientation in the field of medieval drama is toward the low and popular traditions, rather than the ecclesiastic. It is primarily interested in what the Victorians might have termed the contaminations of religious drama. This approach has generally made medieval drama more accessible to the majority of students who have little or no relation to the traditions of medieval spirituality. The students engage the material more profitably from the angle of new historicism or the anthropology of performance than from religious or even theatrical history. That such an approach is not inimical to the realization of religious drama is demonstrated by the Harlotry Players' second connection with a Toronto cycle project, the Towneley plays of May 1985.

We had drawn the Wakefield Master's play *The Buffeting*, and the Comparative Medieval Drama course was reactivated. Since this play is smaller in scope than the Chester *Antichrist*, the course proceeded as a general survey of medieval drama, using Bevington's anthology and focusing on the English cycles, the Towneley plays, the Wakefield Master, and our particular assignment as the semester progressed. Again, extensive ransacking of visual sources complemented the survey of current scholarship on the play and the playwright. The curious overlapping in the iconography of the Fool and the Torturer of Christ proved central to our realization. James H. Marrow's massive work on northern_European Passion iconography, especially its grotesque byways, proved immensely suggestive. From our own work, not following any particular scholarly leads, we detected a deliberate patterning of the Wakefield Master's four main speaking roles on the four humors. This discovery helped the direction in clearly differenti-ating choleric Caiaphas, in red bishop's vestments, from the more calculating (melancholic?) Annas in black. The torturers were treated more in the spirit of Samuel Beckett's Didi and Gogo than as stereotypical heavies, their violent game playing not directed at filling up empty time but at overcoming the unnerving presence of the silent Christ. Our experience with clowning resulted in an even more harrowing scene of torture, leading to an inspired bit of business with a wineskin, a simulated urination on the unconscious Jesus to revive him. Our Christ actor had the difficult task of playing silence. He was introduced to the visceral body acting advocated by Jerzy Grotowski to realize his suffering presence at the center of a whirlwind of physical and verbal abuse. Iconographic research and modern acting theory came together at the moment of removing Christ's blindfold, the cloth becoming, in a long pause, the displayed veil hiding the battered face of Godhead.

We also worked with a scale model of the Toronto mansion to achieve the best balance between broad physical action and such iconic tableaux. On site in Toronto we created our forward playing area by emptying out a circular space in the crowd by means of the long ropes attached to Christ's neck and pinioned hands, thus bringing the brutality of the action directly to the audience. Our players' approach made for a greater relevance and immediacy within the iconographic tradition of the Passion than a traditionally reverent approach perhaps might have done.

To summarize early drama teaching and performance at the Residen-tial College, the following principles have always been foremost:

1. A healthy circulation between scholarly research and publication, theater productions, and new methods and materials for medieval drama teaching, all phases of which involve undergraduates as collaborators
2. Immersion in original materials, texts, and images as much as possible before the assimilation of scholarly commentary in order to encourage fresh observation and analysis
3. Application of contemporary dramatic theory, particularly in the area of acting and particularly the theory of Brecht, to medieval theater reconstruction—potentially a two-way street where one may learn as much about the roots of performance theory as about medieval drama; Brecht and the medieval dramatist both seem to view theatre as the pleasurable demonstration of fundamental contradictions
4. The production of original, stage-oriented translations and reconstructions of previously inaccessible areas of medieval drama—for example, a performance exploration of the romance *King Robert of Sicily*, also the title of several lost English plays

We have no desire at present to pursue the Poculi Ludique Societas model of a semiprofessional, semicommercial theater company. But this reluctance perhaps has its own advantages. The medieval field is one of the few areas of theater today where genuinely original experimental work can be pursued with a minimum of resources. Experiments with entire cycles are within the grasp of only fully fledged theater companies, but the individual modules out of which such theater was built are within the grasp of most teaching units. Access to minor grants and cordial relations with an active theater department are all one needs to begin practical work. The benefits are substantial: for theater people a recognition that much that is currently fascinating in Oriental theater forms is already there in our own pre-Shakespearean tradition; for students of literature, the knowledge that muscle and blood can still be given to the dry bones of our medieval past.

# Festival and Drama

## *Milla C. Riggio*

As much as any single body of literature, medieval drama measures the limits of New Criticism as a primary approach to classroom teaching. Because of the complex verse forms, patterns of imagery, and significant verbal echoes, plays like *The Castle of Perseverance*, *Wisdom*, and the Towneley and York mystery cycles amply reward close textual analysis. Read carefully, the texts tell us much about their places and times of origin and about the nature of their dramatic form. But however closely we listen, medieval play texts, read without references to their cultural context, cannot fully speak for themselves. Performing plays adds an important theatrical dimension to the study of medieval drama. But performing alone is not enough. Understanding medieval religious drama means more than comprehending, even in the most detailed and subtle way, the texts of the plays; it means coming to terms with the social context in which this drama functioned in England, Germany, Italy, and Spain in the fourteenth, fifteenth, and early sixteenth centuries. Seen from this perspective, performance embraces more than a production of a single play; it also involves the re-creation of the festival context in which the play or play cycle functioned.

Getting at that sense of function is the mainspring behind Festival and Drama, a course I teach at Trinity College only when I can find or create a drama festival for students to attend, approximately every two years. Because it depends on the availability of performances, this course changes each time it is taught. Even the concept of festival depends on the circumstances of performance and production. By defining *festivity*, in the terms of Harvey Cox, as "celebrative affirmation" that temporarily alters our ordinary sense of place and time, "help[ing] us affirm dimensions of time we might ordinarily fear, ignore, or deny" (23–24), we treat festival as a form of social or communal celebration, possibly but not necessarily religious, in which joy may be mixed with mourning. It originates in the idea of a shared feast but encompasses other ritualized festivities. For instance, festival may signify private entertainment, such as feasting in a great house, or it may suggest feast days ritually celebrated as part of an annual religious calendar. Three festival and drama courses—one centered on the Macro play *Wisdom* (hence, on morality plays, not usually associated with festival drama), one on the Towneley cycle, and one comparing medieval English cycle plays and Persian passion drama— illustrate the variety of festive settings that comfortably embrace medieval religious plays.

Whatever the focus of the course, the first two weeks are given to analyzing selected representative play texts—of morality plays such as *Wisdom, Mankind,* and *The Castle of Perseverance* or, if the course focuses on cycle drama, selected plays from the York, Chester, Towneley, or N-Town cycles. Slides and videotapes of performances, available for purchase from the University of Toronto Poculi Ludique Societas, enliven and inform the usually disappointing initial reading experience. For a morality play like *Wisdom,* one focuses on dramatic allegory and the drama inherent in expository, presentational dialogue, a point illustrated most easily by comparing Medieval plays with modern morality plays, such as Bertolt Brecht's *Caucasian Chalk Circle* and Caryll Churchill's *Vinegar Tom,* that, whatever their ideological bias, similarly dramatize debates between good and evil.

For cycle plays the textual introduction focuses on ways in which the dramatic subtext weaves historically and typologically, rather than allegorically, through the play cycle. Thus, in place of modern analogies, in the Towneley course I assign a pair of mystery plays in which a single character type appears in a variety of guises—for instance, the *Caesar Augustus* and *Herod* plays, with their comparable types of tyranny. Similarly, when I am comparing medieval cycle drama with Persian passion plays, my initial impulse is to show students how the plays themselves are structured—what kinds of dramatic rhythms move the action forward and what kinds of symbolic or allegorical patterns give the language, the mise-en-scène, and the action a broad frame of linguistic or rhetorical meaning.

All this is done without reference to festival. About three weeks into a thirteen-week course, a new idea appears—the notion of sociological function. We discuss probable audiences—aristocratic or wealthy guests invited to watch *Wisdom* in a great hall after dinner, with servants and others of lower stature perhaps lingering in the hall, a model initially based on Richard Southern's description of the performances of interludes (*Staging* 45–55; Riggio 1–18), or eclectic crowds gathered on the street or in private rooms overlooking outdoor performance areas to watch cycle plays. At this point, the course takes on an overtly ideological cast, as the students begin to understand how entertainment functions not only to amuse and edify its audience but also to reinforce or to challenge basic assumptions about hierarchy and social order.

With *Wisdom,* for instance, we stressed the extent to which the growth of lay piety in the fifteenth century cohabited with the consolidation of monarchical authority in England. Margaret Beaufort, the mother of Henry VII, provides a prime example of a woman whose piety did not in any way interfere with her political ambitions. Risking personal imprisonment to help put her son on the throne of England, even as she pursued a daunting regimen of daily prayer, Beaufort gave royal sanction to a concept of quasi-monastic lay piety. She commissioned William Caxton and Wynkyn de Worde to publish translations of fourteenth-century documents used as blueprints for private contemplation in the fifteenth century, including Walter Hilton's *Scale of Perfection* and *Vita mixta*, both source documents for the play *Wisdom*, which Beaufort had printed together in one volume. (For information on the spread of pietistic manuscripts, see Doyle 1: 1; for the sources of *Wisdom*, see Smart 9–38.)

In a society in which powerful political ambition could be reconciled with essentially cloistered contemplation, wealthy citizens used evening readings or dramatic entertainment to provide both moral instruction and stimulus to personal devotion. For instance, some works, such as *Speculum vitae*, a lengthy poetic explication of the *Pater Noster*, may have been used in place of romances as evening reading. It is not difficult to imagine a play like *Wisdom* as entertainment in a wealthy private home. Beaufort herself may well have presented a play in which Christian allegory converges with and reinforces traditional social authority. The dramatization of Christ as a royal monarch, while in line with standard iconographic portraits, sublimates the connection between monarchical power and divine sovereignty into a condensed visual image of enthroned authority (Riggio 8–16).

Thus, a play like *Wisdom*, which structurally resembles disguisings or masques, serves the function that Stephen Orgel assigns the Renaissance masque; that is, it helps to establish and support the concept of monarchy (42–46). Such an idea is not hard to explain to students, but American students with no symbols of monarchy as points of reference in their own experience can better realize this concept when they see the way in which hosting a lavish dinner and providing a play, even a play of moral instruction, implicitly testifies to the personal power and authority of the host. When God appears in the play dressed in the robes that signify the highest form of secular power in the culture, that of the king, the effect is intensified. For that reason, this course ended with a festival production of the play in a banquet setting, presented before a fictional Edward IV and his queen (Riggio 2–3). Edward at one end of the hall and Christ at the other end— dressed in exactly the same way, as obvious doubles—exemplified the way in which the visual pictures of drama subtly reinforce concepts of power and authority. A videotape of this Trinity production, available for a modest fee on request from the Trinity College English Department, makes it possible to illustrate this process in courses without restaging the play, though for students there is no substitute for the festival.

The great processional festivals of the Middle Ages, particularly Corpus Christi and Whitsuntide, also functioned to reinforce existing social hierarchies, though in a different way. Thus, my Towneley cycle course stressed a different set of sociological referents. When discussing cycle drama, one is able to draw on a body of original documents that do not exist for morality plays. We begin with a few of the documents collected by Peter Meredith and John E. Tailby (47, 48, 56, 71, 188–89). Partly using selected dramatic records, especially those collected in the Records of Early English Drama series, under the general editorship of Alexandra F. Johnston, and *The Revels History of Drama* (Cawley et al., pt. 1, ch. 6), we then discuss the structure and the organization of the religious processional feasts, stressing the variety of possible performance styles (place and scaffold, pageant wagon) while emphasizing the degree to which the trade guilds—for instance, the goldsmiths, the vintners, the mercers—might show off their wares and their wealth through the production of their plays. Such a focus allows one to discuss the economic organization of medieval towns, a key factor in the argument about power and authority.

However, the Towneley cycle—named after an owner of the manuscript, rather than a location for the plays—does not have a single identifiable home. The cycle has long been assumed to belong to Wakefield, but, following the hypothesis developed by dramaturge Alexandra Johnston, the Toronto production of the Towneley cycle conjectured a consolidated West Riding cycle, an idea challenged to some extent by documents collected in *The Revels History* and by Martin Stevens's review of the Toronto production (Johnston, "Notes" 2–3; Cawley et al. 50–58; Stevens, "Processus" 190–92). By tracing this argument, one is able to teach students how much of our own reconstruction of historical reality is based on educated guesses.

After a semester of reading plays and discussing social context, we staged *Caesar Augustus* during the Toronto Towneley festival. What we learned from attending the festival did, as with *Wisdom*, verify the ideas of the course. To choose appropriate costumes, we had studied the possibilities of iconography in costuming—determining, for instance, that Caesar would have been dressed as a medieval king, rather than as a Roman emperor. In Toronto the students were able to judge other productions by what they had learned. By staging the plays on fixed scaffolds around a circle, the production tested Johnston's staging hypothesis (Johnston 2–3; Stevens, "Processus" 190). The students quickly realized that some plays adapted to this staging concept remarkably well, while others—which required changes of set, such as the *Magi* play, produced by Syracuse University—seemed ill at ease in the space allotted them. The disjuncture of theatrical form within the cycle that this difference suggested prepared us for Martin Stevens's interpretation, presented during a symposium session at the festival, of the Towneley manuscript not as a play script but as a coffee-table book, beautifully illustrated and handsomely written but possibly not designed for staging ("Compilation").

Most important, I emphasize festival as a component of the course not only to test hypotheses about the original conditions of production but also to examine ways in which the modern festival fulfills some of the same functions one associates with the original cycles, though in a different, more secular context. As I stressed in the review of the performance I presented during the festival symposium, watching plays together for seven hours a day for two days (at least five hours of which were spent in driving rain), the Toronto audience became temporarily melded into a community of spectators. Friendships were formed among strangers; space was shared and disputed. Time itself took on a different dimension inside the production circle, as spectators hovered between aesthetic pleasure and some form of religious persuasion (Grimes 62–63). My students were mesmerized; though not required to stay the course, they remained through the rain to the end. And two years later they still discussed this experience with other students as a moment out of time. Without consistent civic or religious sponsorship, this modern drama festival did not teach students much about the ways in which the Corpus Christi feasts functioned in Wakefield or in other English cities. Moreover, the plays—organized by colleges, churches, and drama groups—lacked central cohesiveness in costuming and acting styles. And one could not gain from them much information about such problems in early English society. Did guilds in the same city also take the same kind of independent attitude toward production that we did? Did God always change his face and costume radically from play to play? Perhaps, but this festival, which brought acting groups from across America and Canada, could not confirm that fact.

What the festival did was to demonstrate that, even when divorced from its religious origins, a communal event such as this production powerfully creates its own ambience. The festival transcends the particularities of production. There were good plays, bad plays, plays in different styles. But, taken together, the event created a sense of shared community that gave it momentum to absorb weak productions and dramatic inconsistencies. Without knowledge of the plays, no one would have stayed through the production. But the resulting experience was far more than the sum of its parts.

A third Festival and Drama course placed medieval drama in a radically challenging frame of reference. Cotaught in the spring of 1988 with David Parry, former artistic director of the University of Toronto Poculi Ludique Societas, this course compared medieval Christian festivals—particularly those like Corpus Christi and Whitsuntide, which centered on dramatic representations of the Passion of Christ—with modern Shi'ite religious festival rituals called *ta'ziyeh*. *Ta'ziyeh*, or "mourning," processions and plays are celebrated annually in Shi'i culture during the first ten days of the month of Muharram to commemorate the assassination of Husayn, the grandson of Muhammad, on the plain of Karbala in AD 680. (For the only English translation of a full cycle of *ta'ziyeh* plays, see Pelly; for a translation of *Moses and the Wandering Dervish*, performed at Trinity College in April 1988, write to Milla C. Riggio.)

Like the Passion of Christ for Christianity, the martyrdom of Husayn is a central religious event in Shi'ite culture. As commemorative drama that forms the occasion for the renewal of religious faith by reenacting the martyrdom of a central religious figure, *ta'ziyeh* plays resemble medieval cycle plays in their episodic nature, their design as outdoor drama, their focus on the redemptive aspects of human suffering, and their idealization of personal martyrdom. Like European cycle plays, *ta'ziyeh* plays form part of an elaborate processional rite designed to renew Shi'a faith annually.

Students taking this course hosted the *ta'ziyeh* drama festival and conference held at Trinity in the spring of 1988 while studying medieval cycle plays in preparation for the University of Toronto production of the N-Town cycle of mystery plays; under the direction of David Parry, Trinity staged play number 10 in the abridged Toronto production of the N-Town cycle. In this production, our play, which dramatized Joseph's discovery of Mary's pregnancy, was entitled *Joseph's Troubles*. By working with performances in two such radically different traditions, the students were forced to see elements of familiarity in the Shi'ite tradition that, particularly because of processional self-flagellation, seemed initially to be totally foreign, even barbaric. The foreignness was enhanced by differences in theatrical style and dramatic form. In *ta'ziyeh* plays the heroes sing or chant their roles in a style that resembles the chanting of orthodox rabbis; villains shout in unpleasant guttural voices. There are many kinds of *ta'ziyeh* plays; some feature the final day of judgment, whereas others focus, as did the Trinity play, on biblical characters like Moses and Abraham. Such plays are played throughout the year in Iran. But the central *ta'ziyeh* plays, those played specifically during the festival of Muharram, are epic plays centered on military battles. Characters frequently enter and exit on horseback, and, rather than focusing on the life history of Husayn, each day presents the martyrdom of yet another hero on the plain of Karbala.

To identify the common elements among such differences, we not only compared play texts but also stressed the relation between the Qu'ran and the Bible, noting the similarities between the Shi'ite "holy family" of Muhammad, his daughter Fatima—sometimes called the new virgin—and her husband, Ali, and her sons, Hasan and Husayn. Gradually, familiar elements began to emerge from this texture of difference. Students began to perceive the Christian traditions, which they had associated almost entirely with past European history, in the context of ongoing, non-European, non-Christian cultural festivals.

This last course had the deepest influence on the students; it forced them to study two distinctive festival traditions, one from the West and one from the Middle East and then to become aware of lines of intersection between these presumably disparate worlds. Our *ta'ziyeh* had, to some extent, been cut off from its Iranian cultural origins, illustrating the possibilities of reviving a tradition in exile, as our Iranian director did, rather than performing it in its natural habitat. And yet, the students did experience festival as a process of cross-cultural, communal ritual that, even in exile, temporarily creates cohesion among the participants. By focusing on an ongoing religious tradition, such as that in Iran, the students began to understand the swirl of pieties and fears that surround ritual traditions in periods of radical social change. Such a process functions ideologically, as well as theatrically. Understanding this, the students in each festival and drama course perceive cultural rituals and religious beliefs as components in the political and sociological framework of society.

# Tossing Mak Around

*Mícheál F. Vaughan*

A major difficulty facing the teacher of dramatic texts is getting students who are used to reading poems and narratives to realize that the words on the page are not the play itself but, rather, a script for its performance and that any interpretation of the text must take conscious account of the nontextual aspects of that performance. Our understanding, as well as our teaching, suffers if we ignore these necessary complements to the dramatic text. We all have our favorite examples to call students' attention to the necessity of visualizing the performance in order to understand the play. When the action accompanying the words is indicated in the scripted words or in stage directions, we can justify the necessity more readily. However, when these aids to the imagination are absent, we must work harder to summon up the embodiment of the text in action. When we are ignorant or uncertain about the conventions of staging, movement, and delivery—as we generally are about medieval drama—we must work hard to convince ourselves and to inform our students about what must be going on in a play. With a few exceptions, we must try to recover the performance from the scanty evidence of the texts. Unfortunately, most medieval playwrights did not use their dialogue, as Shakespeare and others frequently did, to tell the audience what is happening and where it is occurring; and medieval directors and scribes did not rubricate the text for the benefit of later readers.

The character Mak in the Wakefield *Second Shepherd's Play* provides an effective way to highlight these issues. Discussing his role in the play can lead a class to examine some larger issues about the process and goals of literary criticism, as well as its limits. First, I describe how scholars have offered many interpretations and explanations of Mak: he is an outcast, a Cain figure; a diabolical deceiver; Antichrist or his herald; an emblem of the effects of socioeconomic oppression; a sinner functioning as audience-surrogate. The list can be extended, and the competition among these views is fierce because some resolution of the issue is necessary: without understanding Mak, we cannot understand this play. On the other hand, by focussing on his comings and goings, we can illuminate the idea of the *Second Shepherds' Play*.

The last we see of Mak in the play demands that we engage in acts of dramatic and historical imagination: after his "hee frawde" is uncovered by the three shepherds, they "cast hym in canvas" (Cawley, *Wakefield*, lines 594; 628). This event has been variously interpreted: it is some rough fun, a punishment, an act of ridicule or of forgiveness, an aid to the onset of childbirth (given metaphoric or symbolic weight), or a subtle figuration of the spiritual winnowing of the wheat from the chaff at the eschaton. The disagreements are many, and the subtle refinements in nuances indicate the wide range of critical interpretation, as well as the implied necessity of having this wordless event cohere with interpretative views derived (presumably) from careful readings of the text. The critics' views of the meaning of the canvas tossing depend not on its own significance, externally determined, but on how this neutral or ambiguous sign attains meaning from the context in which it occurs.

However, even after these possibilities are examined, a couple of questions about this event in the play need answering. Whether we opt for one interpretation of the canvasing of Mak or lean toward its being a polysemous symbol, we are left with some unresolved critical matters, which those who have exercised themselves on the canvasing of Mak seem to have almost completely ignored. For example, what happens to Mak after the shepherds have finished tossing him about? Does he lie on the ground? Does he go home? Does he depart the stage altogether (however that might be accomplished)? To choose among these options is to make different sense of the play.

After he is cast in canvas, Mak says nothing more in the play. But where is he when he is silenced? Is silence the dramatic equivalent of nonexistence? Does absence from the ears dictate absence from the eyes? From the mind? This play has a number of entrances but no obvious exits: the three shepherds and Mak all enter at the beginning. On the matter of exits, however, the play remains silent. Movements in and from and to the *plataea* (undifferentiated acting space, usually not distinct from the audience) are reported; likewise for the two *stationes* (fixed, defined settings, associated with one or more of the characters). We are left uncertain, however, about some important matters, such as where Mak comes from when the manuscript reports his entrance: "Tunc intrat Mak" (following line 189)? Our sense of his character and his moral comparability or incomparability to the shepherds dictates our answer. If Mak enters from his *statio* and returns to it at the end, we imply that he operates as some kind of principle of disorder and evil; we align him with the forces of darkness and must take his repentance at the end as a further "frawde."

But I do not find the implication of Mak's moral fixity altogether satisfactory; to imply his damnation goes against what I feel to be the play's presentation of his humanity. He may be morally worse than the three shepherds, but they are not perfect by any means, and it is their moral development that the play charts. So I wonder about Mak and try to get my students to wonder about him: Where does he go when the shepherds go to Bethlehem? Does he go home (because he is unregenerate)? Does he stay in the *plataea* (because he has become a bit more humanized by his experience, on the road to true repentance if not yet ready to enter the ranks of the morally enlightened)? Or does he tag along, silent, behind the shepherds (to suggest that he too has received some moral revelation in the course of his experience and that he has moved from parody to participation, even if he cannot proclaim it with the fluency of the shepherds)? Or does he exit into the audience (and so give pointed effect to the moral lesson of the play)? All these scenarios seem to me possible. But only one of them can be right at any given time for any given performance. The play's director must choose one action. This performance fact I force on my students to make them sharpen their own readings of the play and to help them produce their own conclusions to the play that arise from considerations of its central issues, of its integrity as a work of high art. This fact also provides a way for me to make the case that they cannot hide behind the contemporary critical Laodiceanism: that the text can mean all these things. It certainly didn't when it was performed, and the effort to interpret becomes an act of historical imagining, an effort to find the best solution to a problem that, practically speaking, can admit of only one solution.

I then go on to raise similar questions about the location of Mak and Gyll's house and its relation to the Bethlehem stable. Are these two settings visible throughout, on either side of the *plataea*, with Mary, the Child, and the Angel as present to view as Gyll in her cottage? Or does Bethlehem replace Mak and Gyll's cottage? Such a substitution would raise complications—deciding where Mak goes after the blanket tossing—to say nothing of the moral implications that would arise from a doubling of the parts that some have suggested accompanies this transformation of the cottage into the Bethlehem stable. These are not insignificant questions: a director must make decisions about such matters, and the reader, too, must ask on what grounds such decisions can be made. Then we are left to ask how we test the adequacy or the superiority of any of the options available to us.

Even if we leave aside the problematic question of determining authorial intention, we may find it useful to grapple with historical questions about the actions, movements, and locations likely to have been used at Wakefield. Furthermore, unless we wish to hide from the implications of such questions for our reading and interpretation, we ought not, even in the face of our nearly absolute ignorance, to claim that these questions are insignificant. Since we don't have and may never have the safety net of performance records or reviews or a clear sense of the pertinent theatrical conventions and traditions, we cannot depend on such authorities to guide our choice. We have a text of the play. But it is only an outline, a supplement. In the absence of stage directions or other authority, we fall back on the slippery meaning of the play as the authority for our performance, and where the text is silent, we must still decide: how am I going to deal with Mak's entrance and his exit if I have him exit? To make no decision would be to misread and misrepresent the play as it survives.

After I have raised these questions and critical problems, I try out my solution. By such an interpretative experiment I stimulate my students to question their own solutions, since I am not entirely confident that mine qualifies as the best. Also, I am less interested in arriving at some firm consensus than in raising more questions and in suggesting the kinds of things that could be adduced as evidence to support their decisions. I begin with my two basic axioms: first, that the action of this play, as many have pointed out, operates on parodic principles and, second, that these principles are best served by having Bethlehem on one side of the *plataea* and Mak and Gyll's cottage on the other. With such background, what can we say about the events after the canvasing of Mak? After the shepherds toss Mak around, they lie down to sleep, the second time in the play they do this—a repetition that I argue is structurally and thematically important to the play. In the first instance the shepherds insist that Mak sleep in their midst. In the second, let us presume in the absence of contrary evidence that he, too, is worn out from the exertion and lies down with them. This solution not only applies Occam's razor to the problem but provides a striking punctuation of the play's action, making clear the subdivisions in the play's orderly structuring of the plot.

What happens in the case of the first sleep scene? Mak gets up, chants a magic spell, steals a sheep, and departs for his home, leaving the shepherds to sleep on. What does the text tell us about the second sleep? An angel arrives (the real "sond from a greatt lordyng" [line 202]) and sings the "Gloria"; the shepherds arise, discuss the angelic pronouncement and the prophecies, and depart for Bethlehem. To mark the contrasting actions, I suggest that in the second instance Mak should be the one to remain asleep while the shepherds depart and return. At the level of the play's moral lesson, this works well: Mak has not achieved the shepherds' enlightenment, but he is also not consigned to static anti-Christianity, nor is he consigned to some outer darkness by being off stage. He has reached the *plataea*, has learned something, and seems to be morally improved, but he is not yet fully awake to the spiritual realities that the shepherds now recognize. The play, in this view, is morally optimistic, not Manichaean; reform, even of the deceitful Mak, is possible, but such reform is represented in this play as, first of all, a process within a person; not some transformation arising primarily from external or transcendent revelation.

The attempt to recover this play's meaning gains in force and specificity if it is cast in these performance terms, if the students try, as directors, to choose among the viable options before us for the location and the action of these characters. Does it make a difference if we choose to locate the Bethlehem stable and Mak and Gyll's cottage on opposite sides of the acting area? Or if, to choose the more common alternative, we replace the cottage with the stable for the last scene? Of course it does. Each version has its attractions, but, as directors, we cannot have both. As readers and critics, we may contemplate the two possibilities, but we must be ready to choose between them when the necessity for action replaces the freedom of thought. Likewise, we must do something with Mak—he must come from somewhere, and we must decide what happens to him when he goes silent. On these decisions and through the process of sifting and assessing evidence that permits us to arrive at such decisions, we not only arrive at informed interpretations of the play but also put ourselves more immediately in the presence of the enacted drama and its historical situation. I find that this approach to the *Second Shepherds' Play* leads to a better understanding of the play, and it has the additional benefit of raising crucial and helpful questions about the process of reading and deriving meaning from literary texts. Some of these lessons can be extrapolated from the study of the *Second Shepherds' Play* and applied effectively to other historical, literary, and artistic artifacts.

# L'ENVOI

## Why Teach Medieval Drama?
### David Bevington

The question, finally, is not how to teach medieval drama but why. This drama used to be taught chiefly because it existed as a part of English and medieval literature and because the plays could be presented as the precursors of a greater English drama in the age of Shakespeare. This approach, however much it may have been oversimplified by historical scholars caught up in Darwinian assumptions of progressive development, can in a less doctrinaire form provide a sustained interest for any of us curious to know our own past and how things came to be as they are. Or we can look at the plays as manifestations of medieval culture in various periods. That is, we can approach the plays as documents in social history—as illustrations of marital conflict, class difference, attitudes toward authority, the condition of the poor. The plays can be read and acted, like picture Bibles, as popular theology, reflecting changing attitudes in the medieval period toward the nature of Incarnation. The plays can be seen as vivid indexes of developments in language.

Especially in the early years of medieval drama, these texts provide us a varied workshop in which to study the birth of drama in its complex and even antithetical relation to liturgy. The birth of this drama must afford some insight into the way the drama of ancient Greece first originated. The engendering of dramatic forms and genres, the creation of dialogue, the invention of character and motivation, the devising of a sense of theatrical space, the investing of gesture with theatrical meaning—all these essentials of dramatic representation can be seen as coming into being with virtually no prior literary model, hence testifying to the power and the inventiveness of the mimetic impulse in its quintessential state.

Medieval drama offers us other problems that seldom fail to be interesting in the classroom, problems that deal with what this drama was like and how it was performed. Staging, for example, remains a tantalizing intellectual puzzle. How was it possible to stage all the York pageants on one day—if they were, in fact, done on one day—using individual pageant wagons at a series of acting stations when any short pageant would have had to wait for a long pageant in front of it to finish up at each station? How varied were the conditions of performance at different locales in England and on the Continent? How did town or city governance affect the modes of production? How much did the cycles change from year to year as the guilds themselves changed and as municipalities encountered good times and bad times? How did the cycles begin, and were they essentially translated from existing Latin texts or did Western drama suddenly take a leap forward? When did such changes occur in the various locations in England and on the Continent? How closely related were developments in England to those across the English Channel? The puzzles are still endless, the discoveries constantly new (as reflected, for example, in the ongoing work of the Records of Early English Drama project), the opportunities for research and criticism open-ended.

Medieval drama offers an exciting field to prospective new students, undergraduate and graduate, because they soon discover, if they decide to enter the field as young professionals, that they can be heard at annual gatherings of medievalists if they have something to say. The field is a small one in which people can quickly get to know one another and one another's work. I well remember my own excitement and pleasure in discovering in the early 1960s that the huge Vanity Fair of literary professionals, the Modern Language Association, contained within it a little devoted cell of medieval drama types who met whenever possible to find out the latest from one another. I went to hear Alan Nelson's latest theory about staging, to find out what Martin Stevens and A. C. Cawley were discovering in their editing of the Wakefield cycle, to savor the antagonisms of a musicological-literary debate between William L. Smoldon and O. B. Hardison over the role of music in the taxonomy of early liturgical texts, to listen to Robert Potter's pleading for more careful attention to Dutch drama. The group was young and international and comparativist. Its members dined together, stayed up late in animated conversation, and generally ignored the rest of the conference going on around it, though many who participated were also good medievalists in other areas as well. And a similar experience is still possible today at Western Michigan University's annual medieval conference in Kalamazoo and at other gatherings, as well as at the Modern Language Association.

These are considerations designed to attract potential specialists in the field, but the most important reason for teaching medieval drama is more universal and applies to undergraduate and graduate student alike. No subject more genuinely satisfies the demands of a liberal education: that we attempt to free the mind by enabling students to go well beyond their previous experiences into realms that offer a new perspective on most of the values they have previously encountered. The values I have in mind include the obtaining of some perspective on one's own assumptions, biases, and beliefs, together with a growing awareness of and appreciation for the assumptions of those who occupy an essentially different world from one's own. Medieval drama used to be taught, as O. B. Hardison has shown us, from a Whig Liberal Protestant perspective, as a product of a childish and superstitious medieval world in which the chief value to be found was a purely unconscious anticipation of the greatness of Renaissance drama. In other words, this drama was offered in such a way as not to challenge the prevailing ideology of those who taught and studied. Such an approach is no longer predominant. Instead, we ask our students to consider a civilization that differs strikingly from their own, and we ask them to consider whether a civilization capable of producing the Gothic cathedral and Geoffrey Chaucer could have lacked its own sense of form and coherence. Was not the drama coherent, too, according to an intuitive set of principles owing essentially nothing to classical antiquity and hence not conforming to the rediscovered ideals of neoclassical form so often imposed on Renaissance art by the historical and classically trained scholars of past generations? To find a beauty in a whole genre of literature that had been condescended to by previous scholars and readers as worthy only of antiquarian study is to liberate the mind in a wonderful way.

I was lucky enough to come along at a time when this particular kind of deliverance was at hand, just as, presumably, a similar kind of deliverance is possible for students today. My own background was that of Protestant white middle-western America, even though I was born and brought up in New York City and then in North Carolina; both my grandparents were Methodist ministers, one along the Ohio River and one in upstate New York. At Harvard in the 1940s and 1950s, as an undergraduate and graduate student, I could scarcely find medieval drama in the curriculum except as a background to the drama of the Renaissance. The Latin Middle Ages were similarly neglected. My opportunity came after graduate school in the form of an offer to reedit Joseph Quincy Adams's *Chief Pre-Shakespearean Dramas* for Houghton Mifflin (originally published in 1924). They and I expected it would be a revision in kind: inattentive to the liturgical drama and church drama of the twelfth and thirteenth centuries, selectively interested in the cycles for the comic realism of the Wakefield Master and the York Realist (and definitely not interested in plays about the Marian legends, the Assumption of the Virgin, Antichrist, saints' lives, and such nonbiblical material), paying particular attention to the morality play and its more secular manifestations in the sixteenth century, giving generous representation to neoclassical comedies and tragedies like *Roister Doister* and *Gorboduc*, and so on, toward the culmination of all this historical development in *The Famous Victories of Henry the Fifth*—right at Shakespeare's doorstep. The Vice was there in a play like *Cambises* to be studied as a precursor of Richard III and Iago and Edmund. Never mind that the coverage was not very medieval; the collection had many wonderful plays in it one wouldn't want to give up, including some like John Heywood's *John John* and Richard Edwards's *Damon and Pythias* that were not easily found in print elsewhere.

The trouble was that Adams's collection encouraged the teacher to skim past medieval drama in a rapid journey toward the Renaissance. No other anthology addressed medieval drama in its own right. In other words, I was confronting the issue of canon formation (in more recent times a hot topic of literary criticism) and the way in which the selection of what we read in the classroom affects the view we will have of our traditions, our culture, our values. For better or worse, a new anthology would have to choose whether to reaffirm a previous generation's interest in early English drama as pre-Shakespearean or to focus on some things that appear to have interested medieval dramatists themselves—iconic representations of key moments in Christian history, typological recurrence in the portraying of those key moments, presentational staging in a theatrical space representing the entire cosmos.

As I began reading seriously in medieval drama to consider how an anthology might be put together along different lines, I realized that Adams's format, largely inherited from that of John Matthews Manly (*Specimens of the Pre-Shakesperean Drama*, published in 1897) before him and still others in the late nineteenth century (notably Alfred W. Pollard's *English Miracle Plays, Moralities, and Interludes*, first edition published in 1890), was excluding too much. (For a more detailed consideration of this problem, see my essay "Drama Editing and Its Relation to Recent Trends in Literary Criticism.") Karl Young's *Drama of the Medieval Church*, published in 1933, opened up new vistas, but, I wondered, should one adopt his developmental scheme of placing Easter drama first, even in its most elaborate forms, then Christmas drama, and finally drama of other occasions in the Church year, in disregard (as Young admitted) of the actual chronology of the individual texts? These were some of the questions I pondered in the early 1960s, while I was teaching at the University of Virginia, trying out what for me were new ways to teach medieval drama.

Then in 1965 came Hardison's revolutionary book *Christian Rite and Christian Drama in the Middle Ages*, which made beautifully clear the dissatisfaction I felt with what the Adams collection had to offer. At the University of Chicago in the late 1960s and early 1970s I was fortunate enough to have Alan H. Nelson as a junior colleague and Jerome Taylor as a senior colleague; from them I learned that the brave new world of medieval studies, so new to me, was, in fact, a broadly based movement well underway but in need of a different sort of teaching text. Some graduate students in medieval drama—such as Peter W. Travis and Gordon Kipling, who are by now important leaders in the field—gave new impetus to medieval drama studies, as did some students of the early Renaissance, like Steven Urkowitz, David Kastan, and John Cox. The meetings at the Modern Language Association and at Kalamazoo, among others, provided a forum for the continuing discussion I have already described. It was at these meetings and in new publications that I encountered the work of Stanley J. Kahrl, Lawrence M. Clopper, Glynne Wickham, V. A. Kolve, and many others. Productions of whole cycles and of long plays like *The Castle of Perseverance* at Toronto, inspired and organized by Alexandra F. Johnston and David Parry, became the occasion of biennial pilgrimages in which we could try out staging theories in actual performance. A yearlong seminar at the University of Chicago in 1978–79 sponsored by the National Endowment for the Humanities brought together a group of young scholars who continue to publish joint studies, including Richard K. Emmerson, Pamela Sheingorn, Ronald B. Herzman, Huston Diehl, and Michael Hall; in 1985 most of this group brought out a jointly written study entitled *Homo, Memento Finis: The Iconography of Just Judgment in Medieval Art and Drama*, under the aegis of Clifford Davidson at Western Michigan University (Bevington et al.).

I offer this brief autobiography to describe the genesis of *Medieval Drama*, published by Houghton Mifflin in 1975, as a collaborative effort and as a testimonial to my own liberation, such as it is. *Medieval Drama* is the story, for me, of a search for a medieval drama wholly unknown before in my experience, a drama that my preconceived aesthetic theories could not account for, any more than my Protestant sensibilities could find the significance in medieval Catholicism. Students today, generally predisposed to be tolerant and to grant the value of a pluralistic approach to culture, no doubt find this particular discovery easier and less surprising than I did, though they still have much to learn about the richness and the intellectual complexity of medieval culture. The continual irony of history is such that today's students may well find it hugely liberating to be steeped in the classical training that in earlier generations helped produce an inflexibility toward most things medieval and the shift in canon away from medieval texts. Still, access to the wholeness of medieval culture is something our students today need. If they have learned to be more tolerant, in other ways they are even more distant than I was from what medieval drama has to offer. They need to make new discoveries with the help, presumably, of new anthologies and texts. Probably we should help them move toward greater comparativeness, making more use of Continental drama and of recent methods in interpretation. Whatever the specific choices, the discovery will be as significant as it is liberating. It will once again validate medieval drama as a field in which the teaching of such values as the fuller awareness of a culture very different from our own has an especially important place.

# CONTRIBUTORS AND SURVEY PARTICIPANTS

The following scholars and teachers generously agreed to participate in the survey of approaches to teaching medieval English drama that preceded the preparation of this volume. Without their invaluable assistance and support, the volume would not have been possible.

Robert Alexander, Point Park Coll.; Mark Allen, Univ. of Texas, San Antonio; Frank Ardolino, Univ. of Hawaii, Manoa; Kathleen M. Ashley, Univ. of Southern Maine; Beverly Beem, Walla Walla Coll.; Sidney Berger, Richland Community Coll.; David Bevington, Univ. of Chicago; Karen Bjelland, Catholic Univ. of America; Jane Chance, Rice Univ.; John C. Coldewey, Univ. of Washington; Theresa Coletti, Univ. of Maryland, College Park; Fletcher Collins, Mary Baldwin Coll.; Catherine Corman, Brigham Young Univ.; Clifford Davidson, Western Michigan Univ.; Huston Diehl, Univ. of Iowa; John Elliott, Syracuse Univ.; Grosvenor Fattic, Loma Linda Univ.; Maris Fiondella, Fordham Univ., Lincoln Center; C. Clifford Flanigan, Indiana Univ., Blooming- ton; Peter H. Greenfield, Univ. of Puget Sound; Wilfred Guerin, Louisiana State Univ., Shreveport; Thomas Hahn, Univ. of Rochester; Michael L. Hall, National Endowment for the Humanities; Thomas Hanks, Baylor Univ.; Robert W. Hanning, Columbia Univ.; Elizabeth Hanson-Smith, California State Univ., Sacramento; Kevin Harty, La Salle Univ.; Ronald Heckelman, Univ. of California, Irvine; Ronald Herzman, State Univ. of New York, Geneseo; Paul Hesselink, Covenant Coll.; Julia Bolton Holloway, Southern Methodist; Stanley Kahrl, Ohio State Univ., Columbus; Richard Knowles, Mount Allison Univ.; V. A. Kolve, Univ. of California, Los Angeles; Anne Middleton, Univ. of California, Berkeley; David Mills, Univ. of Leeds; Russell Peck, Univ. of Rochester; Marion Perret, Manhattanville Coll.; Robert Potter, Univ. of California, Santa Barbara; Paul Rathburn, Univ. of Notre Dame; Donnie Rigby, Walla Walla Coll.; Milla C. Riggio, Trinity College, Hartford; Denis Salter, Univ. of Calgary; Gary Schmidt, Calvin Coll.; Pamela Sheingorn, Baruch Coll., City Univ. of New York; Frances Shirley, Wheaton Coll., Wheaton; Martin Stevens, Graduate Center, City Univ. of New York; Lorraine Stock, Univ. of Houston, Houston; Peter W. Travis, Dartmouth Coll.; Míčéal F. Vaughan, Univ. of Washington; John Velz, Univ. of Texas, Austin; Martin W. Walsh, Univ. of Michigan, Ann Arbor; John Wasson, Washington State Univ.; Jerry White, Central Missouri State Univ.; Mary Williams, North Carolina State Univ.; Thomas Wright, Auburn Univ.

# WORKS CITED

## Primary Sources

Abrams, M. H., gen. ed. *Norton Anthology of English Literature*. 5th ed. 2 vols. New York: Norton, 1986.

Adams, Joseph Quincy, ed. *Chief Pre-Shakespearian Dramas*. Boston: Houghton, 1924.

Astington, John, ed. *Everyman*. Poculi Ludique Societas Performance Text. Toronto: Poculi, 1980.

Augustine. *On Christian Doctrine*. Trans. D. W. Robertson, Jr. Library of Liberal Arts. Indianapolis: Bobbs, 1958.

Axton, Richard, and John Stevens, trans. *Medieval French Plays*. Oxford: Blackwell, 1971.

Baker, Donald C., and John L. Murphy, eds. *The Digby Plays: Facsimiles of the Plays in Bodley MSS Digby 133 and e Museo 160*. Leeds Texts and Monographs, Medieval Drama Facsimiles 3. Leeds: U of Leeds, School of English, 1976.

Baker, Donald C., John L. Murphy, and Louis B. Hall, Jr., eds. *The Late Medieval Religious Plays of Bodleian MSS Digby 133 and e Museo 160*. Early English Text Society OS 283. London: Oxford UP, 1982.

Beadle, Richard, ed. *The York Plays*. York Medieval Texts. Baltimore: Arnold, 1982.

———. *The York Plays: A Facsimile of British Library MS Additional 35290*. Leeds Texts and Monographs, Medieval Drama Facsimiles 7. Leeds: U of Leeds, School of English, 1983.

Beadle, Richard, and Pamela M. King, eds. *York Mystery Plays: A Selection in Modern Spelling*. New York: Oxford UP, 1984.

Beuken, W. H., and James H. Marrow, eds. *Spiegel van den leven ons Heren [Mirror of the Life of Our Lord]: Diplomatic Edition of the Text and Facsimile of the 42 Miniatures of a 15th-Century Typological Life of Christ in the Pierpont Morgan Library*. Dornspijk: Davaco, 1979.

Bevington, David, ed. *The Macro Plays*. Folger Facsimiles, Manuscript Series 1. Washington: Folger, 1972.

———, ed. *Medieval Drama*. Boston: Houghton, 1975.

Blackston, Mary A., ed. *Robin Hood and the Friar*. Poculi Ludique Societas Performance Text. Toronto: Poculi Ludique Societas, 1981.

Block, K. S., ed. *Ludus Coventriae: Or, The Plaie Called Corpus Christi*. Early English Text Society OS 120, 1922. London: Oxford UP, 1960.

Brockett, Oscar, ed. *Plays for the Theatre*. 5th ed. New York: Holt, 1988.

Brown, John Russell, trans. *The Complete Plays of the Wakefield Master*. London: Heinemann, 1983.

Burns, Edward, ed. and trans. *The Chester Mystery Cycle: A New Staging Text*. Liverpool: Liverpool UP, 1987.

Caiger-Smith, A. *English Medieval Mural Paintings*. Oxford: Clarendon, 1963.

Cawley, A. C., ed. *Everyman*. Old and Middle English Texts. Manchester: Manchester UP, 1961.

———, ed. *Everyman and Medieval Miracle Plays*. Everyman's Library. New York: Dutton, 1959.

———, ed. *The Wakefield Pageants in the Towneley Cycle*. Old and Middle English Texts. Manchester: Manchester UP, 1958.

Cawley, A. C., and Martin Stevens, eds. *The Towneley Cycle: A Facsimile of Huntingdon MS HM1*. Leeds Texts and Monographs, Medieval Drama Facsimiles 2. Leeds: U of Leeds, School of English, 1976.

Clopper, Lawrence, ed. *Records of Early English Drama: Chester*. Toronto: U of Toronto P, 1980.

Collins, Fletcher, Jr. *Medieval Church Music-Dramas: A Repertory of Complete Plays*. Charlottesville: UP of Virginia, 1976.

Cooper, Geoffrey, and Christopher Wortham, eds. *Everyman*. Nedlands: U of Western Australia P, 1980.

Craig, Hardin, ed. *Two Coventry Corpus Christi Plays*. 2nd ed. Early English Text Society OS 87. Oxford: Oxford UP, 1957.

Creeth, Edmund, ed. *Tudor Plays: An Anthology of Early English Drama*. 1966. New York: Norton, 1972.

Davidson, Clifford, ed. *A Middle English Treatise on the Playing of Miracles*. Washington: UP of America, 1981.

Davies, R. T., ed. *The Corpus Christi Play of the English Middle Ages*. Totowa: Rowman, 1972.

Davis, Norman, ed. *Non-Cycle Plays and Fragments*. Early English Text Society SS 1. London: Oxford UP, 1970.

Davis-Weyer, Caecilia. *Early Medieval Art, 300–1150*. 1971. Medieval Academy Reprints for Teaching 17. Toronto: U of Toronto P, 1986.

Deimling, Herman, and J. Matthews, eds. *The Chester Plays*. Early English Text Society 62, 115. London: Trubner, 1892, 1916.

Dunn, Charles W., and Edward T. Byrnes, eds. *Middle English Literature*. New York: Harcourt, 1973.

Eccles, Mark, ed. *The Macro Plays*. Early English Text Society OS 262. London: Oxford UP, 1969.

England, George, and Alfred W. Pollard, eds. *The Towneley Plays*. Early English Text Society ES 71. London: Oxford UP, 1897.

Erbe, Theodore, ed. *Mirk's Festial: A Collection of Homilies*. Early English Text Society ES 96. London: Trubner, 1905.

Foster, Frances, ed. *A Stanzaic Life of Christ*. Early English Text Society OS 166. London: Oxford UP, 1926.

———— . *The Northern Passion*. Early English Text Society OS 147. London: Oxford UP, 1916.

Garbáty, Thomas J., ed. *Medieval English Literature*. Lexington: Heath, 1984.

Gassner, John, ed. *Medieval and Tudor Drama*. 1963. New York: Bantam, 1971.

Gillespie, Patti P., and Kenneth M. Cameron, eds. *Western Theatre: Revolution and Revival*. New York: Macmillan, 1984.

Greg, W. W. *The Play of Antichrist from the Chester Cycle*. Oxford: Clarendon, 1935.

Happé, Peter, ed. *English Mystery Plays*. New York: Penguin, 1975.

———— , ed. *Four Morality Plays*. New York: Penguin, 1979.

Harris, Markham, trans. *The Cornish Ordinalia: A Medieval Dramatic Trilogy*. Washington: Catholic UP, 1969.

Harrison, Tony. *The Mysteries*. London: Faber, 1985.

Haskell, Ann S., ed. *A Middle English Anthology*. New York: Anchor-Doubleday, 1969.

Hassall, W. O., ed. *The Holkham Bible Picture Book*. London: Dropmore, 1954.

Helm, Alex. *The English Mummers' Play*. Woodbridge, Suffolk: Brewer, 1981.

Hennecke, Edgar, and Wilhelm Schneemelcher, eds. *New Testament Apocrypha*. Philadelphia: Westminster, 1963.

Henry, Avril, ed. *Biblia pauperum: A Facsimile*. Aldershot: Scolar, 1987.

———— , ed. *The Mirour of Mans Salvacioun: A Middle English Translation of Speculum humanae salvationis*. Philadelphia: U of Pennsylvania P, 1987.

Hesbert, René. *Corpus antiphonalium officii*. 4 vols. Rome: Herder, 1963–70.

Hopper, Vincent F., and Gerard B. Lahey, eds. *Medieval Mysteries, Moralities, and Interludes*. New York: Barron's, 1962.

Hussey, Maurice, trans. *The Chester Mystery Plays*. 2nd ed. New York: Theatre Arts, 1975.

James, Montague Rhodes, trans. *The Apocryphal New Testament*. Oxford: Clarendon, 1924.

*Jesus Christ, Superstar*. Dir. Norman Jewison. Screenplay by Melvyn Bragg and Norman Jewison. Music by Andrew Lloyd Webber and Tim Rice. Universal/MCA, 1973. MCA videotape, 1986. 1 hr. 48 min.

Johnston, Alexandra F., and Margaret Dorrell Rogerson, eds. *Records of Early English Drama: York*. 2 vols. Toronto: U of Toronto P, 1979.

Kernan, Alvin. *Character and Conflict: An Introduction to Drama*. 2nd ed. New York: Harcourt, 1969.

Lancashire, Ian. *Dramatic Texts and Records of Britain: A Chronological Topography to 1558*. Toronto: U of Toronto P, 1984.

Lester, G. A., ed. *Three Late Medieval Morality Plays*: Mankind, Everyman, Mundus et Infans. New Mermaid Series. New York: Norton, 1981.

Loomis, Roger S., and Henry W. Wells, trans. *Representative Medieval and Tudor Plays*. New York: Sheed, 1942.

Lumiansky, Robert, and David Mills, eds. *The Chester Mystery Cycle.* 2 vols. Early English Text Society SS 3, 9. London: Oxford UP, 1974, 1986.

———, eds. *The Chester Mystery Cycle: A Facsimile of Bodley 175.* Leeds Texts and Monographs, Medieval Drama Facsimiles 1. Leeds: U of Leeds, School of English, 1973.

———, eds. *The Chester Mystery Cycle: A Reduced Facsimile of Huntington Library MS 2.* Leeds Texts and Monographs, Medieval Drama Facsimiles 6. Leeds: U of Leeds, School of English, 1980.

Luria, Maxwell S., and Richard L. Hoffman, eds. *Middle English Lyrics.* Norton Critical Edition. New York: Norton, 1974.

Mack, Maynard, gen. ed. *The Norton Anthology of World Masterpieces.* 5th ed. New York: Norton, 1985.

Mandel, Oscar, trans. *Five Comedies of Medieval France.* 1970. Washington: UP of America, 1982.

Manly, John Matthews, ed. *Specimens of the Pre-Shakspearean Drama.* 2 vols. 1897. New York: Dover, 1967.

Meiss, Millard, and Marcel Thomas, eds. *The Rohan Master: A Book of Hours.* New York: Braziller, 1973.

Meredith, Peter, ed. *The Mary Play from the N. Town Manuscript.* New York: Longman, 1987.

Meredith, Peter, and Stanley J. Kahrl, eds. *The N-Town Plays: A Facsimile of British Library MS Cotton Vespasian D VIII.* Leeds Texts and Monographs, Medieval Drama Facsimiles 4. Leeds: U of Leeds, School of English, 1977.

Meredith, Peter, and John E. Tailby, eds. *The Staging of Religious Drama in Europe in the Late Middle Ages: Texts and Documents in English Translation.* Early Drama, Art, and Music Monograph 4. Kalamazoo: Medieval Inst., 1983.

Miles, Keith, trans. *The Coventry Mystery Plays.* London: Heinemann, 1981.

Mills, David, ed. *The Chester Mystery Cycle: A Facsimile of British Library MS Harley 2124.* Leeds Texts and Monographs, Medieval Drama Facsimiles 8. Leeds: U of Leeds, School of English, 1984.

Mütherich, Florentine, and Joachim E. Gaehde. *Carolingian Painting.* New York: Braziller, 1976.

Pelly, Lewis. *The Miracle Play of Hasan and Husain: Collected from Oral Tradition.* 2 vols. London: Allen, 1879.

Perrine, Laurence. *Dimensions of Drama.* New York: Harcourt, 1973.

Petroff, Elizabeth Alvida, ed. *Medieval Women's Visionary Literature.* New York: Oxford UP, 1986.

Pickering, Kenneth, et al. *The Mysteries at Canterbury Cathedral.* Worthing: Churchman, 1986.

Plummer, John, ed. *The Hours of Catherine of Cleves.* New York: Braziller, 1966.

Pollard, Alfred W., ed. *English Miracle Plays, Moralities and Interludes.* 1890. Oxford: Oxford UP, 1927.

Purvis, J. S., trans. *The York Cycle of Mystery Plays.* 1957. London: SPCK, 1962.

Robertson, D. W., Jr. *The Literature of Medieval England.* New York: MacGraw, 1970.

Rose, Martial, trans. *The Wakefield Mystery Plays.* 1961. New York: Norton, 1969.

Schell, Edgar T., and J. D. Schuchter, eds. *English Morality Plays and Moral Interludes.* New York: Holt, 1969.

Stone, Brian, trans. *Medieval English Verse.* Baltimore: Penguin, 1973.

Thomas, R. G., ed. *Ten Miracle Plays.* York Medieval Texts. Evanston: Northwestern UP, 1966.

Tiddy, R. J. E. *The Mummer's Play.* Oxford: Clarendon, 1923.

Toulmin-Smith, Lucy, ed. *York Plays.* Oxford: Clarendon, 1885.

Trapp, J. B., ed. *Medieval English Literature.* Vol. 1 of *Oxford Anthology of English Literature.* Gen. eds. Frank Kermode and John Hollander. New York: Oxford UP, 1973.

Tristram, Earnest William. *English Wall Painting of the Fourteenth Century.* London: Routledge, 1955.

Wickham, Glynne, ed. *English Moral Interludes.* Totowa: Rowman, 1976.

Wilkie, Brian, and James Hurt. *Literature of the Western World.* 2nd ed. 2 vols. New York: Macmillan, 1988.

Wilson, Adrian, and Joyce Lancaster Wilson. *A Medieval Mirror: Speculum humanae salvationis, 1324–1500.* Berkeley: U of California P, 1985.

Wilson, Katharina M., ed. *Medieval Women Writers.* Athens: U of Georgia P, 1984.

Wright, John, trans. *The Play of* Antichrist. Toronto: Pontifical Inst., 1967.

Wynkyn de Worde. *Here Begynneth the Byrthe and Lyfe of the Moost False and Deceytfull Antechryst.* London, c. 1528.

Young, Karl, ed. *The Drama of the Medieval Church.* 2 vols. Oxford: Clarendon, 1933.

# Secondary Sources

Ackerman, Robert. *Backgrounds to Medieval English Literature*. New York: Random, 1966.

Adams, Robert. "The Egregious Feasts of the Chester and Towneley Shepherds." *Chaucer Review* 21 (1986): 96–107.

Anderson, M. D. *Drama and Imagery in English Medieval Churches*. New York: Cambridge UP, 1963.

Ashley, Kathleen M. "Divine Power in the Chester Cycle and Late Medieval Thought." *Journal of the History of Ideas* 39 (1978): 1–24.

———. " 'Wyt' and 'Wysdam' in the N-Town Cycle." *Philological Quarterly* 58 (1979): 121–35.

Aston, Margaret. "Huizinga's Harvest: England and *The Waning of the Middle Ages.*" *Medievalia et Humanistica* ns 9 (1979): 1–24.

Auerbach, Erich. "Adam and Eve." *Mimesis* 143–73.

———. "Figura." Trans. Ralph Manheim. 1944. *Scenes from the Drama of European Literature*. 1959. Theory and History of Literature 9. Minneapolis: U of Minnesota P, 1984. 11–76.

———. *Mimesis: The Representation of Reality in Western Literature*. Trans. Willard R. Trask. 1946. Princeton: Princeton UP, 1968.

Axton, Richard. *European Drama of the Early Middle Ages*. Pittsburgh: U of Pittsburgh P, 1975.

Bakhtin, Mikhail M. *Rabelais and His World*. Trans. Helene Iswolsky. Cambridge: MIT P, 1968.

Bal, Mieke. "Sexuality, Sin, and Sorrow: The Emergence of the Female Character (A Reading of Genesis 1–3)." *Poetics Today* 6 (1985): 21–42.

Barkan, Leonard. *Nature's Work of Art: The Human Body as Image of the World*. New Haven: Yale UP, 1975.

Barker, Francis. *The Tremulous Private Body: Essays on Subjection*. London: Methuen, 1984.

Baugh, Albert, et al. *Literary History of England*. 2nd ed. New York: Appleton, 1967.

Berger, Sidney. *Medieval English Drama: A Bibliography of Recent Criticism*. New York: Garland, 1989.

Bevington, David. "Drama Editing and Its Relation to Recent Trends in Literary Criticism." *Editing Early English Drama: Special Problems and New Directions*. Ed. A. F. Johnston. New York: AMS, 1987. 17–32.

———. *From* Mankind *to Marlowe: The Growth of Structure in the Popular Drama of Tudor England*. Cambridge: Harvard UP, 1962.

———. " 'Man, Thinke on Thine Endinge Day': Stage Pictures of Just Judgment in *The Castle of Perseverance.*" Bevington et al. 147–77.

———. "The Staging of Twelfth-Century Liturgical Drama in the Fleury *Playbook.*" Campbell and Davidson 62–81.

Bevington, David, et al. *"Homo, memento finis": The Iconography of Just Judgment in Medieval Art and Drama.* Early Drama, Art, and Music Monograph 6. Kalamazoo: Medieval Inst., 1985.

Blacking, John, ed. *The Anthropology of the Body.* London: Academic, 1977.

Borsay, Peter. "'All the town's a stage': Urban Ritual and Ceremony 1660–1800." *The Transformation of English Provincial Towns 1600–1800.* Ed. Peter Clark. London: Hutchinson, 1984. 228–58.

Briscoe, Marianne G., and John C. Coldewey, eds. *Contexts for Early English Drama.* Bloomington: Indiana UP, 1989.

Brody, Alan. *The English Mummers and Their Plays: Traces of Ancient Mystery.* Philadelphia: U of Pennsylvania P, 1969.

Brooke-Rose, Christine. "Woman as Semiotic Object." *Poetics Today* 6 (1985): 9–20.

Burke, Peter. *Popular Culture in Early Modern Europe.* New York: Harper, 1978.

Burrow, J. A. "Old and Middle English." *The Oxford Illustrated History of English Literature.* Ed. Pat Rogers. New York: Oxford UP, 1987.

Bynum, Caroline Walker. "The Body of Christ in the Later Middle Ages: A Reply to Leo Steinberg." *Renaissance Quarterly* 39 (1986): 399–439.

———. *Holy Feast and Holy Fast: The Religious Significance of Food to Medieval Women.* Berkeley: U of California P, 1987.

———. *Jesus as Mother: Studies in the Spirituality of the High Middle Ages.* Berkeley: U of California P, 1982.

Calkins, Robert G. *Illuminated Books of the Middle Ages.* Ithaca: Cornell UP, 1983.

Campbell, Thomas P. "Eschatology and the Nativity in English Mystery Plays." *American Benedictine Review* 27 (1976): 297–320.

Campbell, Thomas P., and Clifford Davidson. *The Fleury Playbook: Essays and Studies.* Early Drama, Art, and Music Monograph 7. Kalamazoo: Medieval Inst., 1985.

Cashman, Norine. *Teacher's Guide to Classroom Use of Slides for Medieval Studies.* TEAMS pamphlet. Kalamazoo: Medieval Inst., 1985.

Carpenter, Nan Cooke. "Music in the *Secunda pastorum.*" *Speculum* 26 (1951): 696–700. Rpt. in Taylor and Nelson 212–17.

Cawley, A. C. "The 'Grotesque' Feast in the *Prima pastorum.*" *Speculum* 30 (1955): 213–17.

Cawley, A. C., David Mills, Peter F. McDonald, and Marion Jones. *Medieval Drama.* Vol. 1 of *The Revels History of Drama in English.* Gen. ed. Lois Potter. New York: Methuen, 1983.

Chambers, E. K. *The English Folk-Play.* 1933. New York: Russell, 1964.

———. *The Mediaeval Stage.* 2 vols. Oxford: Clarendon, 1903.

Clark, Peter, ed. *The Early Modern Town.* New York: Longman, 1976.

Clark, Peter, and Paul Slack, eds. *Crisis and Order in English Towns, 1500–1700.* Toronto: U of Toronto P, 1972.

_____ , eds. *English Towns in Transition, 1500–1700*. London: Oxford UP, 1976.

Clopper, Lawrence M. "The History and Development of the Chester Cycle." *Modern Philology* 75 (1978): 219–46.

_____ . "The Social Contexts of Civic Religious Drama." Briscoe and Coldewey 703–36.

_____ . "Tyrants and Villains: Characterization in the Passion Sequence of the English Cycle Plays." *Modern Language Quarterly* 41 (1980): 3–20.

Coletti, Theresa. "Devotional Iconography in the N-Town Marian Plays." Davidson, Gianakaris, and Stroupe 249–71.

_____ . "Records of the Drama: Context or Text?" MLA Convention. Washington, DC, 27 Dec. 1984.

_____ . "Sacrament and Sacrifice in the N-Town Passion." *Mediaevalia* 7 (1981): 239–64.

Collins, Fletcher. *The Production of Medieval Church Music-Drama*. Charlottesville: UP of Virginia, 1972.

Conrad, Peter. *The History of English Literature: One Indivisible, Unending Book*. Philadelphia: U of Pennsylvania P, 1987.

Cook, Ann Jennalie. *The Privileged Playgoers of Shakespeare's London: 1576–1642*. Princeton: Princeton UP, 1981.

Cook, William R., and Ronald B. Herzman. *The Medieval World View: An Introduction*. New York: Oxford, 1983.

Coulton, G. R. *Medieval Panorama: The English Scene from Conquest to Reformation*. 1949. New York: Norton, 1974.

Cox, Harvey. *The Feast of Fools: A Theological Essay on Festivity and Fantasy*. Cambridge: Harvard UP, 1969.

Craig, Hardin. *English Religious Drama of the Middle Ages*. Oxford: Clarendon, 1955.

Crosby, Everett U., C. Julian Bishko, and Robert L. Kellogg, eds. *Medieval Studies: A Bibliographic Guide*. New York: Garland, 1983.

Cross, Claire. " 'Great Reasoners in Scripture': The Activities of Women Lollards, 1380–1530." *Medieval Women*. Ed. Derek Baker. Oxford: Blackwell, 1978. 359–80.

Curtius, Ernst Robert. *European Literature and the Latin Middle Ages*. Trans. Willard R. Trask. Bollingen Series 36. 1953. Princeton: Princeton UP, 1973.

Daniélou, Jean. *From Shadows to Reality: Studies in the Biblical Typology of the Fathers*. Trans. Wulstan Hibberd. London: Burns, 1960.

Danker, Frederick E. "Teaching Medieval Literature: Texts, Recordings, and Techniques." *College English* 32 (1970): 340–57.

Davenport, W. A. *Fifteenth-Century English Drama: The Early Moral Plays and Their Literary Relations*. Totowa: Rowman, 1982.

Davidson, Clifford. *Drama and Art: An Introduction to the Use of Evidence from the Visual Arts for the Study of Early Drama*. Early Drama, Art, and Music Monograph 1. Kalamazoo: Medieval Inst., 1977.

——— . *From Creation to Doom: The York Cycle of Mystery Plays.* New York: AMS, 1984.

——— . "The Realism of the York Realist and the York Passion." *Speculum* 50 (1975): 270–83.

——— , ed. *The Saint Play in Medieval Europe.* Early Drama, Art, and Music Monograph 8. Kalamazoo: Medieval Inst., 1986.

Davidson, Clifford, C. J. Gianakaris, and John H. Stroupe, eds. *The Drama of the Middle Ages: Comparative and Critical Essays.* New York: AMS, 1982.

Davidson, Clifford, and David E. O'Connor, eds. *York Art.* Early Drama, Art, and Music Reference 1. Kalamazoo: Medieval Inst., 1978.

Davis, Natalie Zemon. *Society and Culture in Early Modern France.* Stanford: Stanford UP, 1975.

——— . "Women's History in Transition: The European Case." *Feminist Studies* 3 (1976): 83–103.

Denny, Neville. "Arena Staging and Dramatic Quality in the Cornish Passion Play." Denny, *Medieval Drama* 125–54.

——— . ed. *Medieval Drama.* Stratford-upon-Avon Studies 16. London: Arnold, 1973.

Douglas, Mary. "Introduction to Grid/Group Analysis." *Essays in the Sociology of Perception.* Ed. Douglas. London: Routledge, 1982. 1–8.

——— . *Natural Symbols.* London: Cresset, 1970.

Doyle, Ian. "A Survey of the Origins and Circulation of Theological Writings in English in the Fourteeth, Fifteenth, and Early Sixteenth Centuries with Special Consideration of the Part of the Clergy Therein." Diss. Cambridge U, 1954.

Dutka, JoAnna. *Music in the English Mystery Plays.* Early Drama, Art, and Music Reference 2. Kalamazoo: Medieval Inst., 1980.

——— , ed. *Records of Early English Drama: Proceedings of the First Colloquium.* Toronto: U of Toronto P, 1979.

Elliott, John R., Jr. "Medieval Acting." Briscoe and Coldewey 238–51.

Emmerson, Richard K. *Antichrist in the Middle Ages: A Study of Medieval Apocalypticism, Art, and Literature.* Seattle: U of Washington P, 1981.

——— . "Dramatic Developments: Some Recent Scholarship on Medieval Drama." *Envoi: A Review Journal of Medieval Literature* 1 (1988): 23–40.

——— . " 'Nowe Ys Common This Daye': Enoch and Elias, Antichrist, and the Structure of the Chester Cycle." Bevington et al. 89–120.

Enos, Jonathan C. *Teacher's Guide to Classroom Use of 16mm Films and Videocassettes.* TEAMS pamphlet. Kalamazoo: Medieval Inst., 1985.

Falvey, Kathleen C. "Italian Vernacular Religious Drama of the Fourteenth through the Sixteenth Centuries: A Selected Bibliography on the *Lauda dramatica* and the *Sacra rappresentazione.*" *Research Opportunities in Renaissance Drama* 26 (1983): 125–44.

Fifield, Merle. *The Rhetoric of Free Will: The Five-Act Structure of the English Morality Play.* Leeds: U of Leeds, School of English, 1974.

Flanigan, C. Clifford. "The Fleury *Playbook* and the Traditions of Medieval Latin Drama and Modern Scholarship." Campbell and Davidson 1–25.

————. "The Liturgical Drama and Its Tradition: A Review of Scholarship, 1965–1975." *Research Opportunities in Renaissance Drama* 18 (1975): 81–102; 19 (1976): 109–36.

————. "The Roman Rite and the Origins of the Liturgical Drama." *University of Toronto Quarterly* 43 (1973): 263–84.

Foucault, Michel. *Discipline and Punishment: The Birth of the Prison*. Trans. Alan Sheridan. New York: Pantheon, 1977.

Fowler, David C. *The Bible in Middle English Literature*. Seattle: U of Washington P, 1984.

Frank, Grace. *The Medieval French Drama*. Oxford: Clarendon, 1954.

Gardiner, Harold C. *Mysteries' End: An Investigation of the Last Days of the Medieval Religious Stage*. 1946. Hamden: Archon, 1967.

Gash, Anthony. "Carnival against Lent." *Medieval Literature: Criticism, Ideology, and History*. Ed. David Aers. New York: St. Martin's, 1986.

Geertz, Clifford. *Negara: The Theatre State in Nineteenth-Century Bali*. Princeton: Princeton UP, 1980.

Gibson, Gail McMurray. "Bury St. Edmunds, John Lydgate, and the N-Town Cycle." *Speculum* 56 (1981): 56–90.

Girard, René. *Violence and the Sacred*. Trans. Patrick Gregory. Baltimore: Johns Hopkins P, 1977.

Gold, Penny S. "The Marriage of Mary and Joseph in the Twelfth-Century Ideology of Marriage." *Sexual Practices and the Medieval Church*. Ed. Vern Bullough and James Brundage. Buffalo: Prometheus, 1982. 102–17.

Grimes, Ronald L. "Ritual in the Toronto Towneley Cycle of Mystery Plays." *Studies in Religion* 16 (1987): 57–63.

Handelman, Don. "Reflexivity in Festival and Other Cultural Events," *Essays in the Sociology of Perception*. Ed. Mary Douglas. London: Routledge, 1982, 162–90.

Hanning, Robert W. " 'You Have Begun a Parlous Pleye': The Nature and Limits of Dramatic Mimesis as a Theme in Four Middle English 'Fall of Lucifer' Cycle Plays." *Comparative Drama* 7 (1973): 22–50. Rpt. in Davidson, Gianakaris, and Stroupe 140–68.

Happé, Peter, ed. *Medieval English Drama: A Casebook*. London: Macmillan, 1984.

Harbage, Alfred, and Samuel Schoenbaum, eds. *Annals of English Drama 975–1700*. Rev. ed. Philadelphia: U of Pennsylvania P, 1964.

Hardison, O. B. *Christian Rite and Christian Drama in the Middle Ages: Essays in the Origin and Early History of Modern Drama*. Baltimore: Johns Hopkins P, 1965.

Hartung, Albert E., ed. *A Manual of Writings in Middle English, 1050–1500*. Vol. 5. Hamden: Archon, 1975.

Helterman, Jeffrey. *Symbolic Action in the Plays of the Wakefield Master.* Athens: U of Georgia P, 1981.

Henry, Derrick. *The Listener's Guide to Medieval and Renaissance Music.* New York: Facts, 1983.

Herzman, Ronald B. "'Let Us Seek Him Also': Tropological Judgment in Twelfth-Century Art and Drama." Bevington et al. 59–88.

Hoffman, Herbert H., comp. *Recorded Plays: Indexes to Dramatists, Plays, and Actors.* Chicago: American Library Assn., 1985.

Holbrook, Sue Ellen. *Teacher's Guide to Finding Films and Videocassettes for Medieval Studies.* TEAMS Pamphlet. Kalamazoo: Medieval Inst., 1985.

Homan, Richard. "Ritual Aspects of the York Cycle." *Theatre Journal* 33 (1981): 303–15.

Hoppin, Richard H. *Medieval Music.* Norton Introduction to Music History 1. New York: Norton, 1978.

Houle, Peter J. *The English Morality and Related Drama: A Bibliographical Survey.* Hamden: Archon, 1972.

Huizinga, Johan. *The Waning of the Middle Ages.* Trans. F. Hopman. 1924. Harmondsworth: Penguin, 1955.

James, Mervyn. "Ritual, Drama, and the Social Body in the Late Medieval English Town." *Past and Present* 98 (1983): 3–29.

Jardine, Lisa. "Cultural Confusion and Shakespeare's Learned Heroines: 'These are old paradoxes.'" *Shakespeare Quarterly* 38 (1987): 1–18.

—————. *Still Harping on Daughters: Women and Drama in the Age of Shakespeare.* Totowa: Barnes, 1983.

Jeffrey, David. "English Saints Plays." Denny, *Medieval Drama* 69–89.

—————. "Franciscan Spirituality and the Rise of Early English Drama." *Mosaic* 8 (1975): 17–46.

Johnston, Alexandra F. "Notes from the Dramaturge." Towneley production. U of Toronto, May 1985.

—————. "The Plays of the Religious Guilds of York: The Creed Play and the Pater Noster Play." *Speculum* 50 (1975): 55–90.

Johnston, Alexandra F., and Margaret Dorrell. "The Doomsday Pageant of the York Mercers, 1433." *Leeds Studies in English* ns 5 (1971): 29–34.

Jones, Cheslyn, Geoffrey Wainwright, and Edward Yarnold. *The Study of Liturgy.* New York: Oxford, 1978.

Jungmann, Joseph A. *The Mass of the Roman Rite.* Trans. Francis A. Brunner. Rev. ed. New York: Benziger, 1961.

Kahrl, Stanley J. "Secular Life and Popular Piety in Medieval English Drama." *The Popular Literature of Medieval England.* Ed. Thomas J. Heffernan. Knoxville: U of Tennessee P, 1985. 85–107.

—————. *Traditions of Medieval English Drama.* London: Hutchinson, 1974.

Kahrl, Stanley J., and Kenneth Cameron. "Staging the N-Town Cycle." *Theatre Notebook* 21 (1967): 122–38, 152–65.

Kantorowicz, Ernst H. *The King's Two Bodies: A Study in Mediaeval Political Theology.* Princeton: Princeton UP, 1957.

Katzenellenbogen, Adolf. *Allegories of the Virtues and Vices in Mediaeval Art, from Early Christian Times to the Eighteenth Century*. Trans. Alan J. P. Crick. 1939. New York: Norton, 1964.

Kelley, Michael R. *Flamboyant Drama: A Study of* The Castle of Perseverance, Mankind, *and* Wisdom. Carbondale: Southern Illinois UP, 1979.

Knight, Alan E. *Aspects of Genre in Late Medieval French Drama*. Manchester: Manchester UP, 1983.

Knowles, David. *The Evolution of Medieval Thought*. New York: Random, 1964.

Kolve, V. A. *Chaucer and the Imagery of Narrative*. Stanford: Stanford UP, 1984.

———. "*Everyman* and the Parable of the Talents." Sticca 69–98.

———. *The Play Called Corpus Christi*. Stanford: Stanford UP, 1966.

Kristeva, Julia. "*Stabat Mater*." *Poetics Today* 6 (1985): 133–52.

Lacan, Jacques. "Aggressivity in Psychoanalysis." Lacan, *Ecrits* 8–29.

———. *Ecrits*. Trans. Alan Sheridan. New York: Norton, 1977.

———. "The Mirror Stage as Formative of the Function of the I." Lacan, *Ecrits* 1–7.

———. "Of the Gaze as *Object Petit a*." *The Four Fundamental Concepts of Psycho-Analysis*. Trans. Alan Sheridan. New York: Norton, 1978. 67–122.

Lampe, G. W. H. *The West from The Fathers to the Reformation*. Vol. 2 of *The Cambridge History of the Bible*. Cambridge: Cambridge UP, 1969.

Leach, Edmund. *Culture and Communication*. Cambridge: Cambridge UP, 1976.

Leigh, David J. "The Doomsday Mystery Play: An Eschatological Morality." *Modern Philology* 67 (1969–70): 211–33. Rpt. in Taylor and Nelson 260–78.

Lepow, Lauren. " 'What God Has Cleansed': The Shepherds' Feast in the *Prima pastorum*. *Modern Philology* 80 (1982–83): 280–83.

Levin, David Michael. *The Body's Recollection of Being: Phenomenological Psychology and the Deconstruction of Nihilism*. London: Routledge, 1985.

Lewis, C. S. *The Discarded Image: An Introduction to Medieval and Renaissance Literature*. Cambridge: Cambridge UP, 1964.

Lindenbaum, Sheila. "The York Cycle at Toronto: Staging and Performance Style." Happé, *Medieval English Drama* 200–11.

Longsworth, Robert. *The Cornish Ordinalia: Religion and Dramaturgy*. Cambridge: Harvard UP, 1967.

Lubac, Henri de. *Exégèse médiévale: Les quatre sens de l'Ecriture*. 2 vols in 4 pts. Paris: Aubier, 1959.

Lumiansky, Robert, and David Mills. *The Chester Mystery Cycle: Essays and Documents*. Chapel Hill: U of North Carolina P, 1983.

MacAloon, John J., ed. *Rite, Drama, Festival, Spectacle: Rehearsals toward a Theory of Cultural Performance*. Philadelphia: ISHI, 1984.

MacKinnon, Effie. "Notes on the Dramatic Structure of the York Cycle." *Studies in Philology* 28 (1931): 433–49.

MacLean, Sally-Beth, ed. *Chester Art*. Early Drama, Art, and Music Reference 3. Kalamazoo: Medieval Inst., 1982.

———. "King Games and Robin Hood: Play and Profit at Kingston upon Thames." *Research Opportunities in Renaissance Drama* 29 (1986–87): 85–93.

Mâle, Emile. *The Gothic Image: Religious Art in France of the Thirteenth Century*. Trans. Dora Nussey. 1913. New York: Harper, 1958.

Marcus, Leah S. "Shakespeare's Comic Heroines, Elizabeth I, and the Political Uses of Androgyny." *Women in the Middle Ages and the Renaissance*. Ed. Mary Beth Rose. Syracuse: Syracuse UP, 1986. 135–53.

Marrow, James H. *Passion Iconography in Northern European Art of the Late Middle Ages and Early Renaissance*. Brussels: Van Ghemmert, 1979.

Marshall, Mary. "Aesthetic Values of the Liturgical Drama." *English Institute Essays, 1950*. New York: Columbia UP, 1951. 89–115. Rpt. in Taylor and Nelson 28–43.

McGee, Timothy J. "The Liturgical Placements of the 'Quem quaeritis' Dialogue." *Journal of the American Musicological Society* 29 (1976): 1–29.

McLaughlin, Eleanor Commo. "Equality of Souls, Inequality of Sexes: Women in Medieval Theology." *Religion and Sexism: Images of Woman in the Jewish and Christian Traditions*. Ed. Rosemary Radford Reuther. New York: Simon, 1974. 213–66.

McLuskie, Kathleen. "The Patriarchal Bard: Feminist Criticism and Shake-speare: *King Lear* and *Measure for Measure*." *Political Shakespeare*. Ed. Jonathan Dollimore and Alan Sinfeld. Ithaca: Cornell UP, 1985. 88–108.

Medcalf, Stephen. *The Later Middle Ages*. Context of English Literature. London: Methuen, 1981.

Meiss, Millard. *Painting in Florence and Siena after the Black Death: The Arts, Religion, and Society in the Mid-Fourteenth Century*. 1951. Princeton: Princeton UP, 1978.

Meredith, Peter. "Scribes, Texts and Performance." Neuss 13–29.

Meyers, Walter E. "Typology and the Audience of the English Cycle Plays." *Studies in the Literary Imagination* 81 (1975): 145–58.

Michie, Helena R. *The Flesh Made Word: Female Figures and Women's Bodies*. New York: Oxford UP, 1987.

Mills, David. "Characterisation in the English Mystery Cycles: A Critical Prologue." *Medieval English Theatre* 5 (1983): 5–17.

———, ed. *The Staging of the Chester Cycle*. Leeds Texts and Monographs 9. Leeds: U of Leeds, School of English, 1985.

Moi, Toril. *Sexual/Textual Politics: Feminist Literary Theory*. London: Methuen, 1985.

Morris, Desmond. *Bodywatching: A Field Guide to the Human Species*. New York: Crown, 1985.

Muir, Lynette R. "Medieval English Drama: The French Connection." Briscoe and Coldewey 56–76.

———— . "The Saint Play in Medieval France." Davidson, *Saint Play* 123–80.

Mullaney, Steven. *The Place of the Stage: License, Play, and Power in Renaissance England*. Chicago: U of Chicago P, 1988.

Nagler, Alois M. *The Medieval Religious Stage: Shapes and Phantoms*. New Haven: Yale UP, 1976.

Nelson, Alan H. *The Medieval English Stage: Corpus Christi Pageants and Plays*. Chicago: U of Chicago P, 1974.

Neuss, Paula, ed. *Aspects of Early English Drama*. Totowa: Barnes, 1983.

Nicoll, Allardyce. *Masks, Mimes, and Miracles: Studies in the Popular Theatre*. 1931. New York: Cooper, 1963.

Noakes, Susan. *Timely Reading: Between Exegesis and Interpretation*. Ithaca: Cornell UP, 1988.

Ogden, Dunbar H. "The Use of Architectural Space in Medieval Music Drama." *Comparative Drama* 8 (1974): 63-76.

O'Neill, John. *Five Bodies: The Human Species in Modern Society*. Ithaca: Cornell UP, 1985.

Orgel, Stephen. *The Illusion of Power: Political Theater in the English Renaissance*. Berkeley: U of California P, 1975.

Owst, G. R. *Literature and Pulpit in Medieval England*. 2nd rev. ed. Oxford: Blackwell, 1961.

Ozment, Steven. *The Age of Reform, 1250–1550: An Intellectual and Religious History of Late Medieval and Reformation Europe*. New Haven: Yale UP, 1980.

Palmer, Barbara D. " 'Towneley Plays' or 'Wakefield Cycle' Revisited." *Comparative Drama* 22 (1988): 318–48.

Panofsky, Erwin. *Early Netherlandish Painting: Its Origins and Character*. 2 vols. 1953. New York: Harper, 1971.

Patterson, Lee W. " 'For the Wyves Love of Bathe': Feminine Rhetoric and Poetic Resolution in the *Roman de la Rose* and the *Canterbury Tales*." *Speculum* 58 (1983): 656–95.

Pfleiderer, Jean D., and Michael J. Preston, eds. *A Complete Concordance to the Chester Mystery Plays*. New York: Garland, 1981.

———— , eds. *A KWIC Concordance to the Plays of the Wakefield Master*. New York: Garland, 1982.

Phythian-Adams, Charles. "Ceremony and the Citizen: The Communal Year at Coventry, 1450–1550." Clark and Slack 57–85.

———— . *Desolation of a City: Coventry and the Urban Crisis of the Late Middle Ages*. Cambridge: Cambridge UP, 1979.

Platt, Colin. *The English Medieval Town*. New York: McKay, 1976.

Postan, M. M. *Medieval Economy and Society: An Economic History of Britain in the Middle Ages*. Baltimore: Penguin, 1972.

Potter, Robert. *The English Morality Play: Origins, History and Influence of a Dramatic Tradition*. London: Routledge, 1975.

———— . "The Unity of Medieval English: European Contexts for Early English Dramatic Traditions." Briscoe and Coldewey 41–55.

Rackin, Phyllis. "Androgyny, Mimesis, and the Marriage of the Boy Heroine on the English Renaissance Stage." *PMLA* 102 (1987): 29–41.

Rastall, Richard. "'Alle hefne makyth melody.'" Neuss 1–12.

———— . "Female Roles in All-Male Casts." *Medieval English Theatre* 7 (1985): 25–50.

———— . "Music in the Cycle." Lumiansky and Mills, *Essays and Documents* 111–64.

———— . "Music in the Cycle Plays." Briscoe and Coldewey 192–218.

Réau, Louis. *Iconographie de l'art chrétien.* 3 vols. Paris: Presses Universitaires de France, 1955–59.

Reiter, Robert E. "On Biblical Typology and the Interpretation of Literature." *College English* 30 (1969): 562–71.

Rendall, Thomas. "Visual Typology in the Abraham and Isaac Plays." *Modern Philology* 81 (1984): 221–32.

Rickert, Margaret. *Painting in Britain: The Middle Ages.* Pelican History of Art 5. Baltimore: Penguin, 1954.

Riggio, Milla, ed. *The* Wisdom *Symposium: Papers from the Trinity College Medieval Festival.* New York: AMS, 1984.

Robinson, J. W. "The Art of the York Realist." *Modern Philology* 60 (1963): 241–51. Rpt. in Taylor and Nelson 230–44.

Ross, Lawrence J. "Symbol and Structure in the *Secunda pastorum.*" *Comparative Drama* 1 (1967–68): 122–43. Rpt. in Taylor and Nelson 177–211.

Rossiter, A. P. *English Drama from the Early Times to the Elizabethans: Its Background, Origins, and Developments.* London: Hutchinson, 1950.

Roston, Murray. *Renaissance Perspectives in Literature and the Visual Arts.* Princeton: Princeton UP, 1987.

Runnalls, Graham A. "Medieval French Drama: A Review of Recent Scholarship." *Research Opportunities in Renaissance Drama* 21 (1978): 83–90; 22 (1979): 111–36.

Salter, F. M. *Medieval Drama in Chester.* Toronto: U of Toronto P, 1955.

Sanders, Norman. "The Social and Historical Context." *The Revels History of Drama in English.* Ed. Sanders et al. Vol. 2. London: Methuen, 1980. 3–30.

Scarry, Elaine. *The Body in Pain: The Making and Unmaking of the World.* New York: Oxford UP, 1985.

———— , ed. *Literature and the Body: Essays on Populations and Persons.* Selected Papers from the English Institute. ns 12. 1986. Baltimore: Johns Hopkins UP, 1988.

Schell, Edgar. *Strangers and Pilgrims: From* The Castle of Perseverance *to* King Lear. Chicago: U of Chicago P, 1983.

Schiller, Gertrud. *Iconography of Christian Art.* 2 vols. London: Humphries, 1971–72.

Schmitt, Natalie Crohn. "Was There a Medieval Theater in the Round? A Re-examination of the Evidence." *Theatre Notebook* 23 (1968–69): 130–42; 24 (1969–70): 18–25. Rpt. in Taylor and Nelson 292–315.

Sheingorn, Pamela. *The Easter Sepulchre in England.* Early Drama, Art, and Music Reference 5. Kalamazoo: Medieval Inst., 1987.

———. "The Moment of Resurrection in the Corpus Christi Plays." *Medievalia et Humanistica* ns 11 (1982): 111–29.

———. "On Using Medieval Art in the Study of Medieval Drama: An Introduction to Methodology." *Research Opportunities in Renaissance Drama* 22 (1979): 101–09.

———. "The Visual Language of Drama: Principles of Composition." Briscoe and Coldewey 173–91.

Sheingorn, Pamela, and David Bevington. " 'Alle This Was Token Domysday to Drede': Visual Signs of Last Judgment in the Corpus Christi Cycles and in Late Gothic Art." Bevington et al. 121–45.

Showalter, Elaine. "Representing Ophelia: Women, Madness, and the Responsibilities of Feminist Criticism." *Shakespeare and the Question of Theory.* Ed. Patricia Parker and Geoffrey Hartman. London: Methuen, 1985. 77–94.

Sinanoglou, Leah. "The Christ Child as Sacrifice: A Medieval Tradition and the Corpus Christi Plays." *Speculum* 48 (1973): 491–509.

Singer, Milton. *Traditional India: Structure and Change.* Philadelphia: 1959.

Smalley, Beryl. *The Study of the Bible in the Middle Ages.* Oxford: Clarendon, 1941.

Smart, Walter Kay. *Some English and Latin Sources and Parallels for the Morality of* Wisdom. Menosha: Banta, 1912.

Smoldon, William L. "The Melodies of the Medieval Church Dramas and Their Significance." *Comparative Drama* 2 (1968): 185–209. Rpt. in Taylor and Nelson 64–80.

Southern, Richard. *The Medieval Theatre in the Round: A Study of the Staging of* The Castle of Perseverance *and Related Matters.* London: Faber, 1957.

———. *The Staging of Plays before Shakespeare.* New York: Theatre Arts, 1973.

Southern, R. W. *The Making of the Middle Ages.* New Haven: Yale UP, 1953.

Spiegel, Shalom. *The Last Trial: On the Legends and Lore of the Command to Abraham to Offer Isaac as a Sacrifice: The Akedah.* 1967. New York: Behrman, 1979.

Spivack, Bernard. *Shakespeare and the Allegory of Evil.* New York: Columbia UP, 1958.

Steinberg, Leo. *The Sexuality of Christ in Renaissance Art and in Modern Oblivion.* New York: Random, 1983.

Sternberg, Meir. "The Literary Work as a System of Gaps." *The Poetics of Biblical Narrative.* Bloomington: Indiana UP, 1985.

Stevens, John. *Words and Music in the Middle Ages: Song, Narrative, Dance and Drama, 1050–1350.* Cambridge: Cambridge UP, 1986.

Stevens, Martin. "The Compilation of the Wakefield Plays: Some Observations." Paper presented at the Towneley Symposium. U of Toronto, 25 May 1985.

————— . *Four Middle English Mystery Cycles: Textual, Contextual and Critical Interpretations*. Princeton: Princeton UP, 1987.

————— . "Illusion and Reality in the Medieval Drama." *College English* 32 (1971): 448–64.

————— . "*Processus Torontoniensis*: A Performance of the Wakefield Cycle." *Research Opportunities in Renaissance Drama* 28 (1985): 189–200.

————— . "The Reshaping of *Everyman*." *Germanic Review* 48 (1973): 117–31.

Sticca, Sandro, ed. *The Medieval Drama: Papers of the Third Annual Conference of the Center for Medieval and Early Renaissance Studies*. Albany: State U of New York P, 1972.

Stratman, Carl J. *Bibliography of Medieval Drama*. 2nd rev. ed. 2 vols. New York: Ungar, 1972.

Strayer, Joseph R., ed. *Dictionary of the Middle Ages*. 12 vols. New York: Scribner's, 1982–88.

Styan, J. L. *Drama, Stage and Audience*. Cambridge: Cambridge UP, 1975.

————— . *The Elements of Drama*. Cambridge: Cambridge UP, 1960.

Taylor, Henry O. *The Mediaeval Mind: A History of the Development of Thought and Emotion in the Middle Ages*. 4th ed. 2 vols. Cambridge: Harvard UP, 1962.

Taylor, Jerome. "Critics, Mutations, and Historians of Medieval English Drama." Taylor and Nelson 1–27.

Taylor, Jerome, and Alan H. Nelson, eds. *Medieval English Drama: Essays Critical and Contextual*. Chicago: U of Chicago P, 1972.

Travis, Peter W. *Dramatic Design in the Chester Cycle*. Chicago: U of Chicago P, 1982.

————— . "The Social Body of the Dramatic Christ in Medieval England." *Early Drama to 1600*. Ed. Albert H. Tricomi. *Acta* 13 (1985): 18–36.

Turner, Bryan S. *The Body and Society: Explorations in Social Theory*. Oxford: Blackwell, 1984.

Turner, Victor. "Liminality and the Performative Genres." MacAloon 19–41.

Twycross, Meg. " 'Apparell comlye.' " Neuss 30–49.

————— . " 'Transvestism' in the Mystery Plays." *Medieval English Theatre* 5 (1983): 123–80.

Tydeman, William. *English Medieval Theatre, 1400–1500*. London: Routledge, 1986.

————— . *The Theatre in the Middle Ages: Western European Stage Conditions, c. 800–1576*. Cambridge: Cambridge UP, 1978.

Urkowitz, Steven. Rev. of Meredith and Tailby. *Medieval and Renaissance Drama in England* 3 (1986): 335–37.

Vaughan, Míčeál. "The Three Advents in the *Secunda pastorum*." *Speculum* 55 (1980): 484–504.

Walsh, Martin W. "Demon or Deluded Messiah? The Characterization of Antichrist in the Chester Cycle." *Medieval English Theatre* 7 (1985): 13–24.

Watts, Alan W. *Myth and Ritual in Christianity*. Boston: Beacon, 1968.

Weimann, Robert. *Shakespeare and the Popular Tradition in the Theater: Studies in the Social Dimension of Dramatic Form and Function*. Ed. Robert Schwartz. Baltimore: Johns Hopkins UP, 1978.

White, D. Jerry, ed. *Early English Drama*: Everyman *to 1580*. Boston: Hall, 1986.

Wickham, Glynne. *Early English Stages 1300–1600*. 3 vols. in 4 pts. London: Routledge, 1958–81.

———— . *A History of the Theatre*. New York: Cambridge UP, 1985.

———— . *The Medieval Theatre*. 3rd ed. Cambridge: Cambridge UP, 1987.

———— . "The Staging of Saint Plays in England." Sticca 99–119.

Williams, Arnold. *The Characterization of Pilate in the Towneley Plays*. East Lansing: Michigan State Coll. P, 1950.

———— . *The Drama of Medieval England*. East Lansing: Michigan State UP, 1961.

———— . "Typology and the Cycle Plays: Some Criteria." *Speculum* 43 (1968): 677–84.

Wood, Charles T. "The Doctors' Dilemma: Sin, Salvation, and the Menstrual Cycle in Medieval Thought." *Speculum* 56 (1981): 710–27.

Woolf, Rosemary. "The Effect of Typology on the English Medieval Plays of Abraham and Isaac." *Speculum* 32 (1957): 805–25.

———— . *The English Mystery Plays*. Berkeley: U of California P, 1972.

Zesmer, David M. *Guide to English Literature from* Beowulf *through Chaucer and Medieval Drama*. New York: Barnes, 1961.

# INDEX OF DRAMATIC TEXTS

# INDEX OF NAMES